Jennifer Nicolls Sternberg
220 Daniel Low Terrace
Staten Island, NY 10301

Jennifer Nicolls Sternberg
P. O. Box 319
Youngsville, N.Y. 12791

ENGLISH ALIVE

ENGLISH ALIVE

Grammar, Function, and Setting

S E C O N D   E D I T I O N

Gail Fingado
Mary Reinbold Jerome

American Language Program
Columbia University

HEINLE & HEINLE PUBLISHERS
A Division of Wadsworth, Inc.
Boston, Massachusetts 02116

Director: Laurie E. Likoff
Full-Service Manager: Michael Weinstein
Production Coordinator: Cynthia Funkhouser
Text Design: Lucy Leziak Design
Cover Design: Caliber Design Planning
Text Illustrations: Marcie Davis; p. 289, Nancy Mattimore
Photo Research: Jacquelyn Wong
Production: Spectrum Publisher Services
Compositor: Graphic Sciences
Printer and Binder: Malloy Lithographing

Photo Credits: p. 18, The Bettmann Archive; p. 28, Courtesy of the United Nations; p. 46, The Bettmann Archive; p. 85, Courtesy of the United Nations; p. 90, Courtesy of the United Nations; p. 96, Courtesy of the United Nations; p. 138, Courtesy of Colgate University, Hamilton, NY; p. 174, Courtesy of the Congress of the United States; p. 194, Courtesy of the United Nations/B. Lane; p. 204, © Bob Daemmrich/ The Image Works; p. 210, Courtesy of the United Nations; p. 217, Courtesy of Colgate University, Hamilton, NY; p. 270, © Brent Jones; p. 278, *top left*: The Bettmann Archive, all others: UPI/Bettmann.

English Alive: Grammar, Function, and Setting

Copyright © 1991 by Heinle & Heinle Publishers, a division of Wadsworth, Inc. All rights reserved. Printed in the United States of America. No part of this book may be used or reproduced in any manner whatsoever without written permission, except in the case of brief quotations embodied in critical articles and reviews.

ISBN 0-8384-2910-6

Library of Congress Cataloging-in-Publication Data

Fingado, Gail.
    English alive: grammar, function, and setting / Gail Fingado and
  Mary Reinbold Jerome. — 2nd ed.
       p.   cm.
    Includes index.

    1. English language—Textbooks for foreign speakers. I. Jerome,
Mary Reinbold. II. Title.
PE 1128.F48 1991
428.2'4—dc20   90-23710
                                                                                                 CIP

94 93 92 91 9 8 7 6 5 4 3 2

To our parents
Raymond and Dorothy Fingado
Dick and Diana Reinbold

PREFACE TO THE SECOND EDITION

The new revised edition of *English Alive* is designed to make this popular text more user-friendly for both the student and the instructor. It now has a clearer, easier-to-use format. Although the instructor is still encouraged to intersperse grammar lessons with lessons from the function and setting chapters, there are now three separate sections for grammar, function, and setting chapters. The new layout is more attractive, allowing the student's eye to travel more easily over the page. Outdated information has been replaced. In order to provide a better balance with controlled activities such as fill-ins or dialogs, more discussion questions and open-ended or interactive activities have been added. To make the text easier for the instructor to use, comprehension questions now follow every dialog; an audiotape of the dialogs is now available for purchase, allowing the instructor to use the dialogs for listening comprehension. Simple definitions for words in the vocabulary preparation lists preceding readings have been added. Two new integration chapters have been provided, allowing for better review of verb forms. To better meet the needs of a curriculum for low intermediate students, two new grammar chapters have been added: a chapter on the Present Unreal Conditional and one on the Passive Voice with the Simple Past and Simple Present.

The authors are confident that instructors who have enjoyed working with this unique text in the past will find that the revised edition is much improved. Instructors trying *English Alive* for the first time will be delighted to find how easy it is to plan the curriculum around the text.

To the Teacher

This text is intended for low-level adult students of English as a second language. By "low-level students," we mean those who already have had some exposure to basic grammatical structures but have had limited opportunities to practice those structures orally. These students will enjoy the added challenge of learning vocabulary and practicing their discussion skills as they review and learn grammar. *English Alive* is intended to help them attain oral and written mastery of key structures, build their vocabulary, and, at the same time, develop their ability to discuss a wide range of topics. The book provides a full range of classroom activities, from listening comprehension exercises and controlled fill-ins for testing and drilling to freer activities, such as role playing and student presentations. In addition, and perhaps most importantly, the content focus of most of the grammar chapters can be used as a springboard for discussion of such diverse topics as folk remedies for common ailments, street crime, and the existence of ghosts. Even students with limited fluency and vocabulary want and need to have a chance to discuss challenging and possibly controversial subjects. True, the students will make errors, grope for words, and become frustrated at times by their inability to express ideas with ease, but all of this is a very natural part of the language-learning process.

Another unique feature of the text is that, in addition to the grammar-focused chapters, there are chapters on language functions, such as making suggestions or accepting and refusing requests. Moreover, there are chapters on the specific language needed for certain settings, such as a restaurant or a store. These chapters indirectly review and reinforce the grammatical structures that students have learned in previous chapters. Grammar, function, and setting—the three major elements needed to communicate in a language—are thus provided in this text.

This book can be assigned to the student for independent study and review at home or for work in the classroom. The chapters are arranged according to the complexity of the structure, but, for the most part, they can be used in whatever sequence meets the needs of a particular group of students. If you feel that the vocabulary or subject matter of a chapter is too challenging, the grammatical structure can be introduced in a simpler context, and the chapter can be used as a review rather than an introduction.

Chapter Format

Each grammar chapter is introduced with a dialog, cartoon strip, or reading passage that illustrates the target structure. The dialogs consist of conversations among six main characters. Next follows a variety of activities related to the dialog, cartoon strip, or reading passage: comprehension questions, grammar fill-ins, or role playing. The chapter then proceeds to an explanation of the structure, which is highlighted by contextualized examples. Additional exercises follow.

Because *English Alive* is a low-level text, the explanations have been kept as simple and as clear as possible. For example, in the chapter on verbs followed by infinitives and gerunds, not only is the list of verbs limited, but also no mention is made of such problem verbs as *remember* and *forget,* which change meaning according to the verb form that follows. "I forgot to tell him about it" is different in meaning from, "I forgot telling him about it." The intent is to avoid overloading low-level students with information.

The *function* and *setting* chapters have a different format from that of the grammar chapters. The student is given short sample conversations that contain necessary expressions and is then asked to practice these conversations with the aid of dialog guides in which certain parts are left blank.

Suggestions for Using the Grammar Chapters:
Dialogs

Although the dialogs do contain some elements of natural conversation, such as "yeah" instead of "yes," they are not intended to be an accurate reflection of the spoken language. Nor are they meant to be memorized. They are simply intended to provide examples of the use of key structures in spoken English. There are several different ways in which you can introduce the dialog. You may have the students first read it silently and then read it again as you read it aloud. You can then ask them to answer the comprehension questions and do any other follow-up activities for the dialog. If you wish to use the dialog for listening comprehension practice, there is a tape with all the dialogs available for purchase. Start by describing the situation of the dialog and directing the students to preview the comprehension questions in the text, reminding them not to read the dialog. The class will probably need at least two chances to listen before they attempt to answer. If your own voice is your only classroom resource, you can write the names of the characters on the board and shift position when reading each one's lines. Opportunities to use the target structures are then provided through comprehension questions, oral and written fill-in exercises, questions designed to elicit opinions on the issues raised, or, where appropriate, role playing in a situation similar to that of the dialog.

Grammar Explanations and Examples

The explanations for the grammatical structures are given in simple, clear language. Again, since the intent is to avoid overloading the student with information, some explanations may appear to be oversimplified, but students at this level learn best by putting grammar rules into practice, not by reading about them. You may prefer not to take up valuable class time going over the explanations and examples. If so, you can assign them for homework either before or after beginning a chapter, since all of the examples provided relate to the content focus of the chapter.

Exercises

More mileage can be obtained from the grammar fill-ins if they are first used as listening comprehension exercises and then as writing exercises, either in class, where the teacher can provide individual help on the spot, or at home. Many exercises also lead either to general discussions or specific questions that call for student opinions.

In this edition, multipart activities feature an open box (☐) preceding the directions for each part of the activity.

Reading Passages

The reading passages are rich in useful vocabulary. Before each passage is a list of difficult vocabulary items you may wish to preteach. Or you may choose, instead, to go over the pronunciation with the class and then to ask the students to guess meanings from the context of the reading passage. As in the case of the dialogs, the reading passages are followed by various activities. Again, additional use can be made of the passages by dividing them into shorter sections and letting them serve as listening comprehension exercises.

The teachers who have tested this book in their classes at Columbia University's American Language Program and elsewhere have found that it provides a solid core of material for an introductory program of English study and that the variety and substance of the subject matter generate a high level of student interest. It is our belief that the text provides a strong foundation for an accurate and fluent command of the language and makes the study of English an enjoyable and communicative experience.

Acknowledgments

Without the moral support and generous released-time grant given to us by Ward Dennis, dean of the School of General Studies at Columbia University, and Louis Levi, former chair of the American Language Program, this book would not have been possible. We wish to express to both of them our gratitude and appreciation.

We also wish to express our thanks for the advice, criticism, and support received from our colleagues at the American Language Program of Columbia University, expecially Mary Colonna, Irene Schoenberg, Susan Sklar, Thad Ferguson, Diana Berkowitz and Winnie Falcon. Thanks also to Leslie Freeman for her encouragement, to Ellen Lehrberger for her contributions to Chapter 13, and to Kathleen Savage for her special help in editing the manuscript.

We also are grateful for the helpful comments of these reviewers: Erik J. Beukenkamp, Cornell University; Jayne C. Harder, University of Florida; Donna Jurich, San Francisco State University; Patrick T. Kameen, University of Louisville; Robert L. Saitz, Boston University; Ellen Shaw, New York University; and Peter Thomas and Jody Stern, University of California at San Diego.

BRIEF CONTENTS

1. *The Present Continuous Tense* **2**
2. *The Future Tense with* Going to **18**
3. *The Simple Past Tense* **28**
4. Was *and* Were **46**
5. *There Is, There Are, There Was, There Were* **56**
6. *The Simple Present Tense* **68**
7. *Integration of Present Continuous, Simple Present, Simple Past, and Future (*Going to*) Tenses* **90**
8. *Count and Mass Nouns* **96**
9. *The Future Tense with* Will **110**
10. Can *and* Could **121**
11. Should **132**
12. Have to **138**
13. *Verb + Infinitive, Verb + Gerund* **159**
14. *Comparative Forms of Adjectives and Adverbs* **174**
15. *Superlative Forms of Adjectives* **194**
16. *Simple Present Tense Time Clauses* **204**
17. *Simple Past Tense Time Clauses* **210**
18. *Integration of Verb Forms for Chapters 1–17* **217**
19. *The Past Continuous Tense* **222**
20. *The Present Perfect Continuous Tense* **236**
21. *Future Time Clauses* **250**
22. *Real Conditional for Future Events—If, Will* **262**
23. *Present Unreal Conditional* **270**
24. *The Passive Voice with the Simple Past and Simple Present Tenses* **278**
25. *Integration of Tenses and Verb Forms* **289**
26. *Invitations with* Would You Like **295**
27. *Giving Directions* **303**
28. *Making Suggestions with* Let's *and* Why Don't **312**
29. *Requests and Favors* **316**
30. *Travel* **320**
31. *In a Restaurant* **327**
32. *Visiting a Friend's Home* **332**
33. *A Visit to the Doctor* **336**
34. *Using the Telephone* **344**
35. *Shopping for Clothes* **351**
    Appendix: Irregular Verbs in English **357**
    Index **363**

CONTENTS

Preface **vii**
Acknowledgments **x**

1. THE PRESENT CONTINUOUS TENSE   2
    CONTENT FOCUS: INTRODUCTION OF CHARACTERS   3

    Cartoon Strip   3
    The Present Continuous Tense   4
      Statements   4 • Contractions   5 • Questions   9
        Short Answers   10
      Vocabulary   15

2. THE FUTURE TENSE WITH *GOING TO*   18
    CONTENT FOCUS: A TRIP TO WASHINGTON, D.C.   19

    Dialog   19 • Comprehension Questions   19 • Grammar Fill-in   20
    The Future Tense with *Going to*   20
      Questions   20
    Reading—A Trip to Washington, D.C.   22
      Vocabulary   22 • Comprehension Questions   23 • Question Practice—Oral   23 • Question Practice—Written   24 • Dictation   25 • Interview   26
    Using the Present Continuous Tense to Talk about the Future   26

3. THE SIMPLE PAST TENSE   28
    CONTENT FOCUS: A MUGGING   29

    Dialog   29 • Comprehension Questions   29 • Discussion Questions   29 • Grammar Fill-in   30
    The Simple Past Tense   31
      Affirmative Statements   31
        Irregular Verbs   31 • *Regular Verbs*   32 • *Pronunciation*   32
      Negative Statements   33 • Questions   33
        Discussion   35

Reading—The Youngest Bank Robber 42
  Vocabulary 42 • Comprehension Questions 43 • Discussion Questions 43 • Role Playing 43
Irregular Verbs 44

4. WAS AND WERE 46

CONTENT FOCUS: AMERICAN HISTORY 47

  Interview 47 • Vocabulary 47
Was and Were 48
  Statements 48 • Questions 48 • Short Answers 49
  Vocabulary 51 • Vocabulary 53

5. THERE IS, THERE ARE, THERE WAS, THERE WERE 56

CONTENT FOCUS: DISNEYLAND AND CALIFORNIA 57

  Dialog 57 • Comprehension Questions 58 • Dictation 58 • Role Playing 59
There Is, There Are, There Was, There Were 59
  Present Tense 59
    Statements 59
  Vocabulary 60
    Questions 61
  Past Tense 63
    Statements 63 • *Questions* 63
  Listening Comprehension Questions 65

6. THE SIMPLE PRESENT TENSE 68

CONTENT FOCUS: HOLIDAYS IN THE UNITED STATES 69

  Dialog 69 • Comprehension 69
The Simple Present Tense 69
  Statements 70 • Vocabulary 71 • Questions 72 • Short Answers 73 • Frequency 77
    Adverbs of Frequency 77 • *How Often* 78
  The Two Present Tenses of English 82 • Vocabulary 87

7. INTEGRATION OF PRESENT CONTINUOUS, SIMPLE PRESENT, SIMPLE PAST, AND FUTURE (GOING TO) TENSES 90

CONTENT FOCUS: SOME PROBLEMS IN A MARRIAGE 91

  Comprehension Questions 93 • Opinion Questions 93 • Role Playing 94

8. COUNT AND MASS NOUNS — 96

CONTENT FOCUS: FOOD—COOKING AND SHOPPING — 97

Dialog 97 • Comprehension Questions 98 • What about You? 98 • Grammar Fill-in 98

Count and Mass Nouns 99
Large Quantities 100 • Small Quantities 100
Count Nouns 100 • *Mass Nouns* 101
Questions 101
Count Nouns 101 • *Mass Nouns* 101
A Few and *a Little* 103 • *Only a Little* and *Only a Few* 104 • Containers 106

9. THE FUTURE TENSE WITH *WILL* — 110

CONTENT FOCUS: A BIRTHDAY DINNER — 111

Dialog 111 • Comprehension Questions 112 • What Do You Think? 112 • Grammar Fill-in 112

The Future Tense with *Will* 113
Affirmative Statements 113 • Negative Statements 114 • Questions 115

10. *CAN* and *COULD* — 121

CONTENT FOCUS: SPECIAL ABILITIES — 122

Dialog 122 • Comprehension Questions 122 • What about You? 122 • Dictation 123

Can* and *Could 124
Present Tense 124
Statements 124 • *Questions* 124 • *Short Answers* 124
Past Tense 128
Statements 128 • *Questions* 128
Discussion 131

11. *SHOULD* — 132

CONTENT FOCUS: DIFFICULTIES IN LIVING IN A DIFFERENT COUNTRY OR CULTURE — 133

Dialog 133 • Comprehension Questions 133 • What Do You Think? 134 • Role-Playing 134
Should 134

12. *HAVE TO* — 138

CONTENT FOCUS: SCHOOL LIFE — 139

Dialog 139 • Comprehension Questions 140 • What Do You Think? 140 • Grammar Fill-in 140 • Role Playing 141
Have to 142
Vocabulary 143 • Vocabulary 144 • Vocabulary 145 • Negative of *Have to* 150 • *Must* and *Have to* 152 • *Must Not* and *Don't Have to* 152 • Vocabulary 153 • Past Tense of *Have to* and *Must* 155

13. VERB + INFINITIVE, VERB + GERUND 159

CONTENT FOCUS: THE BIG CHOICE—MARRIAGE? CAREER? CHILDREN? 160

Dialog 160 • Comprehension Questions 160 • What Do You Think? 161 • Grammar Fill-in 161 • Role Playing 162
Verb + Infinitive, Verb + Gerund 163
Verb + Infinitive 163
  Role Playing 165
Verb + Gerund 165 • Verb + Infinitive or Gerund 168 • Verb + Object + Infinitive 169 • Role Playing 173

14. COMPARATIVE FORMS OF ADJECTIVES AND ADVERBS 174

CONTENT FOCUS: STEREOTYPES ABOUT MEN AND WOMEN 175

Vocabulary 175
Are Men and Women Equal? 175
Comparative Forms of Adjectives and Adverbs 176
  The Comparative Forms of Adjectives 176
    Short Adjectives 177 • *Two-Syllable Adjectives* 177 • *Long Adjectives* 177 • *Irregular Comparative* 178
  The Comparative Forms of Adverbs 180
    Adverbs with -ly 180 • *Adverbs without -ly* 180 • *Irregular Comparative* 180
  Vocabulary 181 • Expressing Equality 182 • What Do You Think? 183 • What Do You Think? 184 • Expressing Inequality 185 • Vocabulary 185 • Questions with Comparative Adjectives and Adverbs 188
    Who, Which, Whose 188 • Yes/No Questions 188
Reading—Stereotypes about Different Nationalities 190
  Vocabulary 190 • Stereotypes about Americans 191 • Vocabulary 191 • Stereotypes about Japanese 191 • Vocabulary 192 • Stereotypes about Italians 192 • Vocabulary 192 • Stereotypes about Latin Americans 193 • Discussion 193

15. SUPERLATIVE FORMS OF ADJECTIVES — 194
CONTENT FOCUS: FAMOUS PEOPLE — 195

Reading—Abraham Lincoln 195
Superlative Forms of Adjectives 197
 Short Adjectives 197 • Long Adjectives 197 • Irregular Superlatives 197
One of the 199

16. SIMPLE PRESENT TENSE TIME CLAUSES — 204
CONTENT FOCUS: CUSTOMS AND MANNERS IN THE UNITED STATES — 205

Some American Wedding Customs 205
Simple Present Tense Time Clauses 205
 Statements 205 • Questions 206

17. SIMPLE PAST TENSE TIME CLAUSES — 210
CONTENT FOCUS: STORIES FROM THE MAJOR RELIGIONS OF THE WORLD — 211

Reading—The Story of Adam and Eve 211
 Vocabulary 211
Simple Past Tense Time Clauses 212
 Statements 212 • Questions 212
Reading—The Life of Buddha 214
 Vocabulary 214
Reading—The Life of Muhammad 215
 Vocabulary 215
Free Assignment 216

18. INTEGRATION OF VERB FORMS FOR CHAPTERS 1–17 — 217
CONTENT FOCUS: PARENTS AND TEENAGERS — 218

 What Do You Think? 221

19. THE PAST CONTINUOUS TENSE — 222
CONTENT FOCUS: POLTERGEISTS AND GHOSTS — 223

 Dialog 223 • Comprehension Questions 223 • What Do You Think? 224 • Grammar Fill-in 224

The Past Continuous Tense 225
  The Past Continuous Tense with Interrupted Action 225
    When 225 • *While* 226
  Questions with *When* Clauses 226
    Vocabulary 227 • *Vocabulary* 230
  Reading—The Ghosts of King Henry VIII's Wives 233
    Vocabulary 233 • Comprehension Questions 235 • Telling a Story 235

20. THE PRESENT PERFECT CONTINUOUS TENSE 236
Picture Stories 237
  What Do You Think? 238
The Present Perfect Continuous Tense 238
  Statements 238 • Questions 239
    Short Answers 239
  Time Expressions 240
Simple Present Perfect of *Be, Have,* and *Know* 244
  Be 244 • *Have* 244 • *Know* 244
Contrast of Simple Past, Present Continuous, and Present Perfect Continuous Tenses 248

21. FUTURE TIME CLAUSES 250
CONTENT FOCUS: A STORY WITH A MORAL; PROVERBS 251

Reading—"Don't Count Your Chickens before They Hatch" 251
  Vocabulary 251 • Comprehension Questions 252
Future Time Clauses 252
Reading—Proverbs 259

22. REAL CONDITIONAL FOR FUTURE EVENTS— *IF, WILL* 262
CONTENT FOCUS: WORRY 263

  Dialog 263 • Comprehension Questions 263 • What Do You Think? 264 • Grammar Fill-in 264
Real Conditional for Future Events—*If, Will* 265
  Statements 265 • Questions 266

23. PRESENT UNREAL CONDITIONAL 270
CONTENT FOCUS: BAD HABITS 271

  Dialog 271 • Comprehension Questions 271 • How about You? 271
Present Unreal Conditional 272
  Contractions 272
  Questions 275

24. THE PASSIVE VOICE WITH THE SIMPLE PAST AND SIMPLE PRESENT TENSES   278

    CONTENT FOCUS: KNOWLEDGE OF WORLD HISTORY   279

Quiz   279
The Passive Voice with the Simple Past and Simple Present Tenses   281
    Statements   281   •   Questions   285   •   Answers   287   •   Quiz   287

25. INTEGRATION OF TENSES AND VERB FORMS   289

    CONTENT FOCUS: GETTING INTO SHAPE   290

26. INVITATIONS WITH *WOULD YOU LIKE*   295

Would You Like + Noun   296
    How to Offer   296   •   Other Ways to Accept or Refuse   298
Would You Like to + (Base Form of Verb)?   299
    More Ways to Offer   299   •   More Ways to Accept or Refuse   301

27. GIVING DIRECTIONS   303

Questions and Answers   304
Words That Tell Place   308
    Between   308   •   *On the Corner of*   308   •   *Across the Street from*   309   •   *Around the Corner From*   309   •   *Next to*   310

28. MAKING SUGGESTIONS WITH *LET'S* AND *WHY DON'T*   312

29. REQUESTS AND FAVORS   316

30. TRAVEL   320

How to Ask for Directions for the Train and Bus   321
    Dialog Practice   321
How to Ask for Airline Information   322
    Dialog Practice   322
How to Make a Reservation with an Airline   322
    Dialog Practice   323
How to Ask for for Information about a Flight   323
    Dialog Practice   323
Checking in at the Airport   324
    Dialog Practice   324
How to Make Hotel Reservations   324
    Dialog Practice   325

Checking in at the Hotel 326
    Dialog Practice 326
  Role Playing 326

31. IN A RESTAURANT 327
  Making a Reservation by Phone 328
    Dialog Practice 328
  Entering a Restaurant 328
    Dialog Practice 328
  Ordering 329
    Dialog Practice 330
  The Check 330
    Dialog Practice 331
  American Customs 331
    Role Playing 331

32. VISITING A FRIEND'S HOME 332
  When the Guest Arrives 333
    Dialog Practice 333
  At the Dinner Table 334
    Dialog Practice 334
  When the Guest Leaves 335
    Dialog Practice 335
  Role Playing 335

33. A VISIT TO THE DOCTOR 336
  How to Describe Medical Problems 337
  How to Make Appointments 343

34. USING THE TELEPHONE 344
  Long-Distance Calls 345
    Station-to-Station 345
    Dialog Practice 345
    Person-to-Person and Collect 345
    Dialog Practice 346
  Information 346
    Dialog Practice 347
  Wrong Number 347
    Dialog Practice 347
  Busy Signal 348
    Dialog Practice 348
  Leaving a Message 349
    Dialog Practice 349
  Some Important Telephone Numbers 349
  Role Playing 350

35. SHOPPING FOR CLOTHES 351

May I Help You? 352
   Dialog Practice 352
What Size? What Other Colors? 353
   Dialog Practice 353
Trying On 353
   Dialog Practice 354
The Fit 354
   Dialog Practice 354
Paying 355
   Dialog Practice 355
American Sizes 356
   Women's Sizes 356 • *Men's Sizes* 356
   For More Practice

Appendix: Irregular Verbs in English 357
Index 363

ENGLISH ALIVE

Joe
Joe is studying for a master of business administration degree at Columbia University and is working part-time as a waiter to help pay for his courses.

Diane
Diane is studying to become a doctor. She's working at a large hospital. She's a resident there. She and Joe are dating.

Maria
Maria is from Colombia. She is studying for a master's degree in history at Columbia University.

Hiro
Hiro is from Japan. He is studying English at the American Language Program of Columbia University. He and Joe are roommates.

Bill
Bill is an old childhood friend of Joe's. He is a manager at the telephone company. Bill is married to Ruth.

Ruth
Ruth is a social worker and is also taking part-time courses in her field. She and Bill have a son, Billy, Jr.

1 THE PRESENT CONTINUOUS TENSE

Content Focus | **INTRODUCTION OF CHARACTERS**

Cartoon Strip

Read the cartoon strip and pay attention to the verbs in boldface type.

1.
- Oh! Pardon me.
- Ow! You're **standing** on my foot.

2.
- Hey! you're **pushing** me!
- I'm sorry, but the bus is crowded. People **are pushing** me.

3.
- Mommy, what's that boy **doing**? Look, Mommy. He's **writing** on the bus.

4.
- I'm late. This bus **isn't going** very fast.
- No, it **isn't**. The driver **is daydreaming**.

5.

> Are those two boys looking at us?
>
> Yes, they **are**. I think they're cute.

6.

> Why **are** you **reading** my newspaper?

THE PRESENT CONTINUOUS TENSE

Use the present continuous tense to talk about something that is happening now (at the present moment).

Statements

```
I,                    am                    base form
he, she,              is     (not)    +        of       +   -ing
you, we, they         are                   the verb
```

You are pushing me.

Example

> Ow! You're **standing** on my foot.
>
> Oh! Pardon me.

The Present Continuous Tense _____ 5

Contractions

I'm	I'm not		
he's, she's, it's	he's not	or	he isn't
you're, we're, they're	you're not	or	you aren't

ACTIVITY 1A

Fill in the present continuous form of the verb. Write your sentences on the lines below the pictures.

1. (*sleep*)

   SH! The baby *is sleeping*.

2. (*wash*) (*help*)

   Where's Daddy?
   He _____ the car outside. We _____ him.

3. (*wash*)

   John, where are you? Please answer the phone. I _____ the dishes, and my hands are wet.

4. (*study*)

   Please don't turn on the stereo. I _____ for a test.

5. (*snore*)   6. (*demonstrate*)

Wake up, dear. You _____.

Look at all those people over there.
They _____ against nuclear power.

_____

_____

■ Activity 1B

Practice having short telephone conversations with a partner. Follow the example. Choose a verb from the following list to use for the last line of the conversation: *read, study, watch, write, take, wash, look.*

Example

JOHN: Hello?
MARY: Hi, John. This is Mary. How are you?
JOHN: I'm fine. And you?
MARY: Fine, thanks. Are you busy?
JOHN: No, not really. ___*I'm watching*___ TV.

1. STUDENT 1: _____?

   STUDENT 2: Hi, (name). _____ (name).

   How _____?

The Present Continuous Tense

    STUDENT 1: _____ fine. And you?

    STUDENT 2: Fine, thanks. _____
                       busy?

    STUDENT 1: No, not really. _____
                       the newspaper.

2. STUDENT 1: _____?

    STUDENT 2: Hi, (name). _____(name).

                       How _____?

    STUDENT 1: _____ fine. And you?

    STUDENT 2: Fine, thanks. _____
                       busy?

    STUDENT 1: No, not really. _____
                       a letter.

3. STUDENT 1: _____?

    STUDENT 2: Hi, (name). _____(name).

                       How _____?

    STUDENT 1: _____ fine. And you?

    STUDENT 2: Fine, thanks. _____
                       busy?

    STUDENT 1: No, not really. _____
                       English.

Activity 1C

Fill in the present continuous tense of the verb. Make negative statements.

1. (cook)

"Hey! It's 6:30, and you _aren't cooking_ dinner. I'm hungry."

"I'm on strike. You cook!"

2. (drive)

"What's the matter? I _____ fast."

"No, you aren't, but you _____ very well, either."

3. (rain)

"It _____ outside. The window washer is cleaning the windows."

4. (study)

"David, turn off that radio. Your sister is studying."

"She _____. She's talking on the phone."

5. (*work*) (*sweat*)   6. (*talk*)

Come on you guys. You _____ very hard today. You _____. Move! Ten more times around the gym.

Come on, Fatso.
What? Are you talking to me?
No, no. I _____ to you. My dog's name is Fatso.

_____   _____

_____   _____

Questions

Question word + { am / is / are } + subject + base form + **-ing**?

Why are you reading my newspaper?

Example

Mommy, what's that boy **doing**? Look, Mommy. He's **writing** on the bus.

SHORT ANSWERS

When we can answer a question in the present continuous tense with *yes* or *no*, we usually add the subject and *be* to the short answer.

Example

Are those two boys **looking** at us?
    Yes, they **are**.

Yes, I am.   No, I'm not.
Yes, you/we/they are.   No, you/we/they aren't.   or   No, you're not.
Yes, he/she is.   No, he/she isn't.   or   No, he's not.

ACTIVITY 1D

Work with a partner. One student will ask questions with *What* + (*am/is/are*) + (subject) + *doing*? The other student will answer the questions.

1. (*look*)   2. (*make*)

The Present Continuous Tense — *11*

3. (*fix*)

"____ Daddy ____?"
"____ the sink."

4. (*rob*)

"____ those men ____?"
"____ the bank."

_____
_____

_____
_____

5. (*put on*)

"____ you two ____?"
"____ your makeup. We're big now."

_____
_____

Don't ask questions with **doing** here. Use another verb.

❑ Work with a partner. One student will ask questions with *what* + (*am/is/are*) + subject + base form + *-ing?*. The other students will answer the questions.

1. (cook)

"What are you cooking?"
"I'm cooking chicken in red wine sauce."

2. (read)

"_____ you _____?"
"_____ a mystery by Agatha Christie."

3. (watch)

"_____ you _____?"
"_____ a new show. I don't know the name."

4. (listen)

"_____ Sam _____ to?"
"_____ to a new record by U2."

The Present Continuous Tense _____ 13

5. (*make*)

"_____ these people _____ ?"
"_____ shirts."

_____

_____

❑ Work with a partner. One student will ask yes/no questions. The other student will give short answers.

1. (*enjoy*)

"<u>Are</u> you *enjoying* the party?"
"<u>No, I'm not</u>. <u>It isn't a great party</u>."

2. (*come*)

"_____ bus _____ the _____ ?"
"No, _____ ."

_____   _____

_____   _____

3. (*look*)

"_____ the teacher _____ ?"
"No, _____."

4. (*win*)

"_____ the Yankees _____ ?"
"Yes, _____."

5. (*snow*)

"_____ it _____ ?"
"Yes, _____."

Activity 1E

We also use the present continuous tense to talk about the extended present. In sentences about the extended present, *now* doesn't mean "this moment only"; it means "these days" or "nowadays." With verbs such as *study, work,* and *teach,* we often use the present continuous tense to talk about the extended present. In the pictures, you see the people that you will meet in many of the dialogs and activities in this book. Read the information about these people under the pictures. You may need to look at the vocabulary list first.

Vocabulary

waiter: a man who serves customers in a restaurant. A waiter takes orders and brings the food to the table.

date: to go out to the movies, a restaurant, a club, and so on, with a person of the opposite sex

roommate: a person who shares your apartment

manager: a person who directs other workers in a company

social worker: a person who helps people who have problems in the society, for example, poor people, or teenagers who run away from home

resident: a doctor working in a hospital right after graduation from medical school. After a person gets a degree in medicine, he or she must work as a resident in a hospital for a period of time.

Joe
Joe is studying for a master of business administration degree at Columbia University and is working part-time as a waiter to help pay for his courses.

Diane
Diane is studying to become a doctor. She's working at a large hospital. She's a resident there. She and Joe are dating.

Maria
Maria is from Colombia. She is studying for a master's degree in history at Columbia University.

Hiro
Hiro is from Japan. He is studying English at the American Language Program of Columbia University. He and Joe are roommates.

Bill
Bill is an old childhood friend of Joe's. He is a manager at the telephone company. Bill is married to Ruth.

Ruth
Ruth is a social worker and is also taking part-time courses in her field. She and Bill have a son, Billy, Jr.

❑ Draw lines to match the picture of the person with the information about that person. (Don't look back at what you just read.) Then write a sentence to tell what the person is doing.

English
Joe's roommate

Colombia
master's degree in history

a resident at a large hospital

a social worker
part-time courses in social work

master of business administration
waiter

a manager at the telephone company
Ruth
a childhood friend of Joe's

❑ Write questions with *who*. Your answer to each question will be the subject of the sentence. Notice that *who* is the subject of the verb. There is no other subject in the question.

Who + *is* + verb + *ing*?

> **Example**
> *Who is studying* _____ for a degree in business administration?
> Joe is.

1. _____ part-time courses in social work?
   Ruth is.

2. _____ English?
   Hiro is.

The Present Continuous Tense

3. _____ at a hospital?
   Diane is.

4. _____ for the telephone company?
   Bill is.

5. _____ Diane?
   Joe is.

6. _____ for a degree in history?
   Maria is.

Note: *What* questions about the subject of the sentence are similar. Notice that *what* is the subject of the verb. There is no other subject in the question.

> ### *Example*
> JOE: **What's making** that beep-beep noise?
> DIANE: My beeper. They're calling me from the hospital.

2 THE FUTURE TENSE WITH *GOING TO*

The Jefferson Memorial in Washington, D.C.

Content Focus — A Trip to Washington, D.C.

Dialog

(HIRO is from Japan. He's studying English in a high-intermediate class at the American Language Program of Columbia University. JOE is his roommate. He's studying for a master of business administration degree at Columbia University. In the dialog HIRO and JOE are walking on the university campus. Joe is waving to a friend. It is 5:30 P.M.)

HIRO: Who are you waving to?

JOE: That's Maria. She's in my economics class.

HIRO: Hey, she's walking our way. She's really pretty. Introduce me.

JOE: Okay. Maria, come over here and meet my friend. Maria, this is my roommate, Hiro.

MARIA: Hi. It's nice to meet you.

HIRO: Nice to meet you too.

JOE: Listen. **I'm going to say** good-bye. I'm meeting Diane. **We're going to go** to a movie tonight. See you.

MARIA: Bye.

HIRO: See you later.

It's 11:30 P.M. now. JOE is coming into the apartment. HIRO is smiling.)

JOE: What are you so happy about? You're grinning from ear to ear.

HIRO: Maria and I **are going to go** out this weekend.

JOE: Oh, yeah? That's fast work. That's great! Which night **are you going to see** her—Friday or Saturday?

HIRO: **I'm going to see** her Sunday. She **isn't going to be** in town on Friday and Saturday.

JOE: Where's **she going to be?**

HIRO: She's **going to visit** a friend in Washington, D.C.

JOE: What **are you going to do** on Sunday?

HIRO: **I'm going to take** her out to dinner.

JOE: To a Japanese restaurant?

HIRO: Yeah, I think so. Listen, thank you for introducing me to Maria. She's terrific.

Comprehension Questions

1. Who is Hiro going to go out with this weekend?
2. Which night is he going to see Maria?
3. Why isn't he going to see Maria on Friday or Saturday night?
4. Where's Maria going to be on Friday and Saturday?
5. What kind of restaurant is Hiro going to take Maria to on Sunday?

Grammar Fill-in

Read the second part of the dialog again. Pay careful attention to the words in boldface type. Then fill in as many blanks as possible without looking back at the dialog.

JOE: What are you so happy about? You're grinning from ear to ear.

HIRO: Maria and I _____ this weekend.

JOE: Oh, yeah? That's fast work. That's great! Which night _____—Friday or Saturday?

HIRO: _____ Sunday. She _____ in town on Friday and Saturday.

JOE: Where _____?

HIRO: She _____ a friend in Washington, D.C.

JOE: What _____ on Sunday?

HIRO: I _____ her out to dinner.

THE FUTURE TENSE WITH *GOING TO*

When we want to talk about our plans or intentions for a time in the future, we use this pattern.

subject + { am / is / are } **(not) going to** + base form of verb

Hiro is going to take Maria out to dinner.

Questions

(question word) + { am / is / are } + subject + **going to** + base form?

What are you going to do?

The Future Tense with Going To _____ 21

Examples

(This is part of Maria and Hiro's conversation from 5:30.)

HIRO: Say, um... Maria, what **are you going to do** this weekend? Are you free?

MARIA: Well, **I'm not going to be** in town. **I'm going to visit** a friend in Washington, D.C.

HIRO: Oh. Well...uh...uh, how about Sunday? **Are** you **going to be** here Sunday?

MARIA: Yes, I **am.** I'm free Sunday evening.

HIRO: How about dinner Sunday night?

MARIA: That's fine.

These are some of the time expressions that we use with the future tense.

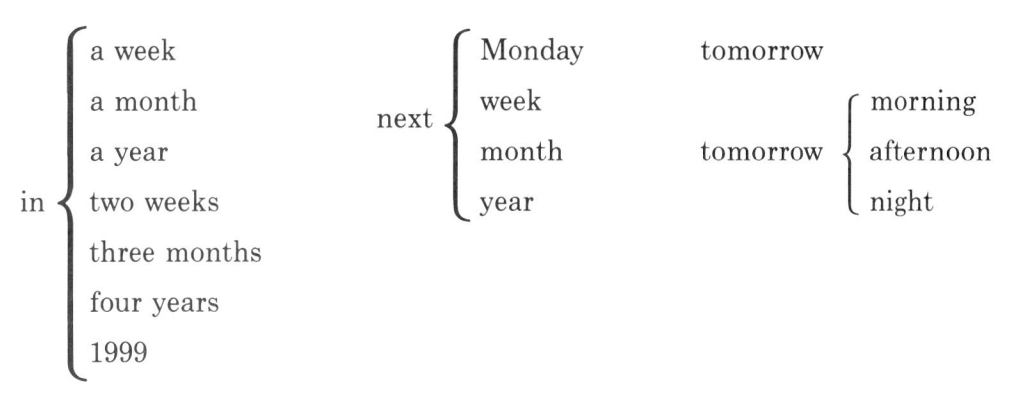

in {a week, a month, a year, two weeks, three months, four years, 1999}

next {Monday, week, month, year}

tomorrow

tomorrow {morning, afternoon, night}

■ ACTIVITY 2A

This exercise continues Joe and Hiro's conversation from the dialog. Use the future tense (going to) with the verb below the blank.

JOE: What __are__ you __going to wear__ on your date with
(wear)
Maria Sunday night?

HIRO: I _____ my new suit.
(wear)

JOE: That's too formal. Wear your jeans and a sports jacket.

HIRO: How about your sports jacket? _____ you

_____ it Sunday night?
(wear)

JOE: No, I _____. Go ahead and wear it.

Hiro: Thanks. What _____ you and Diane _____ this weekend?
(do)

Joe: We _____ a wrestling match Saturday night.
(see)

Hiro: A what?

Joe: A wrestling match. Gorgeous George _____ Ugly Ike.
(fight)

Hiro: Professional American wrestling is a joke.

Joe: I know, but this match Saturday night _____ funny.
(be)

READING—A TRIP TO WASHINGTON, D.C.

Vocabulary

capital: the city where the government offices of a country are located
tourist attraction: a place that many tourists like to visit
monument: a building or statue that makes us remember an important person or historical event
pleasant: nice
(be) in bloom: (to) have flowers (*The cherry trees are in bloom* means "The cherry trees have flowers on them.")
population: how many people a city, state, or country has
employee: someone who works for a company, a government, or a person
federal government: the government of a country
sight-seeing: visiting interesting places
reflection: what you see when you look into a mirror (or into a lake)
complex: a group of related buildings

Maria is going to visit a friend in Washington, D.C., this weekend. A friend of Maria's in New York has a car, and they are going to drive to Washington together. The trip from New York to Washington is four or four and one-half hours by car.

Washington is the capital of the United States. It's a major tourist attraction because many important and beautiful government buildings and national monuments are there. It's a pleasant city with many parks. It's especially lovely in the spring, when Washington's famous cherry trees are in bloom. These trees were a gift from Japan. Washington is not a very large city. The population is about 800,000. About 300,000 people are employees of the federal government.

This weekend, Maria's friend in Washington is going to take her sight-seeing. They are going to visit the White House first. This is the home of the president of the United States. The first two floors are open to the public. One of the rooms is decorated completely in rose. Another room, the Oval Room, is decorated in blue.

After they visit the White House, they are going to see the Washington Monument. It is 555 feet 5⅛ inches (169.3 meters) high, with stairs and an elevator inside. Maria and her friend aren't going to take the elevator; they are going to climb the stairs because it's more fun.

Next, they are going to visit the Lincoln Memorial. It is like a Greek temple with a statue of Abraham Lincoln inside. In front of the building is a pool. In it, you can see the reflection of the Washington Monument.

On Sunday, they are going to visit the Smithsonian Institution. The Smithsonian is a huge complex of buildings with many different museums: the National Museum of Natural History, the National Air and Space Museum, the National Museum of History and Technology, and the National Gallery of Art.

Maria is going to have a lot to talk about with Hiro on Sunday night.

Comprehension Questions

Answer these questions about the reading.

1. What's Maria going to do this weekend?
2. How's she going to get to Washington, D.C.?
3. Why is Washington, D.C., a major tourist attraction?
4. Why is the city especially lovely in the spring?
5. Is Washington, D.C., a very large city?
6. Is Maria's friend going to take her sight-seeing?
7. What are they going to visit first?
8. Are they going to see the Washington Monument? Are they going to take the elevator or the stairs to get to the top?
9. When are they going to visit the Smithsonian Institution—on Saturday or Sunday?
10. What are they going to see at the Smithsonian?

Question Practice—Oral

Don't look back at the preceding questions. Ask a classmate questions about Maria's trip to Washington, D.C., using *going to*. Start with the following words: *What, How, Who, When, Is,* and *Are.*

Question Practice—Written

Write questions about the reading. Look at the answer to the question first, and then write the correct question for the answer. Work in pairs or in groups; your instructor will walk around to help you.

1. _____?
   This weekend.

2. _____alone?
   No, she's going to drive there with a friend.

3. How long _____from New York to Washington, D.C.?
   It's about four hours by car.

4. _____?
   Because many important and beautiful government buildings and national monuments are there.

5. _____?
   No, it isn't. It's not very large.

6. _____the population of Washington, D.C.?
   About 800,000.

7. What _____first?
   They're going to visit the White House.

8. _____all the floors of the White House _____?
   No, only the first two floors are open to the public.

9. _____after the White House?
   The Washington Monument.

10. _____?
    It's 555 feet 5⅛ inches high.

11. _____the elevator?
    No, they're going to climb the stairs.

12. _____the Smithsonian Institution?
    On Sunday.

Dictation

Your instructor will read the story to you. Fill in the blanks.

Maria _____ a friend _____ Washington, D.C., this weekend. A friend of Maria's _____ New York has _____, and _____ Washington together. The trip _____ New York _____ Washington _____ four or four and one-half hours by car.

This weekend, Maria's friend in Washington _____. _____ the White House first. _____ the home of the president of the United States. The _____ two floors _____ to the public.

After they visit the White House, _____ the Washington Monument. _____ 555 feet 5⅛ inches (169.3 meters) high. Maria and her friend _____ the elevator; _____ the stairs because _____ more fun.

Next, _____ the Lincoln Memorial. _____ the building is a pool. In it, you can see the reflection of the Washington Monument.

_____ Sunday, _____ the Smithsonian Institution.

Maria _____ a lot to talk about with Hiro on Sunday night.

Interview

Imagine that you are going to take a vacation next month. Plan a vacation to some place in the world that you really want to visit. First a classmate will ask questions about your plans for the trip. Then you will ask this classmate about his or her plans. Use *going to* in your questions. Take notes about your classmate's plans, because you will tell the class about his or her vacation plans when you finish the interview.

Here are some question words and verbs to use in your questions.

When . . . leave

Where . . . go

alone . . . go

How long . . . stay

Where . . . stay

What famous places . . . visit

How . . . travel

. . . take traveler's checks or cash

How many suitcases . . . take

USING THE PRESENT CONTINUOUS TENSE TO TALK ABOUT THE FUTURE

We sometimes use the present continuous tense to talk about our plans or intentions for a time in the future.

Examples

Maria is talking to Diane about her plans for her trip to Washington, D.C. She can say, "I'm going to go to Washington, D.C., this weekend."

or

"I'm going to Washington, D.C., this weekend."

"My friend and I are going to drive there."

or

"My friend and I are driving there."

Both ways of saying this have a future meaning.

Activity 2B

Diane is asking Maria some questions about her trip to Washington, D.C. Practice using the present continuous tense to talk about the future. Work with a partner. One student will be Diane and ask the questions. The other will be Maria and answer them.

1. DIANE: When _____ for Washington?
   (leave)

   MARIA: I _____ tonight.

2. DIANE: How long _____?
   (stay)

   MARIA: I _____ for two days.

3. DIANE: How _____ there?
   (get)

   MARIA: I _____ there with my friend.
   (drive)

4. DIANE: _____ Hiro _____ with you?
   (go)

   MARIA: No. He _____ in New York this weekend.
   (stay)

5. DIANE: _____ a lot of sight-seeing this weekend?
   (do)

   MARIA: Sure. We _____ to the Washington Monument,
   (go)
   the Smithsonian Institution, the White House, and a couple of other places.

3 THE SIMPLE PAST TENSE

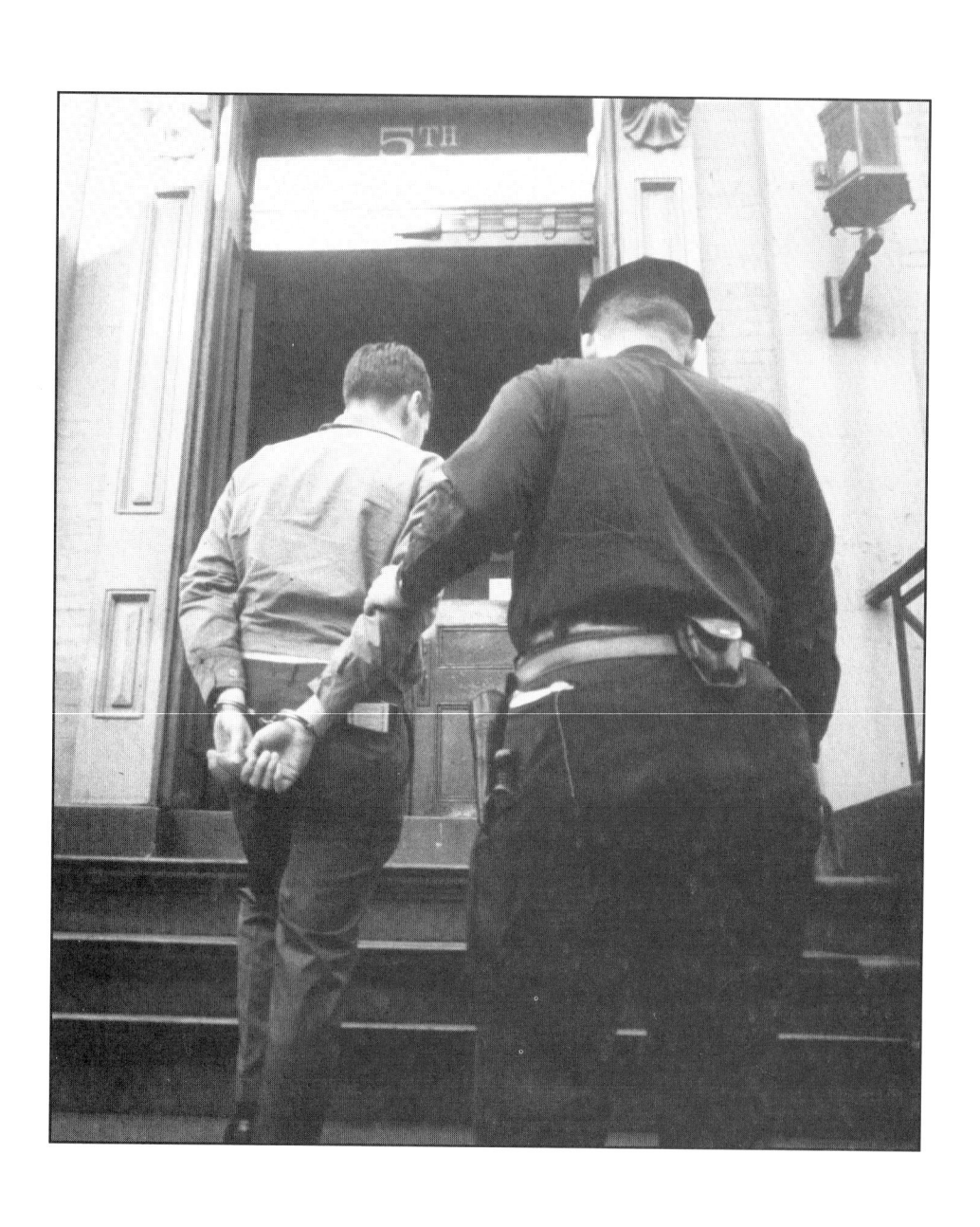

Content Focus — **A Mugging**

Dialog

(It is 9:30 p.m. Diane is Joe's girlfriend. This morning they talked and agreed to meet in front of a restaurant at 9:00 p.m. Joe is worried about Diane because she is half an hour late.)

Joe: Diane, here you are, finally. You're half an hour late. **What happened?** Wow! Your coat is a mess! **Did** you **fall?**

Diane: Yes, **I had** a terrible experience on the subway. Listen to this! A man **came** up to me and **pulled** out a knife. He **pointed** it right at me!

Joe: Oh, no! Are you all right? **Did** he **hurt** you?

Diane: No, he **didn't hurt** me, but he **took** my purse.

Joe: Then what happened? What **did** you **do?**

Diane: I **grabbed** his knife, and he **pushed** me to the floor.

Joe: Oh, no! Why **did** you **grab** his knife? That's dangerous.

Diane: I don't know. I **didn't think**.

Joe: What **did** the other passengers **do? Did** they **help** you?

Diane: Yes, they **did**. Thank God! Two men **ran** after the mugger and **held** him.

Joe: **Did** the police **come?**

Diane: Yeah. The conductor **called** a policeman, and he **arrested** the mugger.

Joe: What a story! Thank God you're all right!

Comprehension Questions

1. A man came up to Diane on the train. Then what did he do?
2. Did he hurt Diane?
3. What did Diane do?
4. Did the other passengers help her? What did they do?
5. Who called the police?
6. Did a policeman arrest the mugger?

Discussion Questions

1. Is Diane's terrible experience typical of life in a big city like New York, Chicago, or Los Angeles? Is it typical of life in the city where you live?
2. Have you heard and read many stories like this one? Do you know anyone who had a bad experience like Diane's?
3. Diane was lucky because the other passengers on the subway helped her. Is this typical, or are most people afraid to help?

Grammar Fill-in

Study this list of verbs from the dialog.

Base Form	Past Tense	Base Form	Past Tense
fall	fell	pull	pulled
have	had	point	pointed
come	came	grab	grabbed
hurt	hurt	push	pushed
take	took	help	helped
think	thought	call	called
run	ran	arrest	arrested
hold	held		

Now read the dialog again. Pay careful attention to the words in boldface type. Then fill in as many blanks as possible without looking back at the dialog.

JOE: Diane, here you are, finally. You're half an hour late. What happened? Wow! Your coat is a mess! _____?

DIANE: Yes, I _____ a terrible experience on the subway. Listen to this! A man _____ up to me and _____ out a knife. He _____ it right at me!

JOE: Oh, no! Are you all right? _____ you?

DIANE: No, he _____ me, but he _____ my purse.

JOE: Then what happened? What _____?

DIANE: I _____ his knife, and he _____ me to the floor.

JOE: Oh, no! Why _____ his knife? That's dangerous.

DIANE: I don't know. I _____.

JOE: What did the other passengers do? _____ you?

DIANE: Yes, they _____. Thank God! Two men _____.

JOE: _____ the police _____?

DIANE: Yeah. The conductor _____ a policeman, and he _____ the mugger.

JOE: What a story! Thank God you're all right!

THE SIMPLE PAST TENSE

We use the simple past tense when we talk about something that happened in the past. These are some of the time expressions that we use with the simple past tense.

yesterday	last night	a second ago	two days ago
	last week	a minute ago	a few years ago
	last year	an hour ago	

Affirmative Statements

There are two major groups of verbs in English: irregular and regular verbs. They form the simple past tense in two different ways.

IRREGULAR VERBS

☐ The past tense form (second form) of most irregular verbs is different from the base form (first form).

Base Form	Past Form	Base Form	Past Form
meet	met	come	came
tell	told	steal	stole

Examples

Diane **met** Joe in front of a restaurant a few days ago. She **told** him about her bad experience on the subway.

Regular Verbs

☐ *Formation:*
Add *-ed* or *-d* to the base form of regular verbs to form the simple past. Sometimes you need to double the last letter of the base form when you add *-ed* or *-d*.

Base Form	Past Form	Base Form	Past Form
grab	grabbed	call	called
push	pushed	arrest	arrested
help	helped		

Examples

Diane **grabbed** the man's knife, but he **pushed** her to the floor. The other passengers **helped** her. Then the conductor **called** a policeman, and he **arrested** the mugger.

Pronunciation

There are three different pronunciations for the *-ed* past-tense ending.

1. /Id/
   Pronounce *-ed* as /Id/ only with verbs that end with these letters or sounds: *t, d.*

   want → wanted   need → needed   arrest → arrested
   　　　　/Id/　　　　　　　　/Id/　　　　　　　　　/Id/

2. /d/
   Pronounce *-ed* or *-d* as /d/ with

   verbs that end with these letters or sounds: *b, g, j, l, m, n, r, v, z*
   　　　grab → grabbed   pull → pulled
   　　　　　　　　/d/　　　　　　　　　/d/

   verbs that end with vowel sounds
   　　　stay → stayed   study → studied
   　　　　　　　/d/　　　　　　　　　/d/

3. /t/
   Pronounce *-ed* or *-d* as /t/ with verbs that end with these letters or sounds: *ch, f, k, p, s, sh, x, ce*
   　　　push → pushed   watch → watched
   　　　　　　　/t/　　　　　　　　　/t/

The Simple Past Tense

Negative Statements

For negative statements, regular and irregular verbs use *did not (didn't)* + base form.

Affirmative	Negative
felt	did not feel
slept	did not sleep
went	did not go

Examples

Diane **didn't feel** well the day after her bad experience. She **didn't sleep** well that night. The next day she **didn't go** to work.

Questions

(Question word) + **did** + subject + base form?

What did you do?

Statement: Diane **stayed** home the next day.

Question: **Did** Diane **stay** home the next day?

Examples

Here is Joe's conversation with Diane on the night after her bad experience.

JOE: Hi, how are you? **Did** you **sleep** okay last night?

DIANE: No, I **didn't**. I woke up about five times. I felt terrible this morning.

JOE: **Did** you **go** to work today?

DIANE: No, I stayed in bed.

JOE: What **did** you **do** all day?

DIANE: I slept and watched TV. In the afternoon I went to the police station.

Some questions use the past tense form of the verb. Notice that in the question *What happened?* we do not use *did*. When we ask a question with *who* about the subject of the verb, we use the past tense form.

Example

Statement: A mugger took Diane's purse. *(subject of the verb: A mugger)*

Question: Who **took** Diane's purse? *(subject of the verb: Who)*

Short Answer: A mugger did.

Activity 3A

☐ Fill in the affirmative or negative form of the past tense.

Here is a list of additional irregular verbs for this exercise. Also review the short lists of irregular verbs for the dialog and the example on pages 30 and 31.

Base Form	Past Tense	Base Form	Past Tense
go	went	make	made
eat	ate	do	did
feel	felt	sleep	slept
drink	drank	put	put
sit	sat	leave	left

After Diane finished her story, she and Joe __went__ into the
                                            (go)
restaurant for dinner and a drink. Diane _____ a big
                                         (negative for **eat**)
dinner because she _____ a headache and _____
                    (have)   (negative for **feel**)
well. She only _____ a salad, and she _____ a glass
                (eat)   (drink)

The Simple Past Tense 35

of wine. Some friends _____ (meet) them in the restaurant and _____ (sit) down at their table. They _____ (listen) to Diane's story and _____ (talk) about it.

The next day, Diane _____ (negative for **go**) to work. She _____ (stay) in bed and _____ (sleep). In the afternoon, she _____ (go) to the police station. The police wanted Diane to identify the mugger. They _____ (put) the mugger in a line with other men, and Diane _____ (point) to him. The police _____ (ask) the mugger a lot of questions, but he _____ (negative for **answer**) them. Then Diane _____ (leave).

DISCUSSIONS

☐ What do you think? What happened to the mugger?

ACTIVITY 3B

Ask questions about Diane's story. Read the answer to the question first. Use the subject and the verb in parentheses after the number.

Example

(*he, do*) A man came up to Diane on the subway and pulled out a knife.

Question: Then what *did he do* _____?

Answer: He took her purse.

1. (*Diane, do*)

    Question: What _____?

    Answer: She grabbed the man's knife.

2. (*the other passengers, help*)

    Question: _____ Diane?

    Answer: Yes, they did. Two passengers caught the mugger.

3. *(the police, come)*

   Question: _____?

   Answer: Yes, a policeman came and arrested the mugger.

4. *(Diane and Joe, go)*

   Question: Where_____after she told her story?

   Answer: They went to a restaurant.

5. *(Diane, eat)*

   Question: _____a big dinner?

   Answer: No, she didn't because she had a headache.

6. *(she, eat)*

   Question: What_____?

   Answer: She only ate a salad.

7. *(Diane, tell)* Some friends met Joe and Diane in the restaurant.

   Question: _____them her story?

   Answer: Yes, she did, and they all talked about it.

8. *(Diane, go)*

   Question: _____to work the next day?

   Answer: No, she didn't. She slept late.

9. *(she, go)*

   Question: When_____to the police station?

   Answer: She went the next day.

The Simple Past Tense _____ 37

10. *(she, identify)*

    Question: _____ the mugger at the police station?

    Answer: Yes. The police put him in a line with other men, and Diane pointed to him.

11. *(the police, do)*

    Question: Then what _____?

    Answer: They asked the mugger a lot of questions.

12. *(the mugger, answer)*

    Question: _____ the questions?

    Answer: No, he didn't.

■ **ACTIVITY 3C**

Write questions beginning with *who*. Remember: Don't use *did* with *who* when you ask a question about the subject of the verb. Use the past tense of the verb.

1. *(drop)* 2. *(break)*

"Who dropped this book?"

"_____ this vase?"

_____   _____

_____   _____

3. *(eat)*

"Hey! _____ all the cake? I didn't get a piece."

4. *(put)*

"Yuk! Salty coffee! _____ salt in the sugar bowl?"

5. *(draw)*

"_____ this?"

6. *(tell)*

"I heard that you got married last week. Congratulations!"

"What? I didn't get married last week. _____ you that?"

The Simple Past Tense — 39

7. *(leave)*

"These aren't my papers. _____ them on my desk?"

8. *(take)*

"_____ this photo of you? It's a great picture."

_____

_____

9. *(take)*

"Where's my eraser? I left it here a minute ago. _____ my eraser?"

_____

_____

■ Activity 3D

- ☐ Work with one or two classmates. Don't look at the dialog or exercises. Tell the story of Diane's bad experience on the train, what she and Joe did in the restaurant, and what she did the next day.
- ☐ Think of a time in your life when you or a member of your family or a friend had a bad experience and felt very afraid. Tell this story to the class.

ACTIVITY 3E

Complete the questions. Read each answer first. Use the list of irregular verbs on pages 44–45.

> **Example**
> STUDENT 1: Boy! I'm tired today.
> STUDENT 2: Why? What _did you do_ yesterday?

1. STUDENT 1: I went to a nightclub last night and danced all night.

   STUDENT 2: Oh, yeah? _____ a good time?

   STUDENT 1: Yeah, I had a wonderful time, but I'm beat[1] today.

   STUDENT 2: What time _____ the nightclub?

   STUDENT 1: I left at about 3:00 A.M.

   STUDENT 2: I'm not surprised that you're tired. Which nightclub

   _____ to?

   STUDENT 1: The Circus. It's on Second Avenue at 53rd Street. It's really nice.

2. STUDENT 1: _____ John in class this morning? I have his book.

   STUDENT 2: No, I didn't see him. He didn't come to class. Where

   _____ his book?

   STUDENT 1: I found it in the library.

3. STUDENT 1: I had tickets to the baseball game last night. It was a great

   game. _____ it on TV?

---

[1] *I'm beat* means "I'm very tired."

The Simple Past Tense _____ 41

STUDENT 2: No, I didn't. I went to the library. Who _____?

STUDENT 1: The Yankees won again. The score was 5 to 3. Their new player from Puerto Rico is really good.

STUDENT 2: _____ a home run?

STUDENT 1: Yeah. He hit two home runs. He's fantastic.

STUDENT 2: Did you have good seats at the game? Where _____?

STUDENT 1: We sat really close.

STUDENT 2: Wow! How much _____ for the tickets?

STUDENT 1: I didn't pay anything. A friend gave me the tickets.

4. STUDENT 1: What _____ this weekend?

STUDENT 2: Well, Saturday my roommate and I drove to a big park about one and a half hours from here.

STUDENT 1: But you two don't have a car, right? _____ one?

STUDENT 2: No. We didn't need to rent one. My uncle lent us his car.

STUDENT 1: What _____ there? _____ a picnic?

STUDENT 2: Yeah. We had a great picnic—hamburgers, hot dogs, potato salad.

How about you? _____ a good weekend?

STUDENT 1: No, I didn't. I had a really rotten weekend. I had the flu.

STUDENT 2: That's too bad. _____ to the doctor?

STUDENT 1: No, I just stayed in bed. I'm okay now.

STUDENT 2: That's good.

READING— THE YOUNGEST BANK ROBBER

Vocabulary

rob:	to steal something from a person, a bank, or some other place
robber:	a person who steals
robbery:	the crime of stealing
teller:	a person who works behind the counter in a bank
holdup:	a robbery. In a holdup, the robber points a gun at people, and they think the robber will shoot if they don't give him or her the money.
hand:	to give
wave:	to hold your hand up and move it in the air to say good-bye or hello
confess:	to say that you did something
drop out of school:	to stop attending school before you have finished
lawyer:	someone who has a degree in law from a law school
blame:	to consider someone responsible for a problem
FBI:	the Federal Bureau of Investigation, a government agency that tries to solve major crimes

On February 25, 1981, a nine-year-old boy named Robert robbed the New York Bank for Savings in Manhattan. He went up to a teller, pointed a gun at her, and said, "This is a holdup. Don't say a word. Give me the money." The teller looked at the boy, looked at his gun, and then handed $118 to him. Robert walked to the door. Then he turned, waved the money in the air, smiled, and said, "Thanks a lot. Good-bye."

Robert spent almost all of the money on hamburgers and french fries and a movie. He also bought a watch for twenty-nine dollars and ninety-five cents. Two days later, with only twenty dollars in his pocket, Robert went to the FBI and confessed. The FBI took the boy to the police.

Nine-year-old Robert dropped out of school in 1980. He stayed home all day and spent hours and hours in front of the TV. The night before the robbery, he watched two programs about police and crime: "The Rockford Files" and "Adam 12." Robert's lawyer blamed TV for the boy's actions. The lawyer also told the newspaper and TV reporters, "Robert did not use a real gun in the robbery. He only had a toy gun."

Comprehension Questions
1. Nine-year-old Robert entered a bank on February 25, 1981. What did he do next?
2. What did he say to the teller?
3. Did the teller give him any money?
4. How much money did Robert take out of the bank with him?
5. Robert walked to the door of the bank and turned around. Then what did he do?
6. What did he do with the money?
7. Robert watched a lot of TV. Why?
8. What kinds of programs did he watch on the night before the robbery?
9. Who or what did Robert's lawyer blame for the boy's crime?
10. Did Robert use a real gun for the robbery?

Discussion Questions
1. The lawyer blamed TV for Robert's crime. What do you think of this? Do you agree?
2. How much responsibility for Robert's crime did the parents have? Do you think that they probably allowed Robert to watch the wrong kind of programs?
3. What do you think the parents did to punish Robert for this crime?

Role Playing
1. Work with a classmate. Imagine that you are the police. Robert came to you to confess just a few seconds ago. Think of some questions that you want to ask him about his crime. For example, "Why did you rob the bank?" "Where did you get that gun?"
2. One student is a policeman who is asking Robert questions about his crime. Another student is Robert. Role play this conversation.

IRREGULAR VERBS

Here is a list of common irregular verbs.

Base Form	Past Tense	Base Form	Past Tense
be (am, is, are)	was, were	eat	ate
become	became	fall	fell
begin	began	feed	fed
bite	bit	feel	felt
break	broke	fight	fought
bring	brought	find	found
build	built	fly	flew
buy	bought	forget	forgot
catch	caught	forgive	forgave
choose	chose	freeze	froze
come	came	get	got
cost	cost	give	gave
cut	cut	go	went
do	did	grow	grew
draw	drew	have	had
drink	drank	hear	heard
drive	drove	hide	hid
hit	hit	shake	shook
hold	held	shine	shone
hurt	hurt	shoot	shot
keep	kept	shut	shut
know	knew	sing	sang
lay	laid	sink	sank
lead	led	sit	sat
leave	left	sleep	slept
lend	lent	speak	spoke
let	let	spend	spent
light	lit	stand	stood

The Simple Past Tense

Base Form	Past Tense	Base Form	Past Tense
lose	lost	steal	stole
lie	lay	swear	swore
make	made	sweep	swept
mean	meant	swim	swam
meet	met	take	took
put	put	teach	taught
read	read	tear	tore
ride	rode	tell	told
ring	rang	think	thought
rise	rose	throw	threw
run	ran	understand	understood
say	said	wake up	woke up
see	saw	wear	wore
sell	sold	win	won
send	sent	write	wrote

4 *WAS* AND *WERE*

The Liberty Bell in Philadelphia, Pennsylvania

Content Focus **AMERICAN HISTORY**

Interview

Vocabulary

independent: not under the control of another country
colony: a group of people who go to live in a new country but stay under the control of the country from which they came
tax: money that people must pay to a government
fair: just. If two children do something bad in a class, but the teacher punishes only one of the children, it's not fair.
revolution: a time when the people of a country fight to change their government
period: a time in history
furious: very, very angry
imaginary: not real
interview: a meeting between two people about something. When a reporter for a newspaper or a TV station asks a person questions, this is called an interview.
vote: to tell the government what you want. Every four years, the citizens of the United States vote for a new president.
patriotic: loving and being ready to fight for your country. A patriotic person shows support for his or her country.

The United States **was** 200 years old in 1976. Before 1776, the United States **was** not an independent country; it **was** a colony of Great Britain. The American colonies **weren't** happy under British control. In 1765, England began to tax many things in the colonies. The Americans said that the taxes **weren't** fair, and they **were** very angry about them. The Boston Tea Party of 1773 **was** the beginning of the American Revolution.

Paul Revere **was** a famous American from this period of American history. On April 14, 1775, the night the American Revolution began, Paul Revere rode his horse through the streets and shouted, "The British are coming! The British are coming!" The following is an imaginary interview with Paul Revere.

INTERVIEWER: Where **were** you on the night of the Boston Tea Party, Mr. Revere? **Were** you there?
PAUL REVERE: Yes, I **was**. Many other patriotic Americans **were** there too.
INTERVIEWER: What **was** the Boston Tea Party? Please tell me about it.
PAUL REVERE: Several British ships **were** in Boston Harbor that day. These ships **were** full of tea with the British tax on it. We Americans **were** angry about this tax.

INTERVIEWER: Why **were** you angry about the tax? **Was** it unfair?
PAUL REVERE: Yes, it **was**. We Americans didn't vote on this tax. Only English people voted on the tax.
INTERVIEWER: **Was** the tax very high?
PAUL REVERE: No, it **wasn't**, but we didn't like it. The night of the tea party, we went onto the ships and threw all of the tea into the sea.
INTERVIEWER: **Were** the British angry? What did they do?
PAUL REVERE: They **weren't** very happy about it. King George III **was** furious. He taxed more things, and he closed Boston Harbor. Two years later, the war between America and England began.

WAS AND *WERE*

The past tense of the verb *be* is *was* or *were*.

Statements

you, we, they	were (not) / weren't
I, he, she, it	was (not) / wasn't

Examples

The Boston Tea Party **was** the beginning of the American Revolution. Americans **were** angry about the British tax on tea. They said the tax **wasn't** fair.

Questions

(question word) **were** { you / we / they } ?   (question word) **was** { I / she / he / it } ?

were { you / we / they } ?   **was** { I / he / it } ?

> ***Examples***
> INTERVIEWER: Where **were** you on the night of the Boston Tea Party?
> PAUL REVERE: I **was** on the ship.
> INTERVIEWER: Why **was** everyone so angry? **Was** the tax on the tea very high?
> PAUL REVERE: No, it **wasn't**, but it **was** very unfair.

Short Answers

When we can answer a question that begins with **was** or **were** with *yes* or *no,* we usually add the subject and *be* to the short answer. Look at the last example above.

Yes, I was.   No, I wasn't.

Yes, he/she/it was.   No, he/she/it wasn't.

Yes, you/we/they were.   No, you/we/they weren't.

ACTIVITY 4A

☐ Answer the following questions about the beginning of the American Revolution.

1. How old was the United States in 1976?
2. Was the United States an independent country in 1750?
3. Were the American colonies happy under British control? Why or why not?
4. Why were the Americans angry about the British taxes?
5. What was the Boston Tea Party?
6. Where was Paul Revere on the night of the Boston Tea Party?
7. Was the tax on the tea very high?
8. The Americans threw all of the tea into the sea. Were the British angry about this? What did they do?

☐ Study the interview with Paul Revere again. Pay careful attention to the examples with *was* and *were*. Then work with a classmate and use this guide to practice the interview.

INTERVIEWER: Where _____ on the night of the Boston Tea Party, Mr. Revere? _____ there?

PAUL REVERE: Yes, _____. Many other patriotic Americans _____.

INTERVIEWER: What _____? Please tell me about it.

PAUL REVERE: Several British _____ Boston Harbor that day. _____ full of tea with the British tax on it. We Americans _____ this tax.

INTERVIEWER: Why _____? _____ unfair?

PAUL REVERE: Yes, _____. We Americans didn't vote on this tax. Only English people voted on the tax.

INTERVIEWER: _____ very high?

PAUL REVERE: No, _____, but we didn't like it. The night of the tea party, we went onto the ships and threw all of the tea into the sea.

INTERVIEWER: _____ angry? What did they do?

PAUL REVERE: _____ very happy about it. King George III _____. He taxed more things, and he closed Boston Harbor. Two years later, the war between America and England began.

❑ Role play the preceding interview. Don't look back at the guide this time. Use your memory, but also feel free to invent some questions. It is not necessary for the interview to be exactly the same as the preceding one.

Activity 4B

Vocabulary

commander:	the most important officer in an army
brilliant:	very smart
soldier:	a person in the army
disappointed:	the feeling you get when you don't get what you thought you would. If you think that a cake looks delicious, but you taste it and it isn't, you feel disappointed. If you wait a long time to get tickets to a show and pay a lot of money, but the show isn't good, you feel disappointed.
terrible:	very bad
loyal:	faithful. Dogs are usually loyal to their masters. If a worker stays with a company, even when times are bad, and his or her pay decreases, the worker is loyal to the company.
battle:	a fight. In a war, there are many battles.
victory:	the opposite of defeat. If you win a battle, you have a victory.
crowded:	with many people close together
cheer:	to yell loudly to show that you like someone or something. People cheer for their favorite team at a baseball game.
peace:	a time without war or fighting
stubborn:	not wanting to change. If a person is stubborn, it is difficult to make that person change his or her mind or to make that person stop trying to do something.

❑ Read the following story about George Washington.

George Washington was the commander of the American army during the American Revolution. He was a brilliant soldier. He was very disappointed with his army at first. The men were brave, but they weren't good soldiers. They were farmers and businessmen, and many of them were very young. They weren't ready to fight a war.

The war with England was long and hard. The winter of 1777 was especially terrible for the American army. The army spent the winter in Valley Forge, Pennsylvania. It was a very cold winter. Washington's soldiers didn't have warm clothing, and many of them didn't have shoes. Many times the army had no food and no pay. Many of the men were sick, and many of them died during that winter. The soldiers were very angry, but they were loyal to Washington and stayed with him through that terrible winter.

The last battle of the war was in 1781. The Battle of Yorktown was a big victory for the Americans. But King George III was a stubborn man, and the English army stayed in New York for almost two more years. In 1783, King George III finally took all of his army back to England. After eight long years, the war was finally over. Washington was a big hero.

In 1787, six years after the last battle, Americans made George Washington their first president. New York City was the capital of the country at this time. On the day that Washington became president, the streets were crowded. Everyone came to see Washington and to cheer him.

Washington's eight years as president were not happy years for him. The country had a lot of problems during this time, and some people weren't happy with Washington as president. They said that he didn't understand the common people because he was from a rich family. Washington was glad to go home to his farm in Virginia in 1795. He died four years later, in 1799. Most Americans were very sad on the day of his death. They said that Washington was "first in war, first in peace, first in the hearts of his countrymen."

❑ Imagine that you are interviewing George Washington. Ask questions using *was* and *were*.

Examples

INTERVIEWER: When *were you the commander of the American army?*

WASHINGTON: During the Revolution.

INTERVIEWER: Why _____ at first?

WASHINGTON: I was disappointed because the American army wasn't very good.

INTERVIEWER: _____?

WASHINGTON: Yes, they were brave, but they weren't good soldiers.

INTERVIEWER: _____ ready to fight a war?

WASHINGTON: No. They were farmers and businessmen. They weren't soldiers.

INTERVIEWER: Why _____ the winter of 1777 _____?

WASHINGTON: Because it was very cold. My men didn't have warm clothing, and many of them didn't have shoes. Many times they had no food and no pay.

INTERVIEWER: _____ angry?

WASHINGTON: Yes, but they were loyal, and they stayed with me.

Was And Were _____ 53

INTERVIEWER: When _____?

WASHINGTON: The last battle of the war was in 1781.

INTERVIEWER: _____ a big victory for the Americans?

WASHINGTON: Yes, it was.

INTERVIEWER: How long _____?

WASHINGTON: It was eight years long. It was finally over in 1783.

INTERVIEWER: Americans made you their president in 1787. What _____ _____ at this time?

WASHINGTON: New York City. I remember the streets were crowded with people.

INTERVIEWER: _____?

WASHINGTON: No, they were not happy years for me.

INTERVIEWER: _____ to go home to your farm in Virginia in 1795?

WASHINGTON: Very glad.

■ ACTIVITY 4C

❏ Read this story about a famous battle from a later period of American history.

Vocabulary

fort: a strong building where soldiers can defend themselves well during a battle
revolt against: to start a revolution to try to change a government
several: more than two but fewer than many
republic: a nation in which the people elect the government officials. There is no king or queen.
originally: at first
stubborn: determined to do what you want to do instead of what others want you to do

The Alamo is in San Antonio, Texas. Originally it was a Spanish church and a school. Later it was an army fort.

Before 1836, Texas was a part of Mexico, but in 1836, Texas revolted against Mexico. The battle for the Alamo was important in the revolution. In this battle, only 150 Texans defended the fort. The name of the Mexican general was Santa Anna. His army had several thousand men. The Texans knew that it was impossible to win, but they were stubborn fighters. It was not an easy victory for Santa Anna. The battle lasted for two weeks, and by the end all the Texans were dead.

Mexico won this battle, but six weeks later Texans fought another battle against Mexico. During the fighting, Texans shouted, "Remember the Alamo!" This time Texas won. It became a separate republic. It was a republic for ten years, and then it became a part of the United States.

❏ Look at the answer to each question first. Then write the correct question for each answer. Use *did, was,* or *were* in the questions.

Examples

QUESTION: *Was Texas* a part of the United States in 1836?
ANSWER: No. It was a part of Mexico.

QUESTION: When *did it become* a separate republic?
ANSWER: In 1836.

1. QUESTION: How long _____ a separate republic?
   ANSWER: For ten years.

2. QUESTION: What _____ originally?
   ANSWER: A Spanish church and a school.

3. QUESTION: _____ important in the revolution against Mexico?
   ANSWER: Yes.

4. QUESTION: What _____?
   ANSWER: Santa Anna.

5. QUESTION: How many men _____?
   ANSWER: Several thousand.

6. QUESTION: _____ that it was impossible to win?
   ANSWER: Yes, they knew, but they continued to fight.

Was And Were 55

7. QUESTION: _____ stubborn fighters?
   ANSWER: Yes.

8. QUESTION: How long _____?
   ANSWER: Two weeks.

9. QUESTION: _____ an easy victory for Santa Anna?
   ANSWER: No.

10. QUESTION: _____ dead by the end of the battle?
    ANSWER: Yes.

11. QUESTION: _____ the battle of the Alamo?
    ANSWER: No, they lost it.

12. QUESTION: When _____?
    ANSWER: Six weeks later.

13. QUESTION: What _____ in this battle?
    ANSWER: "Remember the Alamo!"

14. QUESTION: _____ this battle?
    ANSWER: Yes. They won and became a separate republic.

5
THERE IS, THERE ARE, THERE WAS, AND THERE WERE

Content Focus: DISNEYLAND AND CALIFORNIA

Dialog

BILL and RUTH are on vacation. They are traveling through the western part of the United States. Tonight they are staying in a campground in Yosemite Park in California. It's 11:00 P.M., and they're getting into their sleeping bags.

RUTH: I'm tired. I think we walked about ten miles today.
BILL: Yeah. It was a long day. I'm exhausted. (ZZZzzzz ...)
RUTH: What are we going to do tomorrow?

(BILL doesn't answer. He's asleep.)

Bill? Are you asleep?
BILL: Hmm? What? I was asleep, but now I'm awake. What did you say?
RUTH: What are we going to do tomorrow?
BILL: (ZZZzzzz ...)
RUTH: Bill? Oh, never mind.

(Five minutes later.)

RUTH: Bill, wake up! Wake up!
BILL: What? Hmm? What? What's the matter?
RUTH: **There's** a noise outside the tent. Listen! **Is there** a bear outside? Bill, I think **there's** a bear outside.
BILL: What noise? Listen. It's quiet out there. **There isn't** a sound. **There aren't** any bears around here. Go back to sleep.
RUTH: **There ARE** bears around here. **There was** a story about a bear in the newspaper a week ago.
BILL: Oh?
RUTH: Yes. A bear went into a tent in this campground. **There were** some people in the tent at the time. They yelled and made a lot of noise, and the bear went away. So don't tell me **there aren't** any bears around here.

(CRASH!—a loud noise from outside the tent.)

BILL: What was that?
RUTH: Bill, I'm afraid. Go outside and look.
BILL: I'm not going out there. Maybe you're right. Maybe **there's** a bear outside. Maybe **there are** two bears.
RUTH: Look! The door of our tent is moving. Do something! I think a bear is coming in here.

(A raccoon enters the tent.)

BILL: Look! It's only a raccoon. See? **There's** nothing to be afraid of.
RUTH: Oh. Well, you were afraid too.

Comprehension Questions

1. In what part of the United States are Bill and Ruth traveling?
2. Are they sleeping in a motel tonight?
3. Why is Bill exhausted?
4. Are there any bears around Yosemite Park?
5. Is there a bear outside Bill and Ruth's tent?

Dictation

Study the first half of the dialog for a dictation. Stop studying where Bill says, "Oh?" Then listen to your instructor and write.

RUTH: _____. I think _____ about ten miles today.

BILL: Yeah. _____ a long day. _____. (ZZZzzzz ...)

RUTH: _____?

(Bill doesn't answer. He's asleep.)

Bill? _____ asleep?

BILL: Hmm? What? _____ asleep, but now _____ awake. _____?

RUTH: _____?

BILL: (ZZZzzzz ...)

RUTH: Bill? Oh, never mind.

(Five minutes later.)

Bill, _____! _____!

BILL: What? Hmm? What? What's the matter?

RUTH: _____ a noise outside the tent. _____! _____ a bear outside? Bill, I think _____ a bear outside.

BILL: What noise? Listen. _____ out there.

_____ a sound. _____

_____ any bears around here. _____ back to sleep.

RUTH: _____ bears around here. _____

_____ about a bear in the newspaper _____ .

Role Playing

Study the dialog at home. The next time your class meets, you will role play this situation. You don't have to memorize the dialog; just be ready to have a similar conversation using the same situation. Try to use *there + is/are/was/were* in your conversation.

THERE IS, THERE ARE, THERE WAS AND THERE WERE

Present Tense

STATEMENTS

Use *there + be* (*there is/there are*) when you want to describe something, for example, a picture, a room, a house, a town, or a park.

There is (*not*) + singular noun

There are (*not*) + plural noun

Contractions: *there's, there isn't, there aren't*

> ### *Examples*
> On their vacation in California, Bill and Ruth went to visit Disneyland. **There are** many different parts to Disneyland: Adventureland, Main Street, Frontierland, Tomorrowland, and many others.
>
> In Adventureland, there's a man-made river. Visitors can take boats down the river on a trip through "Africa" and "Asia." **There are** beautiful plants and flowers along the sides of the river, and visitors can see elephants, zebras, tigers, and other animals. But don't be afraid because **there aren't** any real animals in Adventureland. The animals look very real, but they aren't. They are machines.

Activity 5A

Vocabulary

- steam train: an old-fashioned train. Steam from burning coal makes the train go.
- village: a small town
- saloon: a bar like the ones in the Old West
- sound track: the part of a movie with the voices and music
- souvenir: something you can buy to help you remember a place that you visit. When people visit a city, they can buy a T-shirt with the name of the city on it. The T-shirt is a souvenir.
- ice-cream parlor: a shop that sells ice cream and soda
- monorail train: a train with only one rail (track)
- miniature: very small

☐ Fill in the blanks with *there is, there are, there isn't,* or *there aren't.*

In Frontierland _there is_ a steam train to take visitors around. _There are_ also different kinds of boats from America's past to take visitors on a trip down a river. _____ an Indian village near the river. _____ also a small town from the days of the Old West. Visitors can go into the Golden Horseshoe Saloon for a drink. Inside _____ a show with dancing girls and singers.

In Main Street, USA, everything is an example of life in a small American town around 1900. Of course _____ any modern
(negative)
cars or buses. In the theater _____ any movies with a sound
(negative)
track. All the movies are silent films from the old days. _____ stores and shops with souvenirs from the past, and _____ an ice-cream parlor from the old days. Every day _____ a parade down Main Street.

In Tomorrowland _____ a monorail train for visitors to ride. Inside Space Mountain _____ a rocket ship to take you on an imaginary trip through space. For children _____ small sports cars to drive along a miniature superhighway.

☐ Go back and read the passage again. Then tell about the different places and things in Disneyland using *there + is/are*. Don't look back at the exercise. Use the following words to help you.

In Frontierland: *a steam train, boats, an Indian village, a small town, a show*

In Main Street, USA: *modern cars, silent films, stores, an ice-cream parlor, a parade*

In Tomorrowland: *a monorail train, a rocket ship, small sports cars*

QUESTIONS

Reverse the verb *be* (*is/are*) and *there* to form a question.

Is there + singular noun?

Are there + plural noun?

How many + plural noun + *are there?*

> ### Examples
>
> **Is there** a hotel in Disneyland?
>
> No, **there isn't** a hotel right in Disneyland, but the official Disneyland Hotel is very near the park.
>
> **Is there** a swimming pool at the hotel?
>
> Yes, **there is.**
>
> **Are there** tennis courts?
>
> Yes, **there are.**
>
> **How many rooms are there** in the hotel?
>
> **There are** 1,000.

Activity 5B

Make questions with *is there* or *are there*. Then use your imagination to answer the questions. These are typical questions that travelers often need to ask.

> **Example**
> *(campground)*
> _Is there a campground near here_?
> _Yes, there's one about two miles from here._

1. *(wild animals)*

   _____ in this campground?

   _____

2. *(supermarket)*

   _____?

   _____

3. *(drugstore)*

   _____?

   _____

4. *(motel)*

   _____?

   _____

5. *(picnic tables)*

   _____?

   _____

6. *(good restaurants)*

   _____?

   _____

7. *(good beaches)*

_____?

_____

8. *(place to change clothes)*

_____at this beach?

_____

9. *(rooms with a private bath)*

_____in this hotel?

_____

Past Tense

STATEMENTS

Use *there* + *was* or *were* to describe something in the past.

There was (*not*) + *a/an* + singular noun

There were (*not*) + plural noun

> ### Examples
> After visiting Disneyland, Bill and Ruth visited an old Spanish mission in California. California has an interesting history. Before 1760, **there weren't** any European people living in California; **there were** only Indians. After 1760, the Spanish went to live there. They built missions for the Indians and taught them about the Christian religion. On a mission **there was** a church, and **there was** also a school for the Indians. The missions also had a lot of farmland.

QUESTIONS

Reverse the verb *be* (*was/were*) and *there* to form a question.

Was there + singular noun?

Were there + plural noun?

Examples

Were there many missions in California?

Yes, **there were.** In 1823, **there were** twenty-one missions.

Was there a church on every mission?

Yes, **there was. There was** also a school.

Activity 5C

☐ Fill in the blanks with *there was, there were, there wasn't,* or *there weren't*. (Your instructor may want to use this passage for listening comprehension first. If so, read the Listening Comprehension Questions first and keep them in mind as you listen to your instructor read the passage several times. Just listen the first time. Take notes the second and third times. After you answer the questions, go back and fill in the blanks.)

In 1800, *there weren't* (negative) many people in the West. The population was only 386,413, but by 1840 _____ 6,376,972 people in this part of the country. In 1800, _____ (negative) many towns, but forty years later _____ large ranches and cow towns all over the West. Most of these cow towns weren't very big. Sometimes _____ only one hotel, one store, and some houses. Sometimes _____ (negative) a school in the town, but _____ always a saloon where all the cowboys came to drink and play cards. They also came because _____ (negative) many women in these cow towns in the old days, but in the saloon _____ _____ usually a show with a singer and some dancing girls. The cowboys frequently drank too much, so _____ a lot of gunfights in the saloons. In Dodge City, _____ a cemetery called Boot Hill. People gave it this name because almost all of the graves were graves of cowboys who died with their boots on.

Listening Comprehension Questions

1. How many people were there in the West in 1800?
2. Were there many towns in the West in 1800?
3. By 1840, how many people were there in the West?
4. Was there always a school in the small cow towns around the West?
5. There was always one certain kind of building in these cow towns. What was it?
6. All of the cowboys came to the saloon to drink and play cards. Why else did they come there?
7. Why were there a lot of gunfights in the saloons?
8. What famous place from the days of the Old West is there in Dodge City?

❑ After your instructor has corrected this exercise with the class, read it again. Then describe life in the Old West using *there was* and *there were*. Don't look back at the exercise.

■ ACTIVITY 5D

The map below shows a typical small cow town of 1840. The map on page 66 shows the same town as it appears today.

❑ Describe this town as it was in 1840 and as it is today. Use the past and present of *there + be*.

In 1880, the town was very small. _____ only five streets. Today _____ a lot of streets and houses. In 1840, _____ many houses: _____ only
            (negative)
eleven. _____ any cars on the streets in 1840.
      (negative)

_____ only cows, horses, and wagons. Today _____ a big highway near the town, and the streets are crowded with cars. Main Street was very different in 1840. _____ only three buildings: a saloon, a hotel, and a store. Today _____ many buildings on Main Street. In 1840, _____ any houses on Dead Man's Road;
             (negative)
_____ only a jail. Today this street is called Maple Street because _____ a jail there anymore.
                           (negative)

- ❑ Look at the maps and ask a classmate questions about this town in 1840 and today.
- ❑ Is your town, city, or neighborhood different from the way it was when you were a child? Describe these changes using *there + be*.

6 THE SIMPLE PRESENT TENSE

Content Focus

HOLIDAYS IN THE UNITED STATES

Dialog

JOE: Next Thursday is Thanksgiving. I'm going to Boston Wednesday night to spend the holiday with my family. My mother invited you to come.

HIRO: She invited me? Thanks. That's great. I **don't know** very much about Thanksgiving. **Do** all Americans **celebrate** it?

JOE: Yes, it's a national holiday. My whole family **gets** together every Thanksgiving—aunts, uncles, cousins, everyone.

HIRO: **Does** Thanksgiving always **come** on a Thursday?

JOE: Yes, it **does**. It's always the fourth Thursday in November. My mother's Thanksgiving dinner is fantastic. She always cooks a huge meal.

HIRO: What **do** people usually **eat?**

JOE: They almost always **have** turkey and then pumpkin pie for dessert. We all **eat** too much on Thanksgiving.

HIRO: Turkey? We **don't eat** turkey very often in Japan.

JOE: Turkey's delicious.

HIRO: What else **do** people **do** on Thanksgiving?

JOE: Well, some people **watch** football games on TV. Mainly it's a day for families to get together and eat too much.

HIRO: Are you sure that it's okay for me to come?

JOE: Sure. My mother **loves** company. She always **has** a lot of extra food.

HIRO: Okay. Good. Thanks for the invitation.

Comprehension Questions

1. What holiday do Americans celebrate in November?
2. Does Thanksgiving always come on a Thursday?
3. What does Joe's mother do on Thanksgiving?
4. Does she like company?
5. What do Americans eat for Thanksgiving dinner?
6. What else do people do on Thanksgiving?

THE SIMPLE PRESENT TENSE

Use the simple present tense when you want to talk about an action that you repeat—for example, something that you do every day, every year, always, sometimes, usually, or never.

Statements

I you we they	+ base form	he she + base form + it	-s -es
I you we they	+ **do not** + base form (don't)	he she + **does not** + base form it (doesn't)	

Examples

December 25 is Christmas Day. Christmas is a very important holiday in the United States. On this day, most families **get** together for a big dinner. They **exchange** presents and **visit** friends. Joe's little nephew **loves** Christmas. He **doesn't sleep** all night the night before Christmas. He **stays** awake and **thinks** about his presents. The Christmas tree is an important part of the Christmas holiday. Most families **buy** a tree, but Joe **goes** to a tree farm and **cuts** down a tree. His family **decorates** the tree together.

Not all Americans **celebrate** Christmas. For example, some Jewish Americans **don't celebrate** Christmas; they **celebrate** Chanukah, a holiday that **comes** around the same time as Christmas.

Note 1: If a verb ends in *s, z, sh, ch, x,* or *o,* add *-es* for *he/she/it.*
pass → passes   wash → washes   fix → fixes   go → goes
do → does

Note 2: Notice the change in the verb *have* for the third-person singular.

I, you, we, they } have   he, she, it } has

Activity 6A

Listening Comprehension
Your instructor may want to use this exercise for listening comprehension before you read it or fill in the blanks. Listen to your instructor. Then see if you can describe Santa Claus, what he does, and what Jason does.

Grammar Fill-in
Fill in the correct form for the simple present tense.

Vocabulary

Santa Claus: a little fat man with a white beard who wears a red suit
imaginary: not real. Something that your mind invents is imaginary.
beard: hair on a man's face
fur: hair on an animal
sleigh: a kind of vehicle used to travel across snow. A sleigh is usually pulled by horses. (Santa Claus's sleigh is pulled by reindeer.)
land: to arrive on land after traveling by air or water
fireplace: the place where you build a fire to keep a house warm
chimney: the part of a fireplace that carries smoke out through the roof
stocking: a long sock

    Many American children between the ages of two and seven _believe_ (believe) in Santa Claus. Santa Claus is an imaginary person. He _has_ (have) a white beard and _____ (wear) a red suit with white fur. He _____ (live) far away at the North Pole.

    Joe's nephew, Jason, is five years old. He _____ (believe) in Santa Claus. He _____ (believe) that Santa Claus _____ (bring) presents to all good children. Parents always _____ (tell) their children that bad children _____ (negative for get) presents; Santa _____ (bring) presents only to good boys and girls. Every year a few weeks before Christmas, Jason's mother _____ (help) her son write a letter to Santa Claus. In this letter, he _____ (tell) Santa everything that he _____ (want) for Christmas.

    Santa _____ (negative for go) to the houses on Christmas Eve until all the children _____ (go) to bed. Santa _____ (travel) in a sleigh. He _____ (land) his sleigh on the roof. This is because Santa _____ (negative for enter) a house through the door; he always _____ (go) down the chimney.

Jason always _____ a big red stocking on the fireplace before
   (hang)
he _____ to bed. Santa _____ this with fruit, candy, and
    (go)   (fill)
small toys. He _____ the big presents under the Christmas tree. Of
                (leave)
course, he _____ everything that the children ask for.
            (negative for **bring**)

Jason always _____ a plate of cookies for Santa. His parents
             (leave)
secretly _____ them, but they _____ Jason this.
          (eat)   (negative for **tell**)
Jason _____ that Santa ate them.
       (think)

Jason _____ very late on Christmas Day. He
       (negative for **sleep**)
_____ up his parents at about six in the morning because he
 (wake)
_____ to go downstairs to open his presents.
 (want)

Questions

(Question word)	+	**do**	+	I you we they	+	base form?
(Question word)	+	**does**	+	he she it	+	base form?

What else do people do?
What does your mother cook?

Examples

HIRO is asking JOE some questions about Christmas Eve (December 24).

HIRO: What **do** Americans **do** on Christmas Eve? Is that an important day too?

JOE: Some Americans go to church. My father and mother usually invite some friends to come for eggnog and dessert.

The Simple Present Tense 73

> HIRO: What's eggnog? How **do** you **make** it?
> JOE: It's a special Christmas drink. You make it with eggs, cream, milk, rum, and spices. It's delicious.
> HIRO: **Does** your family **exchange** presents on Christmas Eve?
> JOE: No, my family **doesn't**. We do that on Christmas morning, but some families exchange presents on Christmas Eve.

Note: British people sometimes say, "Have you a pencil?" or "Has he a pencil?" People in the United States usually say, "Do you have a pencil?" or "Does he have a pencil?"

Short Answers

When we can answer a question in the simple present with *yes* or *no,* we usually add the subject and *do* or *does* for short answers.

Yes, { I / you / we / they } do.   Yes, { he / she / it } does.

No, { I / you / we / they } don't.   No, { he / she / it } doesn't.

■ ACTIVITY 6B

Ask questions about Diane. Her family is Jewish.

> **Examples**
> (*Diane, celebrate*)
>
> _Does Diane celebrate_ Christmas?
>
> No, she _doesn't_. She and her family celebrate Chanukah.

1. (*Chanukah, come*)

   When _____?

   It comes in December, but the date changes every year.

2. (*Diane, do*)

   What _____ to celebrate Chanukah?

   She lights candles on the eight nights of Chanukah.

3. (*she, exchange*)

   _____ presents with her family?

   Yes, she _____.

4. (*she, get*)

   _____ together with her family on Chanukah?

   Yes, she usually goes home for the first night of Chanukah.

   ❑ Ask a classmate questions about a holiday in his or her country. Your classmate will answer. When you finish, your classmate can ask you the same questions.

   Example
   (*your country, have*)

   Does your country have a national holiday?

   Answer: _____

1. (*people, celebrate*)

   When _____ this holiday?

   Answer: _____

2. (*people, celebrate*)

   Why _____ this holiday? What is its origin?

   Answer: _____

3. (*people, eat*)

   _____ a big dinner on this holiday?

   Answer: _____

The Simple Present Tense

4. (*people, cook*)

   What special dishes _____ on this day?

   Answer: _____

5. (*people, exchange*)

   _____ presents on this day?

   Answer: _____

6. (*people, visit*)

   _____ their friends and relatives on this day?

   Answer: _____

7. (*people, do*)

   What else _____ on this day?

   Answer: _____

8. (*stores and offices, close*)

   _____ on this day?

   Answer: _____

9. (*people in your country, celebrate*)

   _____ Christmas?

   Answer: _____

■ Activity 6C

❑ When we don't understand the meaning of a word, we can ask this question.

   What does _____ mean?

Now practice this question. Ask questions about these words.

sad	filthy	cheap
difficult	poor	skinny

Answer them with these words.

not expensive	the opposite of happy
not easy	very thin
very dirty	the opposite of rich

> *Example*
>
> *What does sad mean _____?*
> *It means the opposite of happy.*

❑ When we don't know how to pronounce a word, we can ask this question.

How do you pronounce _____?

Now practice this question. Ask a classmate about these words.

1. thought
2. found
3. shirt
4. thousand
5. caught
6. dangerous

> *Example*
>
> *How do you pronounce the first word _____?*
>
> The student who answers will say the word. Then he or she will ask you about the second word.

❑ When we don't know how to spell a word, we can ask this question.

How do you spell _____?

Now practice this question. Ask a classmate to spell these:

1. his or her name
2. the name of his or her country

3. the instructor's name
4. the names of some famous people
5. some difficult words in English

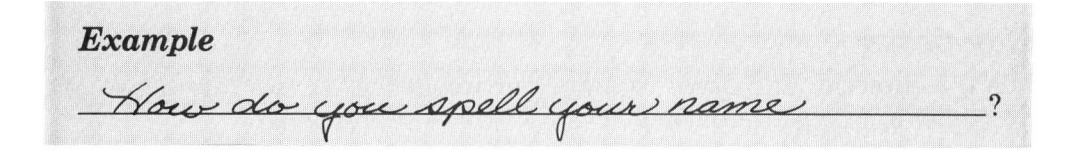

> **Example**
>
> *How do you spell your name* ?

Frequency

ADVERBS OF FREQUENCY

100%	always
	almost always
	usually
	frequently, often
	sometimes
	seldom
	almost never
0%	never

These frequency adverbs usually come after *am*, *is*, and *are*, and before all other verbs.

> **Examples**
>
> Christmas **is always** a happy day for children.
>
> They **usually get up** very early on Christmas morning.

Sometimes can also come at the beginning of a sentence.

> **Examples**
>
> Children **sometimes** have stomachaches from eating too much candy on Christmas.

or

Sometimes children have stomachaches from eating too much candy on Christmas.

How Often

Use the question *How often?* to ask about frequency. Answer questions with *how often* by using a frequency adverb or these expressions.

$$\left.\begin{array}{l}\text{once}\\\text{twice}\end{array}\right\} \text{a} \left\{\begin{array}{l}\text{day}\\\text{week}\\\text{month}\\\text{year}\end{array}\right. \qquad \left.\begin{array}{l}\text{three}\\\text{four}\\\text{five}\\\text{six}\end{array}\right\} \text{times a} \left\{\begin{array}{l}\text{day}\\\text{week}\\\text{month}\\\text{year}\end{array}\right.$$

$$\text{every} \left\{\begin{array}{l}\text{day}\\\text{week}\\\text{year}\end{array}\right. \qquad \text{all the time}$$

Examples

HIRO: **How often** do you visit your parents in Boston?
JOE: I visit them about **four or five times a year**. But my mother wants me to come home more often. She calls me **once a week**. How often do you write to your parents?
HIRO: I write a letter **every week**.

Activity 6D

☐ Rewrite the sentences and put the frequency adverbs in the correct position.

Example

(*always*)
In the United States, offices are closed on New Year's Day (January 1).

In the United States, offices are always closed on New Year's Day.

The Simple Present Tense 79

1. (*usually*)
   Office workers go home early on New Year's Eve (December 31).
   _____

2. (*usually*)
   People go out to a party or out to dinner at a restaurant on New Year's Eve.
   _____

3. (*often*)
   Restaurants and nightclubs are full this night.
   _____

4. (*often*)
   It's difficult to get a reservation in a restaurant or a nightclub on New Year's Eve.
   _____

5. (*usually*)
   At midnight on New Year's Eve, people make a lot of noise and kiss each other.
   _____

6. (*seldom*)
   People exchange gifts on New Year's Day.
   _____

7. (*often*)
   People make New Year's resolutions.
   _____

☐ Choose a frequency adverb and write a sentence about yourself.

Example
(be) tired in the morning
I'm almost always tired in the morning.

1. fall asleep in class _____
2. get up late _____
3. cry in sad movies _____
4. eat breakfast _____
5. dance a lot at parties _____
6. (be) late to class _____
7. tell lies _____
8. (be) nervous before a test _____
9. sing in the shower _____

❑ Write questions with *How often* and answer them with *all the time, never, every (day/week/month),* or *(once, twice, three times) a (day/week/month/year).*

Example

(MARIA is writing a letter.)

HIRO: Who are you writing to? To your family?
MARIA: Yes, to my sister.
HIRO: I like to receive letters, but I don't like to write them. *How often do you write* to your family?
MARIA: *Oh, I don't know. I probably write a letter once or twice a month.*

1. (BILL met JOE by chance a minute ago.)

   BILL: I see you're wearing your running suit. Are you going to the park to jog?

   JOE: Yeah. It's a great day to jog.

   BILL: _____? Every day?

   JOE: Well, not every day. _____

The Simple Present Tense

2. (Today is Friday.)

   JOE: Hey, Bill. What are you going to do tomorrow?

   BILL: Oh, I don't know. Wash the car maybe.

   JOE: Wash the car? You just washed it last weekend. _____

   _____?

   BILL: _____

3. BILL: I love my car.

   JOE: You really take good care of that car. _____

   _____ it to the garage for a tune-up?

   BILL: _____.

4. (In a supermarket in the meat section.)

   DIANE: Look at the price on that steak!

   RUTH: I know. It's terrible. Steak is so high now.

   DIANE: I love steak.

   RUTH: _____?

   DIANE: Not very often. _____

   _____.

5. (Joe hung up the telephone a second ago.)

   HIRO: Who was that on the phone? Was your mother calling long distance from Boston again?

   JOE: Yeah. Again.

   HIRO: She just called you the night before last. _____

   _____?

   JOE: _____.

   I think my parents' phone bill is about sixty dollars a month.

The Two Present Tenses of English

Some languages have only one present tense. English has two present tenses. They frequently have very different meanings. In general, when you talk about the present moment (right now), use the present continuous: *be* + verb + *-ing*. When you talk about an action that you repeat (every day, usually, sometimes, once a week), use the simple present: base form or base form + *-s* or *-es*.

Study the difference between these two present tenses in the examples.

> ### *Examples*
> (HIRO and JOE are at a New Year's Eve party.)
> HIRO: Why **are** people **wearing** those funny little hats?
> JOE: I don't know. We always **wear** funny hats on New Year's Eve.
> HIRO: Everybody **is kissing**. **Do** you always **kiss** on New Year's Eve?
> JOE: Yes. Everybody **kisses** at midnight on New Year's Eve.

These are some verbs that you don't often see used in the present continuous form.

have[1]	want	know	see[1]
agree	remember	forget	understand
hear	like	love	need
cost	believe	prefer	belong
own			

When you use these verbs to talk about the present moment (now), use the simple present form of the verbs.

Correct: I **want** a cup of coffee now.

Incorrect: I **am wanting** a cup of coffee.

Correct: Do you **know** the answer now?

Incorrect: **Are** you **knowing** the answer now?

---

[1] When you see the verbs *have* or *see* in the continuous form, they have a special meaning.

I **have** a car.   I'm **having** a good time.
I **see** some money on the floor.   The doctor **is seeing** a patient now.

The Simple Present Tense _____ 83

■ ACTIVITY 6E

❑ Choose the correct present tense: present continuous or simple present.

Every year, the United States government __*puts*__ up a gigantic
                                                      (put)

Christmas tree outside near the Washington Monument in Washington,

D.C. The tree is always decorated with colored lights and ornaments. The

president _____ this tree in a special ceremony every year. Across
               (light)

the nation, TV stations _____ this ceremony.
                             (show)

❑ Imagine that you are a reporter for a TV station. You are at the ceremony now. You are describing it to the TV audience. Continue to choose between the present continuous or simple present tenses.

REPORTER: I'm here at the annual tree-lighting ceremony in Washington,

D.C. I'*m standing* in a big crowd of people. We
       (stand)

_____ for the president to come and light the
     (wait)

tree. Many other people _____ by the area
                                 (pass)

now, but _____. They _____
         (negative for stop)   **(rush)**

to finish their Christmas shopping. Most stores

__*stay*__ open until 9:00 or 10:00 during the
   (stay)

Christmas season. Hundreds of people _____ here
                                       (come)

every year to watch the ceremony. The tree _____
                                                  (be)

always a big one—about fifty feet high. It's cold out here

tonight. The wind _____, and a little snow
                   (blow)

_____. It usually _____ very
  (fall)   **(negative for snow)**

hard at this time of the year in Washington, D.C. Severe

winter weather usually _____ in January or
                       (come)

February. But let me tell you, it's really cold out here

tonight. I _____ gloves, and my hands
        (negative for wear)

_____(freeze). People _____(stamp) their feet to keep warm. There's some snow on the ground, and some children _____(throw) snowballs. There's a choir over near the tree. They _____(sing) "Silent Night." Every year, a choir _____(sing) traditional Christmas carols[2] at the tree-lighting ceremony. Ladies and gentlemen, I think I _____(hear) the president's car now. Yes, now I _____(see) him. Now the president _____(walk) toward the microphone in front of the tree. Let's listen to the president.

❑ Again imagine that you are the reporter. Don't look back at the fill-in exercise. Describe the ceremony to the TV audience.

Activity 6F

❑ Prepare a talk for your class. Describe an important holiday in your country. Don't write the talk and memorize it. Just use your dictionary to find words that you need, and practice your talk at home before you give it to your class.

❑ Describe a person in your family (your father, mother, sister, brother, husband, or wife). Is the person tall or short? What color hair and eyes does he or she have? How old is he or she? Describe the daily routine of this person. Describe any unusual habits that this person has. How are you similar to, or different from, this person?

❑ Look at the accompanying photo. The life of this woman is probably very different from the lives of people who live in large cities around the world. Tell how her life is different. How does she get food to eat? Does she shop in supermarkets? Does she eat frozen foods? Where does she get water? Does she have electricity in her home? How does she cook meals? Does she go to school? What does she do in her free time? Where does she get clothes? What time does she get up in the morning and go to bed at night? How does she travel from her village to the next? In what other ways is her life different?

---

[2]*Carol* means "song."

The Simple Present Tense _____ 85

Example

This woman probably doesn't have any supermarkets in her village. She probably has chickens and a garden in her yard, or perhaps she buys food from farmers in her village. People in large cities go to supermarkets for food. They eat many frozen and prepared foods.

■ ACTIVITY 6G

The following are typical questions that people ask when they meet a person from another country for the first time (at a party, for example) and want to make conversation.

1. Look at the answer. Then ask the correct question for the answer.

   a. _____?
      I live at Broadway on 95th Street.

   b. How _____the United States?
      I like this country very much. It's very interesting, but sometimes I miss my country very much.

   c. _____?
      I think some Americans are friendly, but others are not. It's the same in any country.

   d. _____?
      Yes, I have a son and two daughters.

   e. _____?
      Yes, I have two brothers and three sisters.

   f. How many _____?
      I speak Arabic and French and a little English.

   g. _____when you watch TV in English or when people speak English to you?
      I only understand about fifty percent.

   h. What kind of _____?
      I like rock music and jazz.

   i. _____?
      I go to the movies about once or twice a week. It's good for my English.

   j. _____any musical instruments?
      Yes, I play the piano.

   k. _____any hobbies or special interests?
      I like to swim. I also paint a little.

   l. What _____?
      I'm an engineer, but right now I'm a student.

   m. What _____your wife/husband/father/mother _____?

2. Now ask a classmate these questions. Your classmate will give his or her own answers.

Activity 6H

Vocabulary

dream: an image or idea that occurs in the mind while we sleep
emotion: feeling—for example, anger, happiness, sadness
decision: making up your mind. When you like two pairs of shoes but finally decide which pair to buy, you have made a decision.
quiz: a short test
sluggish: slow; lazy; without much energy
alert: awake and aware of everything around you
nightmare: a bad dream
vivid: bright; full of life. Orange is a vivid color.
powerful: strong. Superman is powerful.
score: the number of points that you get in a game or on a quiz like the one that follows

☐ Some people believe that dreams are very important. They believe that dreams help you in your real life. They help you understand your feelings and emotions better. Sometimes they help you make important decisions. Everyone's dreams are different. Some people's dreams help them more than other people's. This is a little quiz to tell you if your dreams help you or don't help you.[3] Circle the number of each of your answers.

1. How often do you remember your dreams?
   (1) never   (2) once or twice a year   (3) a few times a month
   (4) three or four times a week   (5) every night—one or two dreams

2. Do you ever think about your dreams?
   (1) never   (2) seldom   (3) sometimes   (4) frequently

3. Do you ever talk about your dreams to your friends?
   (1) never   (2) seldom   (3) sometimes   (4) frequently

4. Do you ever write your dreams down on paper so that you can remember them?
   (1) never   (2) seldom   (3) sometimes   (4) frequently

5. How long does it take you to get to sleep?
   (1) 30 minutes to 1 hour   (2) I can't sleep without a sleeping pill.
   (3) one hour or more   (4) 15 to 20 minutes   (5) 15 minutes or less

[3]This quiz has been adapted from the Dream Capabilities Assessment Test, © 1976 The Center Foundation. No part of the test may be reproduced or used without consent of The Center Foundation. (The complete Dream Capabilities Assessment Test appears in *The Dream Makers: Discovering Your Breakthrough Dreams*, by Richard Corriere and Joseph Hart, © 1977 by Richard Corriere and Joseph Hart. Published by Funk & Wagnalls, Inc.)

6. When you wake up in the morning, are you usually
   (1) sluggish?   (2) tired?   (3) awake?   (4) awake and alert?
   (5) awake and happy?

7. Do you ever have the same dreams again and again?
   (1) frequently   (2) sometimes   (3) seldom   (4) never

8. Do you ever have nightmares?
   (1) never   (2) infrequently   (3) sometimes   (4) frequently

9. Are your dreams in color?
   (1) I don't know.   (2) They are usually black and white.
   (3) sometimes   (4) usually   (5) frequently in strong, vivid color

10. How much feeling and emotion are there in your dreams?
    (1) no feeling (The dreams are about things that don't carry feeling or emotion for me.)   (2) a little feeling   (3) some feeling
    (4) strong feeling   (5) very intense feeling (the feeling is more important than anything else in the dream).

11. Do you ever do wonderful, powerful things like Superman in your dreams?
    (1) never   (2) I did once.   (3) seldom   (4) sometimes
    (5) frequently

12. Are your dreams very clear and easy to understand?
    (1) never   (2) They were once.   (3) seldom   (4) sometimes
    (5) frequently

13. Do you ever have dreams that you can't forget and remember all your life?
    (1) never   (2) I did once.   (3) seldom   (4) sometimes
    (5) frequently

14. Do your friends ever help you in your dreams?
    (1) never   (2) They did once.   (3) seldom   (4) sometimes
    (5) frequently

15. Do your dreams ever tell you what to do in the future?
    (1) never   (2) They did once.   (3) seldom   (4) sometimes
    (5) frequently

16. Are your dreams ever helpful to you in real life? (Do they teach you things?)
    (1) never   (2) They were once.   (3) seldom   (4) sometimes
    (5) frequently

Now add all of the numbers that you circled. If your score is between 17 and 40, your dreams don't help you with your real life. You don't pay very much attention to your dreams.

If your score is more than 40, your dreams help you understand your real life. They teach you something about it and help you make decisions.

❏ Make complete sentences about yourself and your dreams, putting the frequency expression in the correct position; for example, "I remember my dreams a few times a month." Or interview a classmate and make complete sentences about the classmate and his or her dreams.

❏ Discuss the following questions.

1. Do you believe that dreams are important? Why or why not?
2. Tell about a particularly unusual, beautiful, or frightening dream that you once had.
3. Some people believe that dreams can come true. Do you believe this? Tell about a dream of yours or a friend's dream that came true.
4. Some people believe that dreams can predict the future. Do you believe this? Do many people in your country believe this? What are some superstitions about dreams in your country?
5. There are many stories about people who dreamed that a member of the family far away in another country or city was sick, dying, or in some kind of danger. When they woke up and telephoned this relative, they found that the dream was true. Do you know any stories like this?

7 INTEGRATION OF PRESENT CONTINUOUS, SIMPLE PRESENT, SIMPLE PAST, AND FUTURE (*GOING TO*) TENSES

A romantic spot for a honeymoon.

Content Focus | **SOME PROBLEMS IN A MARRIAGE**

In this chapter, you will practice using the four basic tenses that you have learned in the preceding chapters.

ACTIVITY 7A

Fill in the blank with the correct tense of the verb. Choose from the present continuous, simple present, simple past, or future (*going to*) tenses. For some of the questions, you must fill in the subject also.

(DIANE is talking to RUTH on the telephone.)

DIANE: Hello, Ruth? This is Diane.

RUTH: Hi. How are things?

DIANE: Oh, fine. _____ you _____ a minute to talk? What
         (have)
_____ now?
   (do)

RUTH: I _____ at some old photographs. Just a minute.
        (look)
I can't hear because the radio is too loud. I _____ it off.
                                                (turn)

(RUTH leaves and then comes back to the phone.)

Okay, I'm back.

DIANE: What photographs _____ at?
                        (look)

RUTH: Oh, some photos of me and Bill on our honeymoon.

DIANE: I guess those photos bring back wonderful memories for you.

Where _____ on your honeymoon?
       (go)

RUTH: We _____ a week in Bermuda. It _____ so nice.
        (spend)   **(be)**
We _____ a wonderful time. But you know something,
    (have)
Diane? These photos make me feel a little sad.

DIANE: Why?

RUTH: Well, because Bill _____ so romantic before our marriage.
 (be)
He _____ me flowers. We _____ each other every
 (bring) (see)
night after work. We _____ every free moment together.
 (spend)
We _____ out dancing. We _____ to movies. But
 (go) (go)
these days he never _____ me flowers. We never
 (bring)
_____ out dancing. We seldom _____ to movies.
 (go) (go)
We really _____ very much time together. Bill
 (negative for spend)
_____ home until 10:00 two nights a week
 (negative for come)
because he has classes, and I _____ home until 9:00 one
 (negative for get)
night a week because I have a class—we're so busy all the time.

DIANE: Tonight is Friday. Bill _____ class tonight. Where
 (negative for have)
_____ now?
 (be)

RUTH: He's at a friend's house. They _____ the baseball
 (watch)
game on TV. I'm a little upset about it because we _____
 (negative for have)
much time together, and tonight is one of our free nights. And you

know, Diane, tomorrow is my birthday.

DIANE: Oh, happy birthday. What _____ you and Bill

_____ to celebrate tomorrow? _____ Bill
 (do)
_____ you out to dinner?
 (take)

RUTH: I _____. To tell you the truth, Diane, I'm almost
 (negative for know)
sure that he _____ that tomorrow is my birthday.
 (negative for remember)

DIANE: Oh, no. I'm sure that he remembers. Maybe he

_____ you tomorrow.
 (surprise)

RUTH: Well, maybe you're right.

DIANE: Listen, Ruth. Why don't you talk to Bill? _____ you and Bill ever _____ about your problems?
(talk)

RUTH: Sometimes I _____, but Bill _____ to
(try)   (negative for **like**)
talk about our problems. He always _____ that we
(say)
_____ any problems. He _____
(negative for **have**)   (negative for **think**)
that there is anything wrong between us.

DIANE: Well, everyone can see that Bill _____ you very much.
(love)

RUTH: Oh, I _____ that he _____ me, and of course I
(know)   (love)
_____ him, but all couples _____ problems. I
(love)   (have)
_____ that it's very important to talk about how you feel.
(think)

DIANE: I _____. Why don't you and Bill go away for a weekend?
(agree)
Then you can have a chance to really talk.

RUTH: That's a good idea. I _____ that suggestion tomorrow.
(make)
Thank you for talking to me about this, Diane.

Comprehension Questions

1. Why do the photos of Bill and Ruth's honeymoon make Ruth feel sad?
2. In what way was Bill different before they got married?
3. Why is Ruth a little unhappy with their relationship now?

Opinion Questions

1. Does love between a man and a woman change over the years? How? Why? Does marriage change this love? Do children change a marriage? How?
2. Do all married couples have problems? What kinds of problems?
3. Is it important for a married couple to keep romance in their marriage? What do husbands and wives do to keep romance in a marriage? Is it important for husbands to bring flowers to their wives or to plan a special vacation without the children? What do wives do? Is it important for a wife to cook her husband's favorite dinner? Is it important for a wife to go to sports events with her husband? What else?

Role Playing

☐ Study the dialog between Diane and Ruth again. Then role play using a similar conversation.

☐ Working with a classmate, write a dialog between Ruth and Bill. In the conversation, Ruth is talking to Bill about why she is unhappy with their relationship. After your instructor checks your dialog, role play it for your class without reading it.

ACTIVITY 7B

A friend of Diane's, Neal, is asking Diane about her interest in sports. Look at Diane's answers to help you form the correct questions. Choose from the four tenses that you are reviewing in this chapter.

NEAL: _____ sports?
            (like)

DIANE: Yes. I especially like tennis and karate.

NEAL: _____ tennis a lot?
            (play)

DIANE: Yes, but I'm not Martina Navratilova.

NEAL: _____?
                        (play)

DIANE: In the summer, I play twice a week, but, in the winter, only about once a month.

NEAL: How _____ ? _____ lessons?
              (learn)   (take)

DIANE: My brother taught me, and I also took lessons a few years ago.

NEAL: The Wimbledon tennis matches are going to on TV tomorrow. _____ them?
            (watch)

DIANE: Yes. I'm going to go over to Joe's apartment because my TV is broken.

Activity 7C

Bill is asking Hiro questions about his family. Follow the directions for Activity 7B.

BILL: _____ any brothers or sisters, Hiro?
(have)

HIRO: I have a sister. She's in high school in Japan.

BILL: _____ to the United States to study after
(come)
high school?

HIRO: No, I don't think so. She applied to a college in Japan.

BILL: When _____ your parents _____ here to visit you?
(come)

HIRO: Maybe next year. My father is very busy at work now.

BILL: What _____ ?
(do)

HIRO: He has an import-export business.

BILL: What about your mother? _____ too?
(work)

HIRO: Yes. She teaches, but she's going to retire at the end of this year.

8 COUNT AND MASS NOUNS

Content Focus / **FOOD—COOKING AND SHOPPING**

Dialog

(MARIA invited some friends to her apartment for dinner. HIRO is helping her prepare the dinner now.)

MARIA: Hiro, I'm really glad you're here. This meal is going to be a disaster.[1] I need **a lot of** help with this dinner. I'm a terrible cook.

HIRO: Don't worry. Your dinner is going to be delicious. **How many** people did you invite?

MARIA: **A lot.** Let me think a minute. . . . Ten people.

HIRO: Okay. What can I do to help?

MARIA: Cut up some carrots for me, please.

HIRO: Okay. **How many** do you want?

MARIA: **Not many.** I only want **a few** for the salad. Please try this chicken.

(HIRO tastes some chicken. His face turns red, and he begins to cough and choke.)

HIRO: Water! Water!

MARIA: Hiro, are you all right? What's the matter? Here, drink **a little** water.

(She gives him a glass of water.)

HIRO: I'm sorry, Maria, but it's very spicy. Wow! **How much** pepper did you put on that chicken?

MARIA: I did**n't** put **much** on it. I only used **a little.** Let me taste it. Wow! Yes, it's too hot!

HIRO: Maybe you forgot and put the pepper on it twice.

MARIA: Maybe I did.

HIRO: It's good except for the pepper.

MARIA: Good? This chicken isn't good. It's terrible! What am I going to do? I'm not going to serve this for dinner.

(MARIA opens the oven.)

MARIA: Oh, no! The baked potatoes exploded in the oven. What am I going to do? No chicken, no potatoes!

HIRO: **How much** time do we have? Maybe we can run out to the supermarket and get something we can cook fast.

MARIA: No, we do**n't** have **much** time. Wait a minute! I have an idea. I'm going to call the pizza place and order four pizzas.

HIRO: But what are you going to do with your chicken?

MARIA: Throw it in the garbage!

[1] *A disaster* means "something very bad."

Comprehension Questions

1. What is Hiro helping Maria do in this dialog?
2. How many people did Maria invite for dinner?
3. Is she a good cook?
4. Does Hiro like the chicken?
5. Why is the chicken so spicy?
6. What other problem did Maria discover when she opened the oven?
7. Is Maria going to serve the chicken and potatoes to her guests?

What About You?

1. Do you know how to cook? Do you like to cook? How much time do you spend in the kitchen?
   Is your mother or father a good cook? What are some of her or his favorite recipes?
2. Do many men cook in your country? In most countries, women do the cooking at home, but most famous chefs are men. Why?
3. Talk about food in your country. What are some typical dishes? Do people in your country eat a lot of meat? Is it good for people to eat a lot of meat? Why or why not?
   Do people in your country eat a lot of sugar? Is it good for people to eat a lot of sugar?
   How much coffee do people in your country drink? Is coffee good for you?
   Is food from your country very spicy? Do you like spicy food?
4. What do you think of American food? What is typical American food?

Grammar Fill-in

Study the words in boldface type in this dialog. You can stop where Maria says, "Wow! Yes, it's too hot!" Then fill in the blanks. Don't look back at the dialog.

MARIA: Hiro, I'm really glad you're here. This meal is going to be a disaster. I need _____ with this dinner. I'm a terrible cook.

HIRO: Don't worry. Your dinner is going to be delicious. _____ did you invite?

MARIA: _____. Let me think a minute.... Ten people.

HIRO: Okay. What can I do to help?

MARIA: Cut up some carrots for me, please.

HIRO: Okay. _____ do you want?

MARIA: Not _____. I only want _____ for the salad.

Please try this chicken.

(HIRO tastes some chicken. His face turns red, and he begins to cough and choke.)

HIRO: Water! Water!

MARIA: Hiro, are you all right? What's the matter? Here, drink _____ water.

(She gives him a glass of water.)

HIRO: I'm sorry, Maria, but it's very spicy. Wow! _____ did you put on that chicken?

MARIA: I didn't put _____ on it. I only _____.

Let me taste it. Wow! Yes, it's too hot!

COUNT AND MASS NOUNS

There are two major groups of nouns in English: count nouns and mass nouns. Count nouns have a plural form that usually ends with *-s* or *-es*. They can have a number in front of them.

> ### *Examples*
> a book, two books, a box, four boxes

Mass nouns usually do not have a plural form or a number in front of them.

> ### *Examples*
> milk, wine, sugar, gasoline

Use *a* or *an* with singular count nouns. Don't use *a* or *an* with mass nouns.

This is *an* apple. What's this?
It's *an* apple.

This is sugar. What's this?
It's *sugar.*

Large Quantities

For everyday conversation, use *a lot of* to talk about large quantities of count nouns and mass nouns. To vary your conversation, use *a great deal of* with mass nouns and *a great many* with count nouns. These two expressions are often more formal than *a lot of.*

> ### Examples
>
> *Count Nouns*
>
> Maria used **a lot of** pots when she cooked dinner.
>
> Japan exports **a great many** cars to other countries.
>
> *Mass Nouns*
>
> Hiro tasted Maria's chicken. Then he drank **a lot of** water because she put **a lot of** pepper on it.
>
> Americans eat **a great deal of** sugar.

Many students make this mistake:

> He drank *much* water.

Much is too formal in this sentence. Use *a lot of* for conversational English.

Small Quantities

COUNT NOUNS

not $\begin{Bmatrix} \text{many} \\ \text{a lot of} \end{Bmatrix}$ + plural count noun

> ### Example
>
> HIRO: There aren't **many** napkins in this package. Do you have any more?
> MARIA: There's another package in the closet.

Mass Nouns

$not \begin{Bmatrix} much \\ a\ lot\ of \end{Bmatrix}$ + mass noun

> **Examples**
> HIRO: There **isn't much** ice in the freezer. Do you have more?
> MARIA: No. I forgot to buy ice at the supermarket. Can you go out and buy a bag, please? Please hurry because we **don't** have **much** time.

Questions

Count Nouns

How many + plural count noun?

or

Are there $\begin{Bmatrix} many \\ a\ lot\ of \end{Bmatrix}$ + plural count noun?

> **Example**
> RUTH: Bill, do we need more potatoes? Look in the refrigerator. **How many** potatoes are there in that bag?
> BILL: A lot.[2] Don't buy any more potatoes.

Mass Nouns

How much + mass noun?

Is there $\begin{Bmatrix} much \\ a\ lot\ of \end{Bmatrix}$ + mass noun?

> **Example**
> RUTH: **How much** milk do we have? Do we need more?
> BILL: Yes. There isn't much left.

---

[2]With a short answer, don't use *of* after *a lot*.

Activity 8A

Fill in the blanks with *much, many, a lot of,* or *a lot*. Also add *-s* or *-es* to form the plural if the noun is a count noun. For some blanks, you must choose between *it* and *them* or *is* and *are*.

In this dialog, Bill is in Joe's kitchen. Joe is making a special healthful drink, and Bill is watching.

BILL: That looks disgusting![3] What are you making?

JOE: It's a carrot and yogurt drink.

BILL: Carrots and yogurt! Yuk! Every time I see you, you have a carrot in your mouth. How _____ carrot____ do you eat each day?

JOE: I don't know. Carrot _____ good for you. I eat _____
(is/are)
_____.
(it/them)

BILL: I can't stand[4] _____. By the way, how do you drink a
(it/them)
carrot? How _____ juice____ do you get from one carrot?

JOE: Not _____, but I use about ten carrots to make the juice.

BILL: Well, I guess I'm just a junk-food[5] addict.[6] Give me a chocolate milk shake any day.

JOE: A milk shake? Milk shakes have _____ sugar____ in them. How _____ sugar____ do you take in from all this junk food each day?

BILL: _____. I put sugar in my coffee, I eat a doughnut every morning, candy bars after lunch, milk shakes . . .

JOE: Candy bars? There's nothing good for you in a candy bar.

---

[3]*That looks disgusting* means "I feel sick when I look at that. (It can be very impolite to say this. Bill and Joe are good friends, so Joe knows Bill is joking.)
[4]*Can't stand* means "hate; don't like."
[5]*Junk food* means "foods such as french fries, candy, and potato chips that don't have many vitamins."
[6]*Addict* means "a person who cannot live without something." Some people are coffee addicts, some are cigarette addicts, and some are drug addicts.

Count and Mass Nouns — 103

BILL: Don't look so horrified. I eat _____ hot dog___, too, and _____ meat___. You probably don't eat _____ meat___, right?
(much/many)

JOE: I don't eat any meat. Meat is really bad for you.

BILL: No meat? How do you get enough protein?

JOE: Well, I eat _____ egg___ and cheese and nuts. There is a lot of protein in those kinds of food.

BILL: Eggs, cheese, and nuts. You are a nut![7]

JOE: Maybe I'm a nut, but I'm going to live to be ninety years old. How's your health? How _____ cold___ do you get a year?

BILL: Maybe two or three. How about you?

JOE: Well, to tell the truth, I think I'm catching a cold today. I don't feel so great.

(Bill takes a candy bar out of his pocket and gives it to Joe.)

BILL: Here. Have a candy bar. Candy bars are great for a cold.

A Few and *a Little*

Use { *a few* + plural count noun / *a little* + mass noun } to talk about small quantities.

Examples

(HIRO is setting the table.)

HIRO: I need more wine glasses. There are only nine.
MARIA: There are **a few** glasses in that cabinet over there. Here's the wine. Oh, no! I spilled some wine on my blouse.
HIRO: Put **a little** salt on it. Salt takes out red wine.

---

[7] *You are a nut!* means "You're crazy."

Activity 8B

Fill in the blanks with *a few* or *a little*. Add *-s* or *-es* to the noun if it is a count noun.

HIRO: You know, except for the pepper, the chicken was very good. How did you make it?

MARIA: First, I put _a little_ butter____ and oil____ in a pan. Then I cut up _a few_ onion_s_ and cooked them in the oil and butter for _____ minute____. Next, I put _____ flour____ on the chicken and put it in the pan. Then I cut up _____ tomato____ and _____ carrot____ and added them to the chicken. I added _____ white wine____ and cooked everything for an hour and a half. Near the end, I cut up _____ big mushroom____ and added them to the chicken.

Only a Little and *Only a Few*

Use *only a little* + mass noun and *only a few* + count noun to talk about very small quantities. The meaning is similar to *not much* and *not many*.

> ### Examples
>
> *Count Nouns*
> HIRO: There are **only a few** napkins in this package. Do you have any more?
>
> *Mass Nouns*
> HIRO: There's **only a little** ice in the freezer. Do you have any more?

Activity 8C

Imagine that your roommate, wife, or husband is going to the supermarket. Make a sentence with *We only have (a little/a few),* and ask her or him to buy some more. Add *-s* or *-es* to form the plural of count nouns.

Count and Mass Nouns _____ 105

> **Example**
> (Coca-Cola)
> *We only have a little Coca-Cola left. Please buy some more.*

1. (*onion*)

2. (*honey*)

3. (*sugar*)

4. (*egg*)

5. (*coffee*)

6. (*salt*)

7. (*cookie*)

Containers

You can also answer the question, "How much . . . ?" or "How many . . . ?" with the following expressions.

a cup of coffee

a glass of water

two bottles of wine

a pound of meat

a kilo of flour

five boxes of matches

four packs of cigarettes

> ### *Examples*
> HIRO: How much seltzer did you buy?
> MARIA: **Two bottles of** plain seltzer and **two bottles of** orange seltzer.

Here are some other containers or measurements that we use.

a tube (a tube of toothpaste)

a pack (a pack of cigarettes)

a roll (a roll of film)

a carton (a carton of milk, a carton of eggs)

a can (a can of tomatoes)

a bag (a bag of potatoes)

a teaspoon (a teaspoon of sugar)

a tablespoon (a tablespoon of honey)

a gallon (a gallon of gas)

ACTIVITY 8D

Answer the following questions. Use a container or measurement in your answer. Choose from *cup, pound, gallon, bottle, carton, teaspoon,* and *glass*.

1. How much coffee (or tea) do you drink each day?
2. How much sugar do you usually put in your coffee or tea?
3. How much gas does a small car (a Volkswagen, for example) need to go a hundred miles?
4. Ruth's friend Nancy has four young children. How much milk do you think Nancy buys every week?

Count and Mass Nouns ———————————————————————————— 107

5. Joe invited five friends to come to his home for dinner tomorrow evening. How much wine does he need to buy for six people?

6. He's going to serve fish for dinner. How much fish does he need to buy for six people?

7. Doctors say that it is important to drink a lot of water. How much water do you drink each day?

■ ACTIVITY 8E

Ask your classmates the following questions. Complete the questions with *much, many, a lot of,* or *a great deal of.* Add *-s* or *-es* to count nouns to form the plural. (Remember to change *y* to *i* before you add *-es.*) For some questions, you must choose between *is* and *are.* Answer the questions with a number or *not much, not many, a lot of, a great deal of, a great many, thousands of,* or *millions of.* (Remember not to use *of* when you give a short answer that doesn't repeat the noun.)

Here is a list of count and mass nouns to study before you work on the questions.

Count Nouns		Mass Nouns	
beach	country	rain	rice
mountain	car	snow	wine
river	person (people)	oil	money
natural resource	worker	coffee	traffic
museum	tourist	sugar	time
hotel	language	wheat	
restaurant	day		
nightclub	week		
city	hour		

1. How _____ oil____ does Venezuela export each year?

   _____

2. How _____ oil____ does France produce each year?

   _____

3. How _____ car____ does Japan export each year?

   _____

4. How _____ coffee____ does Colombia export each year?

_____

5. Does Japan have _____ natural resource____?

_____

6. Does France export _____ wine____ to other countries?

_____

7. _____ there _____ traffic____ in Rome?

_____

8. How _____ time____ does it take to drive about ten blocks during rush hour in Tokyo?

_____

9. _____ there _____ foreign worker____ in
   (is/are)
Switzerland?

_____

10. How _____ official language____ do people speak in Switzerland?

_____

11. Do _____ people____ speak English in India?

_____

12. _____ there _____ inexpensive hotel____ in
    (is/are)
Paris?

_____

13. How _____ snow____ does Zurich get during the winter months?

_____

Count and Mass Nouns _____ 109

14. _____ there _____ beautiful beach ____ in
        (is/are)
    Brazil?

    _____

15. How _____ money____ does a person need to visit (name

    of a classmate's city) for a week?

    _____

16. How _____ Arabic-speaking country ____

    _____ there in the world?
        (is/are)

    _____

17. Do _____ student____ from (name of classmate's country)

    come to the United States to study?

    _____

18. How _____ people____ in China speak the Cantonese

    dialect of the Chinese language?

    _____

19. How _____ rain____ does Cairo get during the year?

    _____

20. How _____ tourist____ visit New York each year?

    _____

9 THE FUTURE TENSE WITH *WILL*

Content Focus — A BIRTHDAY DINNER

Dialog

(BILL and RUTH are going to have dinner in a restaurant because today is BILL's birthday.)

HEADWAITER: Good evening. May I help you?

BILL: Yes, we have a reservation for two people at 8:00. The name is Johnson.

HEADWAITER: Follow me, please. I'**ll show** you to your table.

(Now they are at the table looking at the menu.)

RUTH: What are you going to order? Don't forget that it's my treat.[1]

BILL: Don't worry, I **won't.** I'm going to have steak.

RUTH: That sounds delicious. I'm trying to make up my mind[2] between the shrimp and the steak.

BILL: Order the shrimp. I'**ll give** you some of my steak.

RUTH: Okay. I'**ll give** you some of my shrimp.

BILL: Ruth, watch out!

(Just at this moment, a customer at the next table gets up, and the WAITRESS spills a tray of drinks all over RUTH.)

RUTH: Oh, no! What am I going to do? My dress is soaking wet.[3]

WAITRESS: I'm very sorry. Just a minute. I'**ll get** some towels for you.

RUTH: Never mind. I'**ll use** our napkins. I know it wasn't your fault, but my dress is ruined. What can I do?

WAITRESS: I'**ll call** the headwaiter. Just a moment.

HEADWAITER: We apologize for what happened to your dress. It was an unfortunate accident.

RUTH: I know it was an accident, but this is a brand-new[4] dress. **Will** the restaurant **pay** the dry-cleaning bill?

HEADWAITER: I'm sorry, but it's not our policy. These accidents happen in a restaurant.

RUTH: It's not your policy? I can't understand that. You can cancel our orders. We're going to leave.

HEADWAITER: Very well, I **will.**

[1] *It's my treat* means "I'm going to pay for this."
[2] *Make up my mind* means "decide."
[3] *Soaking wet* means "completely wet."
[4] *Brand-new* means "very new."

Comprehension Questions

1. Why are Bill and Ruth going to have dinner in a restaurant? Is today a special occasion?
2. Did they make a reservation for dinner?
3. Who's going to pay for the dinner?
4. Why did the waitress spill a tray of drinks all over Ruth?
5. Is Ruth upset about her brand-new dress? What does she want the restaurant to do?
6. Is the restaurant going to do what Ruth asks?
7. Are Bill and Ruth going to stay and have dinner in this restaurant?

What Do You Think

1. Who is right in this situation? Is the restaurant responsible for the dry-cleaning bill? Why or why not?
2. Can you remember any time when a waiter or a manager in a restaurant or a salesperson in a store was rude or unfair to you? Tell about it.
3. Why do salespeople or waiters sometimes become impatient with, or even rude to, customers? Is their job difficult?
4. Is it difficult for you to stand up for your rights (defend yourself when someone is unfair or rude to you) in English? How do you feel?
5. Do you think there is a difference between salespeople and waiters in your country and those in the United States? In which country are salespeople and waiters more courteous?
6. What kinds of behavior are impolite in restaurants in your country? What is the polite way to call a waiter? Do you leave a tip? Does the man usually give the order to the waiter when a man and a woman are eating in a restaurant?

Grammar Fill-in

Study the words printed in boldface type in the dialog. Use *will* or *won't* in these parts from the dialog.

1. HEADWAITER: Follow me, please. I _____ you to your table.

2. RUTH: What are you going to order? Don't forget that it's my treat.

   BILL: Don't worry, I _____. I'm going to have steak.

3. RUTH: That sounds delicious. I'm trying to make up my mind between the shrimp and the steak.

   BILL: Order the shrimp. I _____ you some of my steak.

RUTH: Okay. I _____ you some of my shrimp.

4. RUTH: Oh, no! What am I going to do? My dress is soaking wet.

   WAITRESS: I'm very sorry. Just a minute. I_____ some towels for you.

5. RUTH: I know it was an accident, but this is a brand-new dress. _____ the dry-cleaning bill?

   HEADWAITER: I'm sorry, but it's not our policy. These accidents happen in a restaurant.

6. RUTH: It's not your policy? I can't understand that. You can cancel our orders. We're going to leave.

   HEADWAITER: Very well, I _____.

THE FUTURE TENSE WITH *WILL*

In Chapter 2, you learned that we usually use *be going to* to talk about our plans or intentions for the future. *Will* + base form is another structure that you use to talk about future time. When you want to offer your help to someone or to make a promise, use *will*.

Affirmative Statements

> subject + **will** + base form
>
> *I will call the headwaiter.*

Examples

Ruth and Bill left the first restaurant and went to a different one to celebrate Bill's birthday. They had a nice dinner. Then they met Joe and Diane to have some dessert at home.

DIANE: Oh, it's raining! Joe, we don't have an umbrella.
BILL: Here, I'**ll give** you mine. Ruth and I **will share** her umbrella.
JOE: How are we going to get home—taxi or subway?
BILL: We have our car. We'**ll give** you and Diane a ride.
JOE: Fantastic. I forgot about your car.

Negative Statements

When a person says, "Please don't do that" or "Don't forget to do that," you can answer, "I won't." This means "I will not do that" or "I will not forget to do that."

---

subject + **will not** + base form

I will not forget.
I won't forget.

Examples

Now Diane and Joe are at Bill and Ruth's home for some birthday cake and ice cream. Ruth is in the kitchen with Diane. They are putting candles on Bill's birthday cake.

DIANE: I'm going to light the candles now. Don't forget to turn off the lights in the dining room.

RUTH: Okay, I **won't.** I'll turn them off now.

(Now they are all in the dining room. The cake is on the table in front of Bill. Ruth, Diane, and Joe are singing "Happy Birthday.")

RUTH, DIANE,
AND JOE: Happy Birthday to you,
Happy Birthday to you,
Happy Birthday, dear Bill,
Happy Birthday to you.

RUTH: Blow out the candles, and don't forget to make a wish.

BILL: I **won't.** I'm going to wish for $1 million.

DIANE: Ruth, your cake looks delicious, but I'm really full from dinner. I don't think I can eat another bite.

RUTH: Oh, come on, Diane. I **won't give** you a big piece. Have some.

Questions

Use *Will you . . . ?* when you want to ask for help or a favor.

> **Will** + subject + base form?
>
> *Will you help me?*

Examples

DIANE: Your cake is delicious, Ruth. **Will** you **give** me the recipe?

RUTH: Sure. Bill, **will** you please **bring** me a piece of paper and a pen from the desk?

BILL: Okay. I'll get it in a minute. I'm going to wash my hands.

Note: If someone asks for a favor with *Will you . . . ?* and you want to say no, don't say, "No, I won't." This is too strong. Answer with, "I'm sorry, but I can't right now because. . . ."

Activity 9A

Write sentences with *will* or a contracted form of *will ('ll)*.

Example

BILL: I can't open the door. My hands are full.

RUTH: Just a minute. *I'll open it.*

1. RUTH: I burned my hand when I was cooking. Look at all these dishes. How can I wash them?

   BILL: _____.

2. JOE: I saw Bob this morning, but I forgot to tell him about my party next weekend.

   BILL AND RUTH: We're going to see Bob tonight. He's going to come to our place for dinner. We _____

   _____.

3. JOE: I forgot to buy a newspaper when I was out.

   HIRO: I'm going to the store now. _____.

4. HIRO: I have to return this book to the library, but I don't feel very well.

   JOE: Diane and I are going to the library tonight. We _____
   _____.

5. RUTH: I need the sugar. It's on the top shelf, and I can't reach it. The shelf's too high.

   BILL: _____.

■ ACTIVITY 9B

Write questions with *will*.

> *Example*
> MARIA: I have a bad headache. *Will you get me* a couple of aspirin, please?
> HIRO: Sure, I'll get you some now.

1. JOE: I can't find my pen. _____?

   HIRO: Of course. Here's one.

2. HIRO: I can't understand this homework from my English class. You know more English than I do. _____
   _____?

3. BILL: I don't have time to go out for lunch. Are you going out now?

   COWORKER: Yes, I'm going to the delicatessen on the corner.

   BILL: _____ a sandwich?

   COWORKER: Sure. I'll be glad to.

4. RUTH: I can't open this window. It's stuck. _____
   _____?

   BILL: Okay. I'll open it in a minute.

The Future Tense with Will

ACTIVITY 9C

Joe's mother worries about her son all the time. This weekend Joe was visiting his parents in Boston. He is getting ready to drive back to New York City now. It is January, and there was a big snowstorm last night, so his mother is very nervous and worried about his trip back to New York City.

Write sentences with *won't*.

MRS. HALEY: Joe, I'm terribly worried. There's a lot of snow on the roads. They're very slippery.

JOE: Mom, please don't worry. I *won't drive* fast. I *won't have* an accident.

MRS. HALEY: And don't stop for any hitchhikers. I think it's very dangerous to pick up hitchhikers.

JOE: Okay, I _____ any hitchhikers.

MRS. HALEY: Joe, you're yawning. It's very dangerous to drive when you're sleepy.

JOE: Don't worry. I _____ asleep when I'm driving.
(fall)

MRS. HALEY: It's very wet outside.

JOE: I know. I _____ to wear my boots.
(forget)

MRS. HALEY: And don't forget to call me as soon as you get to New York.

JOE: I _____. I'll be fine. Now, Mom, let me tell you something. I'll be okay. Don't worry. You worry too much.

MRS. HALEY: All right. I _____.

ACTIVITY 9D

Decide carefully which one is more correct for each sentence—*will* or *going to*. There are no really incorrect answers here, but remember that we usually use *going to* for a plan or intention and *will* to offer help or to make a promise.

Examples

(JOE, BILL, and RUTH are all at DIANE's apartment.)

JOE: Come on, everybody. Let's go. _We're going to go_ to a nightclub tonight. Remember?

DIANE: I'll be ready in a minute. I _'m going to change_ my shoes.

RUTH: Where are our coats?

JOE: I _'ll get_ them. Diane, don't forget your keys.

DIANE: I _won't_.

1. Hiro and Maria's friend is in the hospital.

    HIRO: _____ Helen in the hospital tonight?
               (visit)

    MARIA: Yes, I _____.

    HIRO: I want to go, too, but I can't. Joe invited some friends over for dinner tonight, and I _____ for them.
               (cook)

    MARIA: I _____ hello to Helen for you.
         (say)

    HIRO: Thanks. And _____ you _____ me a favor?
                 (do)

    _____ you _____ Helen some flowers for me, please?
             (buy)

    MARIA: Sure. I _____ glad to do that.
         (be)

    HIRO: Thanks. I don't have any money right now, but I _____ it to you tomorrow.
                                  (give)

    MARIA: Don't worry about it.

    HIRO: When _____ Helen _____ the hospital?
                         (leave)

    MARIA: In about three or four days.

    HIRO: Oh, that's good. Don't forget to buy the flowers.

    MARIA: I _____.

The Future Tense with Will _____ *119*

2. DIANE: I _____ a party next Friday. Would you and Bill
(have)
like to come?

   RUTH: Thank you. What kind of party? How many people _____
   you _____?
   (invite)

   DIANE: I _____ about thirty or forty people.
   (ask)

   RUTH: What _____?
   (wear)

   DIANE: I _____ my purple dress, but you can wear jeans
   (wear)
   if you want.

   RUTH: What time _____ people to come?
   (ask)

   DIANE: At about 9:00.

   RUTH: Do you need anything for the party? Is there anything I can do to help?

   DIANE: Well, I don't have many glasses. Do you have some extras?

   RUTH: Sure. I _____ you them. If you want me to, I
   (lend)
   _____ early on Friday to help you get everything
   (come)
   ready for the party.

   DIANE: That's wonderful. I appreciate it. Please don't forget the glasses.

   RUTH: I _____.

3. MARIA: What _____ tonight?
   (do)

   HIRO: I _____ English. I don't understand some of the
   (study)
   verb tenses.

   MARIA: I _____ over to your place and help you. What
   (come)
   time _____?
   (start)

   HIRO: About 8:00.

MARIA: Okay, I _____ there at about 7:45.
       (be)

HIRO: Fine. I _____ you out for some dessert when we
             (take)
      finish.

■ ACTIVITY 9E

Look at the short dialogs in Activity 9A. With a classmate, write a similar short dialog about the following situations, using *will* to ask for help, to offer help, or to make promises.

1. A friend of yours is sick. This friend lives alone, so he needs help doing the laundry, grocery shopping, cooking, and other things.

2. A friend of yours has a TV that is not working well. You are very good at fixing things.

3. You are reading a good book. A friend of yours is interested in this book, too, and is asking you about it.

4. You are a parent. You are talking to your eight-year-old child, who is upset and crying because she is having a lot of trouble with schoolwork and also she has broken a favorite toy.

10 CAN AND COULD

Diane in a karate class.

Content Focus: SPECIAL ABILITIES

Dialog

MARIA: Hey, Diane, I heard that you got your brown belt last week. Congratulations! Come on, give me a karate demonstration. **Can** you **break** this table with a karate chop?

DIANE: No, I **can't** do that, but my instructor **can**. He **can chop** a brick in half with his bare hand.

MARIA: What **can** you **do?** Show me something.

DIANE: Okay. Pretend that you're attacking me. Put your hands around my neck. I **can escape** in a second. Watch this!

(MARIA puts her hands around DIANE's neck. DIANE escapes.)

MARIA: Wow, that's great! I **can't do** that.

DIANE: Yes, you **can**. Come with me to my next karate class. You **can watch** for an hour. Maybe you **can join** a beginners' class.

MARIA: Oh, no! Me—study karate? I'm not athletic. I **can't** even **throw** a ball.

DIANE: Oh, come on.[1] I don't believe you.

MARIA: It's true. I took tennis classes about a year ago. At the end of the course, I still **couldn't hit** the ball.

DIANE: **I can understand** that. Tennis is a difficult sport.

MARIA: Then I went skiing a few months ago. I took lessons for a week.

DIANE: How did you do? **Could** you **ski** a little at the end of the week?

MARIA: Oh, **I could ski,** but I **couldn't stop.** I skied into a tree three times.

Comprehension Questions

1. What color belt in karate does Diane have?
2. Can she chop a brick in half with her bare hand?
3. Can she escape if someone has his or her hands around her neck?
4. Is Maria athletic?
5. Is she a good tennis player?
6. Maria took ski lessons a few months ago. At the end of the week, could she ski?

What about You?

1. Are you athletic? What sports can you play? If you say that you are not athletic, why do you say that? What can't you do?

---

[1] *Oh, come on.* We often say this when we mean "I don't really believe you. I think you're joking."

Can and Could   123

2. Do you know very much about karate or kung fu? Tell what you know. Are kung fu movies very popular in your country? Bruce Lee was a famous actor in kung fu movies. Tell about some things that he could do.
3. What are your special talents or abilities? Can you play a musical instrument? Can you sing? Can you cook well? Do you know anyone who has a special or unusual talent? Tell about this person.

Dictation

Study the second half of the dialog for a dictation. Begin studying where Maria says "Wow, that's great!" Then listen to your instructor and fill in the blanks.

MARIA: Wow, _____ great! _____ that.

DIANE: Yes, you _____. _____ to my next karate class. _____ for _____ hour. Maybe you _____ a beginners' class.

MARIA: Oh, no! Me—study karate? _____. I _____ even _____ a ball.

DIANE: Oh, come on, I _____ you.

MARIA: _____. I _____ tennis classes about a year ago. At the end of the course, I still _____ the ball.

DIANE: _____ that. Tennis is a difficult sport.

MARIA: Then _____ skiing _____. I took lessons for a week.

DIANE: _____? _____ a little at the end of the week?

MARIA: Oh, I _____, but I _____. I skied into a tree _____.

CAN AND COULD

Present Tense

Use *can* with the base form of a verb to talk about ability or possibility in the present.

STATEMENTS

subject   + **can** + base form
(I, you, he, she,
it, we, they)

I can ski.

subject   + **cannot** + base form
               (can't)

I can't ski.

QUESTIONS

Can + subject + base form?

Can you ski?

(Question word) + **can** + subject + base form?

What can you do?

SHORT ANSWERS

When we answer a question that starts with *can* with *yes* or *no*, we usually add the subject and *can* or *can't* to the short answer.

Yes, + subject + can.

Yes, she can.

No, + subject + can't.

No, she can't.

Can has several different meanings.

❑ Use *can* to say that someone has the ability to do something.

Examples

Diane's karate instructor is very strong. He **can tear** a thick phone book in half.

Diane is studying karate, but she **can't do** that.

Can you **tear** a phone book in half?

Yes, I **can.**   or   No, I **can't.**

❑ Also use *can* to say that it is possible to do something.

Examples

Americans are very interested in the martial arts from oriental countries—karate, judo, and kung fu. A person **can find** classes in these arts in almost every city in the United States.

❑ Sometimes we use *can* when we want to ask for, or give someone, permission to do something. Here *can* has the same meaning as *may*.

Examples

DIANE: Mr. Noguchi, **can I bring** a friend to class next week?
INSTRUCTOR: Of course you **can.**

Note: Many students make these mistakes.

I can **to** play baseball.

Remember: There is no *to* after *can* or *can't*.

She can**s** play baseball   or   She can play**s** baseball.

Remember: With *can*, don't use *-s* for *he, she,* or *it.*

■ ACTIVITY 10A

❑ Which of these things can you do? Which things can't you do? Write a sentence about yourself using *can* or *can't*.

Examples

(*play*)

I can't play _____ soccer.

I can play _____ baseball.

1. (*lift*)

   _____ a hundred pounds (forty-five kilos) over my head with one hand.

2. (*swim*)

   _____ well.

3. (*run*)

   _____ five miles.

4. (*drink*)

   _____ a whole bottle of whiskey in half an hour.

5. (*stand*)

   _____ on my head.

☐ Joe's friend John is a bodybuilder. He lifts weights every day to develop his muscles. He's in great physical condition and is very strong. What are some things that he can do? Use your imagination to answer.

1. _____
2. _____
3. _____
4. _____

Can and Could — 127

☐ Bill is out of shape.[2] Use your imagination to write some sentences about the things that he can't do.

1. _____
2. _____
3. _____
4. _____

☐ Ask a classmate a question. Your classmate will give a short answer.

Example
(play)

Can you play _____ tennis?

Answer: _____

1. (ride)

    _____ a horse?

    Answer: _____

2. (ski)

    _____?

    Answer: _____

3. (touch)

    _____ your toes?

    Answer: _____

4. (run)

    How far _____?

    Answer: _____

[2] *Out of shape* means "not in good physical condition"—usually because a person doesn't exercise regularly.

Past Tense

When you talk about ability, the past tense of *can* is *could*.

STATEMENTS

> subject + **could (not)** + base form
> **(couldn't)**
>
> *Harry Houdini could do wonderful things.*

QUESTIONS

> **Could** + subject + base form?
>
> *Could he escape from anything?*
>
> (Question word) + **could** + subject + base form?
>
> *How could he do that?*

Examples

Harry Houdini was a famous magician. He was born in 1874 and died in 1926. He was famous all over the world. He **could escape** from anything. He **could escape** from a locked box under water, he **could get** his hands out of handcuffs, he **could escape** from chains, and he **could escape** from any prison.

There were many other magicians in Houdini's time. **Could** they **do** all these things? No, they **couldn't.** No one **could understand** how Houdini escaped.

Houdini died tragically. One night he gave a show in a big theater. He was upside down in a tank of water with chains and locks all around the tank. He **couldn't get** out of the tank, so he drowned. Houdini's friends believed that he was sick on that day, and that is why he **couldn't escape.**

Can and Could

■ **ACTIVITY 10B**

☐ Which of these things could you do when you were a child? Which things couldn't you do? Complete the following sentences. Use the words in parentheses in the sentence.

Example

(*walk*) When I was three years old, _I could walk_.

1. (*read*) _____ when I was three years old.

2. (*tie*) _____ my own shoes when I was five years old.

3. (*ride*) When I was five years old, _____ bicycle.

4. (*swim*) _____ when I was four.

5. (*cross*) When I was five, _____ the street alone.

☐ Ask your classmate questions. Your classmate will give a short answer.

Example

(*speak*)

Question: _Could you speak_ at two years of age?

Answer: _____

1. (*drive*)

   Question: _____ a car when you were fourteen years old?

   Answer: _____

2. (*stay up*)

   Question: _____ until midnight when you were seven years old?

   Answer: _____

3. (*smoke*)

   Question: _____ when you were thirteen years old, or did your parents punish you if they saw you with a cigarette?

   Answer: _____

■ ACTIVITY 10C

Fill in the blanks with *can, can't, could,* or *couldn't* and the verb below the blank. (JOE and DIANE are talking on the telephone.)

JOE: How was your day today, Diane?

DIANE: Not great. This morning I _____ my car, so I was
 (negative for **start**)
about fifteen minutes late to work.

JOE: What's the matter with your car?

DIANE: I don't know. _____ over here now and look at it?
 (**come**)
Maybe you _____ it.
 (**fix**)

JOE: Sure.

DIANE: Joe, _____ a little louder? I _____ you
 (**speak**)   (negative for **hear**)
very well. What's the matter with your voice? Do you have a cold?

JOE: Yeah. I feel lousy. I _____ last night because I
 (negative for **sleep**)
_____. Today I _____. I'm losing my voice.
 (negative for **breathe**)   (negative for **talk**)

DIANE: Well, look. I don't want you to come out in this cold weather. You stay in. I'm going to come over to your place.

JOE: Okay. _____ at the drugstore and buy some
 (**stop**)
cough medicine for me?

DIANE: Sure. I'll be there in about half an hour.

Discussion

1. What could you do when you were in your country that you can't do now? Example: "When I was in my country, I could speak my own language all the time, but here I can't."

2. Tell about some things that you couldn't do when you were in your country but that you can do here. Example: When I was in my country, I couldn't see many movies in English, but here I can.

3. How was life different 200 years ago? Tell about some things that people couldn't do 200 years ago that we can do today. Are there some things that people could do 200 years ago that we can't do today? What are they?

4. How is country life different from city life? What can people who live in the country do that people in the city can't do? What can people in the city do that people in the country can't do?

11 SHOULD

Content Focus

DIFFICULTIES IN LIVING IN A DIFFERENT COUNTRY OR CULTURE

Dialog

(MARIA is meeting HIRO for a cup of coffee after class. It's a very cold day, and HIRO has a cold.)

MARIA: Hiro, you look sick. What's the matter?

HIRO: I have a cold. I have a sore throat, a runny nose, a cough—I feel miserable.

MARIA: That's too bad. You **shouldn't be** out in the cold. You **should go** home and go to bed.

HIRO: I think I'll do that. I'm really down[1] today too.

MARIA: Why? What's wrong?

HIRO: Everything is wrong. I'm homesick. Sometimes I really hate the United States. And my English is lousy, too, so I can't get into graduate school next semester.

MARIA: What are you talking about? Your English isn't lousy. It's good.

HIRO: My writing and grammar are okay, but my comprehension isn't very good. What do you think? What **should** I **do**?

MARIA: Well, one problem is that you spend a lot of time with your Japanese friends. It's important to use your English.

HIRO: I know I **shouldn't speak** Japanese all the time, but it's difficult to meet Americans, and I'm embarrassed when I speak English with Americans.

MARIA: I know. Some Americans don't try very hard to understand foreigners. Listen! I have an idea. You **should find** an American girlfriend.

HIRO: What? Are you joking? You're my girlfriend.

MARIA: Yes. I'm joking. But here's a good idea. There are a lot of Americans in my photography club. Why don't you come to the next meeting with me?

HIRO: Okay. That's a good idea.

Comprehension Questions

1. What's the matter with Hiro today?
2. Why is he down today?
3. How does he feel about living in the United States?
4. How does he feel about his English?
5. Does he have many opportunities to speak English? Why or why not?
6. Why can't he get into graduate school next semester?

[1] *I'm down* means "I'm unhappy and depressed."

What Do You Think?

1. Hiro says he is homesick. Why do people feel homesick? Describe how people feel when they are homesick. Are you homesick? What should a person do when he or she is homesick?

2. Is it difficult to live in another country or culture? Why? Is your culture very different from the culture of the United States? How is it different? Give some examples. What customs or manners in the United States are difficult for you to understand?

3. What about food? Do you sometimes get homesick for food from your country? Do you like American food? Why or why not?

4. Hiro says that his writing and grammar in English are okay but his comprehension isn't very good. What are your problems in English? How much do you understand when people speak to you or when you watch TV or a movie? What TV programs are easy for you to understand? Is the English that you study in class the same as the English that you hear on the streets? How do you feel when you speak English? Do you feel embarrassed? How about when you make mistakes? Does this make you feel like a child? How do you feel about your progress in learning English? Are you happy with your progress, or do you think you are learning very slowly?

5. Do you or any of your classmates have an American boyfriend or girlfriend? Does this help your English? What else should you do to improve your English?

6. Do some people learn languages faster than others? Why do some people learn faster than others?

Role Playing

Study the dialog at home. The next time your class meets, you will role play this situation. You don't have to memorize the dialog; just be ready to have a similar conversation using the same situation. Try to use *should* in your conversation.

SHOULD

We use *should* when we want to give someone advice—to say, "In my opinion, I think it is good for you to do this." We also use *should* to express what society thinks is good.

	Subject + **should (not)** + base form
(shouldn't)	*You should go home.*
	Should + subject + base form?
	Should I do that?
	Yes, (subject) **should.**
	No, (subject) **shouldn't.**

Examples

A few days ago, Hiro talked to Maria about his problems with English and with meeting Americans. Today he feels better because he received some good news in the mail. He's going to spend two weeks with an American family in Arizona. The Experiment in International Living[2] arranged the visit for him. He's talking with Joe about this trip.

HIRO: I'm really excited about my trip to Arizona. I'm going to get my plane ticket now.

JOE: Are you going to fly round trip? Maybe you **should take** the bus or train one way so you can see the country.

HIRO: Yes, I'm going to take the train on the way back. Tell me about Arizona. What **should** I **see** there?

JOE: Well, the Grand Canyon is fantastic. You **should see** that. I also think you **should visit** the Painted Desert. It's beautiful.

HIRO: Okay. Thanks for your advice.

ACTIVITY 11A

Use *should* or *shouldn't* to offer advice about these medical problems. Note: In these questions, *you* has a general meaning. Here *you* means "a person" (any person). Don't answer with *I*. Start your answer with *you*.

1. What should you do when you have a headache? What shouldn't you do?
2. What should you do when you have a stomachache? What medicines should you take? What food should or shouldn't you eat? Should you drink alcohol?
3. What should you do when you have a fever?

---

[2]The Experiment in International Living is an organization that arranges for foreign students to visit American families for two or three weeks. For information, write to The Experiment in International Living, Kipling Road, Brattleboro, Vermont 05301 USA

4. What should you do if you burn your hand (not seriously—just a small burn, for example, from touching a hot pan when you're cooking)? What should or shouldn't you put on it? Butter? Toothpaste? Cold water? A bandage?

5. What should you do if you want to lose weight? What should or shouldn't you eat? What about exercise?

6. What should or shouldn't you do when you have a hangover? (You get a hangover when you drink too much liquor, and the next day you feel bad; you have a headache or a stomachache.)

ACTIVITY 11B

Use *should* or *shouldn't* to give advice about these situations.

1. Ruth is in a supermarket. She's watching an old lady who looks very poor. The old lady is stealing food. She's hiding some bread and fruit under her coat. What should Ruth do? Should she tell the security guard? Should she tell the old lady that what she is doing is wrong? Should she just look the other way? Is there anything else she should do?

2. Diane is in a very expensive department store. She's watching a lady who is wearing nice, expensive clothes. The lady is stealing some clothes from the store. She is putting an expensive sweater under her coat. What should Diane do? Should she tell the store detective or the salesperson? Should she say anything to the lady? Should she look the other way? Is this situation different from the first one?

3. Maria is taking a history examination. A classmate gave her a piece of paper a few seconds ago. The piece of paper says, "Please give me the answers to questions 3, 10, 14, and 17. The professor is not watching us now." What should Maria do? Should she give her classmate the answers? Should she tell the professor? What should she say to her classmate after the exam? What should teachers do when they catch a student who is cheating? Is it ever right to cheat?

4. Joe found a wallet on the street a few minutes ago. The wallet has $500 in it. It also has the name and address of the owner in it, and the address is in a rich neighborhood. Joe is a waiter and a student. He is trying to decide what he should do with the wallet and the money now. What do you think? Should he keep the money? Should he take the wallet and money to the police? Should he call the owner?

5. Ruth and Bill frequently argue about the housework. Bill doesn't think he should help with the housework because he has a full-time job. Also, he says that housework is women's work. Ruth thinks Bill should help her because she works part-time and goes to school and is very busy. What's the solution to their problem?

6. One of Ruth's clients does not know what to do about her marriage. She and her husband don't love each other. They fight all the time. Her husband goes out with other women. She wants to get a divorce, but they have three young children, and she has no work experience. What should she do?

■ Activity 11C

Use *should* or *shouldn't* to give your opinion.

1. If you want to live a long, happy, and healthy life, what should you do? What shouldn't you do? Talk about food, liquor, exercise, work, friends, and anything else you can think of.
2. In some countries, it is not the custom for young people to date. In other countries, such as the United States, most young people date several different people before they think about getting married. What are your opinions about dating? Should people date before they get married? At what age should they begin to date? Is it important for a chaperone to go with the young couple on a date? Should a girl or a woman ever ask a boy or a man for a date? What are the rules for good manners on a date? What should or shouldn't people do? For example, should the man always pay for everything on a date?

■ Activity 11D

Give advice to a classmate who is planning to visit your country for the first time. This classmate can stay for only two weeks. What places should he or she visit? How long should he or she stay in each place? How much money should the classmate plan to bring? Is there anything he or she should be careful not to do? What things should the classmate be sure to buy to bring back to his or her country? One person can ask the questions, and the other can give advice using *should* or *I think it's a good idea to . . .* or *It's important (to/not to) . . .* or *I advise you to. . . .*

12 HAVE TO

Content Focus — SCHOOL LIFE

Dialog

(Joe's younger sister, BETTY, is sixteen years old. She's a high-school student. In this dialog, BETTY is getting ready to go out on a date with her boyfriend, Jeff. Her FATHER and MOTHER are sitting in the living room.)

BETTY: Mom, where's my new sweater? I can't find it. I **have to hurry.**

MOTHER: It's in your closet. Look again.

FATHER: Are you going out with Jeff tonight? You have school tomorrow.

BETTY: I'm not going to stay out late. Jeff and I are going to a party.

FATHER: Oh, no you aren't. Your grades were terrible last semester—D in history and F in math. And you **have to get up** early for school tomorrow.

BETTY: But, Dad, I finished all my homework tonight.

FATHER: You spent about half an hour on your homework. Sit down and study an hour more. No dates on school nights.

BETTY: But Mom gave me permission to go out tonight. Mom, tell him.

MOTHER: That's right, dear. Today is Jeff's birthday.

FATHER: Well, all right. But in the future, no dates on school nights. And don't stay out late tonight.

BETTY: Okay, Dad. What time **do I have to be** home?

FATHER: Tell Jeff that he **has to bring** you home at 11:00.

BETTY: 11:00? Dad, I'm sixteen years old. My friends don't **have to be** home so early. Kathy **doesn't have to come** in until 1:00. Mom, **do I have to come** in so early?

MOTHER: I agree with your father. When I was your age, I **had to be** home at 10:00.

BETTY: Oh, Mom. That was a hundred years ago. Things are different now.

FATHER: Don't talk to your mother that way. And wait a minute—what about the dishes, young lady? You **have to wash** them before you go out.

BETTY: The dishes! Why **do I have to wash** the dishes? Kathy **doesn't have to wash** the dishes. Joe **didn't have to wash** the dishes when he was in high school.

FATHER: I don't care about Kathy. And Joe **had to do** other things to help.

BETTY: But I don't have time now. I **have to get** ready.

FATHER: No dishes, no date.

BETTY: Oh, all right.

Comprehension Questions

1. Where is Betty going tonight?
2. Does her father want her to go out tonight? Why or why not?
3. What time does she have to be home tonight?
4. Do her friends have to be home at that time too?
5. What time did Betty's mother have to be home when she was sixteen?
6. What does Betty have to do before she can go out tonight?
7. Did Joe have to do things to help around the house when he was Betty's age?

What Do You Think?

1. What do parents and teenagers usually disagree about? Do they usually disagree about schoolwork? Housework? Friends? Clothes? Music?
2. When you were a teenager, what time did you have to come in at night?
3. Did you have to help your parents with the housework when you were a child? What did you have to do? Wash the dishes? Take out the garbage? Clean your room? Make your bed? Take care of your younger brothers and sisters?
4. Do you have children? If so, what rules do they have to follow? For example, do they have to finish all their homework before they can watch TV? Are there some kinds of food that they don't like? Do they have to eat these foods? Do they have to help with the housework? What do they have to do? What time do they have to come home at night?

Grammar Fill-in

Read the last half of the dialog again beginning where Betty's father says, "Well, all right. But in the future...." Pay careful attention to the words in boldface type. Then fill in as many blanks as possible without looking back at the dialog.

FATHER: Well, all right. But in the future, no dates on school nights. And don't stay out late tonight.

BETTY: Okay, Dad. What time _____ I _____ home?

FATHER: Tell Jeff that he _____ you home at 11:00.

Have To   141

BETTY: 11:00? Dad, I'm sixteen years old. My friends _____ _____ home so early. Kathy _____ _____ in until 1:00. Mom, _____ _____ in so early?

MOTHER: I agree with your father. When I was your age, I _____ home at 10:00.

BETTY: Oh, Mom. That was a hundred years ago. Things are different now.

FATHER: Don't talk to your mother that way. And wait a minute—what about the dishes, young lady? You _____ them before you go out.

BETTY: The dishes! Why _____ the dishes? Kathy _____ the dishes. Joe _____ the dishes when he was in high school.

FATHER: I don't care about Kathy. And Joe _____ other things to help.

BETTY: But I don't have time now. I _____ ready.

FATHER: No dishes, no date.

BETTY: Oh, all right.

Role Playing

Study the dialog at home. The next time your class meets, you will role play this situation. You don't have to memorize the dialog; just be ready to have a similar conversation using the same situation. Try to use the different forms of *have to* in your conversation.

HAVE TO

Use *have to* when you want to talk about something that is necessary to do.

$\left.\begin{array}{l}\text{I}\\\text{you}\\\text{we}\\\text{they}\end{array}\right\}$ + **have to** + base form $\left.\begin{array}{l}\text{he}\\\text{she}\\\text{it}\end{array}\right\}$ + **has to** + base form

I have to hurry.   *Jeff has to bring you home by 11:00.*

Examples

Betty's father is angry with her because she got bad grades in school last semester. She can't go out on school nights. She **has to come** home right after school. She **has to study** from 7:00 to 9:00 every night. On the weekends, Betty and her boyfriend **have to leave** parties early because she **has to be** home at 11:00.

(Question word) **do** + $\left\{\begin{array}{l}\text{I}\\\text{you}\\\text{we}\\\text{they}\end{array}\right\}$ + **have to** + base form?

Why do I have to wash the dishes?

(Question word) **does** + $\left\{\begin{array}{l}\text{he}\\\text{she}\\\text{it}\end{array}\right\}$ + **have to** + base form?

When does Kathy have to come home?

Examples

Betty has to help her parents with the housework.

What **does** she **have to do?**

She has to wash the dishes.

Does she **have to do** anything else?

Yes, she does. She has to clean her room, and she has to cook two nights a week.

ACTIVITY 12A

Vocabulary

military: the army
academy: school
strict: hard; severe. A strict school has many hard rules that students must follow.
obey: to follow a rule or an order
upperclassman: a student in the third or fourth year of college

Betty and Joe's brother Tom is eighteen years old. He's in his first year at West Point. West Point is the U.S. Army Military Academy. West Point is a very good military school and university. It is a very strict school, and there are many rules. Students at West Point are called cadets.

This is a letter from Tom to his brother Joe about life at West Point. Close your book. Your instructor will read short sections of Tom's letter to the class. After you listen to each section, open your book and fill in the blanks.

Section 1

Use *have to* and one of these verbs: *do, put, obey, run.*

Dear Joe,

How are you doing? Well, here I am at West Point. Life here is very difficult. We're busy every minute of the day. We *have to obey* a thousand rules. A first-year cadet is nothing at West Point. We

_____ everything that an upperclassman tells us to

do. On the first day, upperclassmen always tell the new cadets to do a

lot of crazy things. For example, we usually _____

down our suitcases and pick them up again about fifty times. And we

_____ up and down the stairs ten times. We can't

say no. We _____ these crazy things.

Section 2
Use *have to* and one of these verbs: *look, obey, be, wear, polish.*

Vocabulary

    uniform: special clothes that make everyone look the same. Police and people in the military wear uniforms.
    perfect: without any fault or mistake
    polish: to clean something until it shines
  reflection: what you see when you look into a mirror or lake
  complain: to say that you are unhappy or dissatisfied with something

The cadet uniform is very important. Our uniforms

_____ perfect at all times. I _____

my shoes about three times a day. If an upperclassman can't see his

reflection in our shoes, we _____ them again. We

_____ different uniforms on different days. Every

morning, a cadet puts up a flag. This flag tells the cadets which uniform to

wear that day. We _____ out our windows every morning

to see the flag. If the day is a beautiful sunny day and the flag says, "Wear

your raincoat," we _____ our raincoats. We complain all

the time, but we _____ the rules.

Section 3
Use *have to* and one of these verbs: *tell, stand, sit, memorize, run, touch, get.*

Vocabulary

stand at attention: to stand very straight with your hands at your sides
memorize: to study something until you can say every word of it

Cadets _____ at attention when they speak to upperclassmen. When we stand at attention, our chins _____ our chests. We even _____ at attention when we eat our meals. You won't believe some of the other stupid things that we have to do for upperclassmen. We _____ the menu for lunch and dinner every day. If an upperclassman asks, "What's for dinner?" we _____ him the complete menu: "Roast chicken, potatoes, carrots, salad, and apple pie, sir." Also, if an upperclassman wants a Coke, we _____ to the soda machine and _____ a Coke for him.

Section 4
Use *have to* and one of these verbs: *go, tell, be.*

Vocabulary

honest: truthful
honor: good reputation for being honest
lie: to say something that is not true
cheat: to try to win a game or pass a test in a way that is not honest. If you look at your neighbor's test paper and copy the answers, you cheat.
commander: the officer in charge

Honor is very important at West Point. Cadets _____ honest in everything they do at West Point. For example, if you know that another cadet lied or cheated on a test, you _____ the commander.

I don't have time to write any more. I _____ to class now. Please write to me. Sometimes I'm very lonely here. It's very different from high school and home.

See you at Christmas,

Tom

■ Activity 12B

Look at each picture that follows and make a sentence about it. Tell what Tom *has to do* at West Point.

1.

2.

3.

4.

5.   6.

(comic panels: 5. Cadet reciting "Roast chicken, potatoes, carrots, salad, and apple pie, sir." 6. Officer saying "Get me a Coke." Cadet replying "Yes, sir." running to Coke machine.)

▪ **ACTIVITY 12C**

Write questions about West Point using *do/does* + subject + *have to* + base form.

> **Example**
>
> (*cadets, pay*)
>
> *Do cadets have to pay* for their education at West Point?
>
> No, *they don't*. The government pays for their education.

1. (*cadets, serve*)

   _____ in the army after they graduate

   from West Point?

   Yes, they _____. This is the way they pay back the

   government for their education.

2. (*students, get*)

   _____ good grades in high school if they

   want to go to West Point?

   Yes, _____. West Point accepts only very good students.

3. (*students, take*)

   _____ an entrance examination to get into West Point?

   Yes, _____ .

4. (*Tom, attend*)

   _____ all of his classes?

   Yes, _____ . The instructors report all students who are absent.

5. (*he, study*)

   _____ hard?

   Yes, he has to spend a lot of time studying.

6. (*cadets, be*)

   Why _____ in excellent physical condition?

   Because they have to march long hours with heavy equipment.

7. (*cadets, do*)

   What _____ when they leave West Point for the weekend?

   They have to sign out when they leave and sign in when they come back.

8. (*Tom, live*)

   _____ in a dormitory all four years at West Point?

   Yes, _____ .

Activity 12D

Look at this sentence.

Tom doesn't like to sit at attention when he eats meals, but he has to.

Write sentences like the one above.

> **Example**
> (get)
>
> *Tom doesn't like to get* Cokes for the upperclassmen, but *he has to*.

1. (memorize)

   _____ the menu, but _____.

2. (polish)

   _____ his shoes, but _____.

3. (attend)

   _____ all of his classes, but _____.

4. (sign)

   _____ out and sign in on the weekends,

   but _____.

Activity 12E

What are some things you don't like to do but have to do? Wash the dishes? Go to the dentist? Get up early? Do exercises? Write four or five sentences similar to the sentences above.

Negative of *Have to*

The negative of *have to* means "It is not necessary."

I
you   + **do not have to** + base form
we
they

Betty's friends don't have to come home at 11:00.

he
she + **does not have to** + base form
it

Kathy doesn't have to come home at 11:00.

Examples

Joe and Betty have another brother, Mike. Mike is in his third year at a small university in Massachusetts. His school life is completely different from Tom's life at West Point. Mike's school doesn't have many rules. Mike **doesn't have to live** in a dormitory. He lives in an apartment near the campus. The professors do not take attendance in class, so the students **don't have to attend** class if they don't want to. Mike **doesn't have to sign out** or sign in for the weekend; he can leave the university at any time.

Activity 12F

☐ Make a negative sentence using *don't have to/doesn't have to*.

Example

HIRO: How much is the admission to the museum—a dollar and a half?

MARIA: It's free for students. We <u>*don't have to pay*</u>.

Have To   151

1. BETTY: Wow! The teacher gave us a lot of homework—six pages of exercises!

   JEFF: But the teacher said we can have two days to do this assignment. We _____ all six pages tonight. You can do half tonight and half tomorrow night.

2. MARIA: My class is planning a party for next Saturday. All of the students are going to cook something and take it to the party. What can I make? I'm a terrible cook.

   HIRO: You _____. You can buy some cake or fruit and take that to the party.

3. RUTH: Would you like to come for dinner at our place tomorrow night?

   DIANE: That sounds great. Thanks.

   RUTH: Bill will pick you up at about 7:00.

   DIANE: Oh, I can take the bus. Bill _____. It's only a short ride.

   RUTH: Are you sure?

   DIANE: Of course. Listen, what can I bring? Can I bring some dessert?

   RUTH: I know you're very busy. You _____ anything.

   DIANE: It's no trouble. I'll make a pie.

   RUTH: Okay. Thanks.

4. JEFF: What time do you have to be home tonight—11:00?

   BETTY: No, I have special permission to stay out late tonight. I _____ until 1:00.

5. INSTRUCTOR: Please write a composition about your family.

   BETTY: How long does it have to be—two pages?

   INSTRUCTOR: It _____ two pages. It can be only one page if you want.

6. HIRO: Do you know the telephone number for bus reservations? I'm going to Boston by bus tomorrow.

   JOE: You _____ a reservation for the bus. There are always extra seats.

7. MARIA: Do you have the correct change for this machine? A soda costs eighty-five cents, and I have one dollar.

HIRO: Let me see. No, I don't have any change. But that's okay. You _____ the correct change for this machine. Put in your dollar, and the machine will give you fifteen cents back.

☐ There are many things children do not like to do. Imagine a wonderful special place, a paradise for children, where children don't have to do anything they don't like to do. Make some sentences similar to the following example.

> ### Example
> Most children don't like to eat spinach. In paradise, children **don't have to eat** spinach.

Must and *Have to*

Look at the following two dialogs.

1. *have to*

    JEFF: Can you go to the movies with me tonight?
    BETTY: I'd like to go, but I can't. I **have to study** tonight.

2. *must*
    In the following dialog, Betty's mathematics instructor is talking to her.

    INSTRUCTOR: Betty, I'm worried about you. I was surprised that you failed math last semester. If you want to pass math this semester, you **must study** harder.

Why do we use *have to study* in dialog 1 and *must study* in dialog 2? *Must* and *have to* have the same meaning, but people in the United States use *have to* in more situations. We can use *must* in dialog 2 because a person in authority is speaking; for example, a doctor can give orders to a patient with *must*. In informal conversational English, as in dialog 1, we use *have to*.

Must Not and *Don't Have to*

Must not and *don't have to/doesn't have to* have very different meanings. *You must not do this* means "It is against the rules" or "I forbid you to do this." We often use *cannot* or *can't* to express the same meaning as *must not*.

Study the following examples.

Have To _____ *153*

You **must not drive** through a red light. It's against the law and is very dangerous.

CHILD: Mommy, I'm not hungry. Do I have to eat my vegetables?
MOTHER: Well, you **don't have to eat** all of them, but eat some.

ACTIVITY 12G

Vocabulary

spaceship: a vehicle (something like a rocket or airplane) that travels in outer space
land: to come down to earth (or another planet) from the sky or space
planet: one of the bodies that moves around the sun. Earth, Jupiter, Mars, and Saturn are some of the planets.
crew: the people who work on an airplane, spaceship, or ship
explore: to travel through a new territory to discover what is there
helmet: a special kind of hat that protects the head

☐ Imagine that you are the commander of a spaceship. Your ship has just landed on a strange new planet. You are giving orders to your crew, which will soon leave the ship to explore this new planet. Use *must not* with the verb below each blank.

COMMANDER: Listen to me carefully. The temperature on this planet is very different from the temperature on Earth. It's very hot during the day; the sun is very strong. You _must not stay_
(stay)
out in the sun very long, or you will die. You

_____ anything, or you will burn your hand.
(touch)

You _____ your special sunglasses, or the
(take off)

sun will burn your eyes. The days are very hot, but the nights

are very cold here. You _____ the ship at
(leave)

night, or you will freeze. When you are outside the ship, you

_____ your helmet. The air on this planet
(take off)

will kill you. You _____ the water here, and
(drink)

you _____ any plants that you see, or you
(eat)

will die.

☐ After you correct this exercise with your instructor, imagine that you are the commander and give orders with *must not*. Don't look at the preceding exercise. What about the sun? What about the special sunglasses? What about the nights? What about the helmets? What about the water and the plants?

▪ ACTIVITY 12H

Think about the meaning of each sentence. Then fill in the blank with *must not* or *doesn't have to/don't have to* and the verb below the blank.

Example

Young children _must not play_ with matches. It is dangerous.
                    (play)

1. When U.S. citizens travel to most countries, they have to have a passport. Canada is different. U.S. citizens can show a driver's license for identification when they travel to Canada. They _don't have to take_ a passport.
   (take)

2. In many parks, you _____ on the grass.
                         (walk)

3. Many people in India believe in the Hindu religion. Hindus believe that cows are holy and that they _____ a cow, so they don't eat beef.
                                                        (kill)

4. (A house painter is talking to a little boy.)

   Painter: Hey, be careful! That's wet paint! You _____ the wall now.
                                                      (touch)

5. Some very intelligent students _____ very hard to
                                    (study)
   get good grades. Some students can get a good grade on a test with only half an hour or an hour of studying.

6. You _____ at a gas station because of the danger of explosion.
        (smoke)

7. Many famous actors and actresses cannot act very well. For example, Daryl Hannah is very famous, but many people say she isn't a good

actress. You _____ a good actress or actor if you want to be
         (be)
famous.

8. At the dinner table, many parents tell their children, "You

   _____ with your mouth full. It's impolite."
        (talk)

9. In Saudi Arabia, people _____ high prices for gas. Gas is
                                  (pay)
   cheap there because Saudi Arabia has a lot of oil.

■ **ACTIVITY 12I**

Imagine that you are a high-school teacher. It is the first day of school, and you are telling your students the rules for your class. Use *must*, *have to*, and *must not* with the following: *come late, talk, chew gum, cheat on tests, copy your homework from other students, do your homework, study hard, raise your hand*.

Past Tense of *Have to* and *Must*

The past tense of *have to/has to* and *must* is the same—*had to*.

subject + *had to* + base form

subject + *didn't have to* + base form

(Question word) + *did* + subject + *have to* + base form?

> ### *Examples*
> (Betty's father is speaking to her about her schoolwork.)
>
> FATHER: What's the matter with you? Why don't you study more? Don't you like school?
> BETTY: I hate school. I hate to study. I hate to get up early.
> FATHER: Get up early? When I was your age, **I had to get up** at 5:00 in the morning. **I had to milk** the cows and clean the barn, and then I **had to walk** five miles to school in the snow and rain, and I was never absent.
> BETTY: Five miles! Why **did** you **have to walk?** Wasn't there a school bus?
> FATHER: No. We lived far out in the country. School was very important to me. My parents **didn't have to tell** me to study. When I was in high school, I studied three hours every night.
> BETTY: Well, I'm sorry, Dad, but I don't like school.

Activity 12J

One hundred years ago, schools were very different, especially in the country. Many schools had only one room. Sometimes the nearest school was many miles away. Tell how life was different for schoolchildren one hundred years ago. Make sentences with *had to*.

> *Example*
> There were no school buses in those days.
> *Children had to walk many miles to school.*

1. There were no school cafeterias to serve hot lunches to the students.

   _____

2. The students had to show respect for their teachers.

   _____

3. The teachers were strict, and the punishments were severe in those days.

   The students _____ when they did something bad.

4. When students left school, they couldn't just go out to play. They had to help with the farm work after school.

   For example, _____

5. The children had no electric lights to use when they studied at night.

   _____

6. Paper was very expensive in those days. Many families could not afford to buy it.

   _____

7. Because some schoolhouses had only one room, teachers often had children of all ages in the same class.

   _____

Have To

ACTIVITY 12K

☐ Answer the following questions. Talk about when you were in high school or elementary school.

1. Did you have to walk to school? How far did you have to walk?

   _____

2. Did you have to get up early for school? What time did you have to get up?

   _____

3. Did you have to wear a uniform to school? What kind of uniform did you have to wear?

   _____

4. Did you have to raise your hand when you wanted to speak in class?

   _____

5. Did you have to do a lot of homework? How many hours did you have to spend on your homework each night?

   _____

6. For which classes did you have to study especially hard?

   _____

7. When you were absent from school, did you have to bring a letter from your parents to explain why you were absent?

   _____

☐ After you answer these questions, close your book and ask a classmate the same questions.

Activity 12L

Work with a classmate. One person will ask questions with *Did you have to ...*, and the other person will answer. Talk about the things you had to do before you left your country to come to the United States.

Example
(get)

Did you have to get a passport?

Answer: _____

1. (get)

   _____ a visa?

   Answer: _____

2. (stand)

   _____ in a long line to get your visa?

   Answer: _____

3. (wait)

   How long _____ before you received your visa?

   Answer: _____

4. (get)

   _____ any injections before you came here?

   How many injections _____?

   Answer: _____

5. (buy)

   _____ new clothes to come here? What new clothes?

   Answer: _____

13 VERB + INFINITIVE, VERB + GERUND

Content Focus

THE BIG CHOICE—MARRIAGE? CAREER? CHILDREN?

Dialog

(Today is February 14, Valentine's Day. Valentine's Day is a special day for people who are in love. On this day, boyfriends, girlfriends, husbands, and wives usually exchange presents.)

JOE: Happy Valentine's Day. Here's a little present for you.

DIANE: Oh, thank you. What a surprise! Is today Valentine's Day? Oh, no! I **forgot to get** you a present.

JOE: That's okay. Come on. I **want you to open** your present right now.

(DIANE opens the package and finds an engagement ring.)

DIANE: Joe! It's beautiful. What a beautiful diamond ring! I ... uh ... I ... I don't know what to say.

JOE: That's easy. Say yes. I **want you to be** my wife. I love you.

DIANE: Joe, I love you, too, but ... I don't know ... I'm not sure that I'm ready for marriage.

JOE: But why? Diane, what's the matter? Don't you **want to marry** me?

DIANE: Yes ... no ... oh, I don't know. I think we **need to talk** about this.

JOE: Why do we **need to talk**? I love you. You love me. That's all we **need to know**, right?

DIANE: Oh, Joe. I love you, but sometimes I'm **afraid of getting** married. I **enjoy living** alone. I'm **worried about losing** my freedom.

JOE: Losing your freedom? What do you mean?

DIANE: Oh, I don't know. Sometimes after a hard day at work, I **like to be** alone.

JOE: Well, sometimes I **enjoy doing** things alone too.

DIANE: But I'm not ready for marriage and a family. I'm so busy at work all the time. Some days I don't **stop running** from 6:00 in the morning to midnight. I **have trouble finding** even a few minutes for myself.

JOE: Sometimes I don't understand you. I thought you loved me. Maybe it's better for us to break up.

DIANE: Oh, Joe. Don't get angry. Please try to understand. Let's have a cup of coffee and talk about this some more.

Comprehension Questions

1. What did Joe buy Diane for a Valentine's Day present?
2. What did Diane get for Joe for Valentine's Day?
3. Joe wants Diane to marry him. How does Diane feel? Does she want to marry Joe?

4. Diane says that she is afraid of getting married. What does she mean? Why is she afraid of getting married?
5. Does Joe understand why Diane is afraid of getting married?
6. Does he really want to break up with Diane?

What Do You Think?

1. When people get married, do they lose their freedom? Explain your answer.
2. Do you like to be alone? Do you enjoy doing things alone? What things? Do you enjoy living alone? Why or why not?
3. Diane says that she is not ready for marriage and a family because she's so busy at work all the time. When a woman wants to have a family and a job at the same time, is this difficult? What problems does she have? Is it good for children when their mothers work? Explain your answer. Did your mother work when you were a child? How did you feel about it? In your country, do mothers usually stay at home and take care of the children, or do they often work outside the home?
4. Diane is single. She lives alone. In the United States, many single women live alone. Do many single women live alone in your country, or do they usually live with their families?

Grammar Fill-in

Study the dialog again, paying careful attention to the words in boldface type. When you are ready, fill in as many blanks as possible without looking back at the dialog.

JOE: Happy Valentine's Day. Here's a little present for you.

DIANE: Oh, thank you. What a surprise! Is today Valentine's Day? Oh, no! I forgot _____ you a present.

JOE: That's okay. Come on. I want _____ your present right now.

(DIANE opens the package and finds an engagement ring.)

DIANE: Joe! It's beautiful. What a beautiful diamond ring! I ... uh ... I ... I don't know what to say.

JOE: That's easy. Say yes. I want _____ my wife. I love you.

DIANE: Joe, I love you, too, but ... I don't know ... I'm not sure that I'm ready for marriage.

JOE: But why? Diane, what's the matter? Don't you want _____ me?

DIANE: Yes . . . no . . . oh, I don't know. I think we need _____ about this.

JOE: Why do we need _____? I love you. You love me. That's all we need _____, right?

DIANE: Oh, Joe. I love you, but sometimes I'm afraid _____ married. I enjoy _____ alone. I'm worried _____ my freedom.

JOE: Losing your freedom? What do you mean?

DIANE: Oh, I don't know. Sometimes after a hard day at work, I like _____ alone.

JOE: Well, sometimes I enjoy _____ things alone too.

DIANE: But I'm not ready for marriage and a family. I'm so busy at work all the time. Some days I don't stop _____ from 6:00 in the morning to midnight. I have trouble _____ even a few minutes for myself.

JOE: Sometimes I don't understand you. I thought you loved me. Maybe it's better for us to break up.

DIANE: Oh, Joe. Don't get angry. Please try to understand. Let's have a cup of coffee and talk about this some more.

Role Playing

Role play using a similar conversation. Your conversation does not have to be exactly the same as the dialog.

VERB + INFINITIVE, VERB + GERUND

Look at these two sentences.

1. Joe **wants to marry** Diane.
2. Diane **enjoys living** alone.

Notice that sentences 1 and 2 both have two main verbs (*want* + *marry*; *enjoy* + *live*). In sentence 1, the second verb (*marry*) is in the infinitive form: *to* + base form. In sentence 2, the second verb (*live*) is in the gerund form: base form + *-ing*.

This chapter will look at only a short list of verbs + infinitive and verbs + gerund. There are much longer lists for these verbs in other texts, but you will become confused if you try to learn all of them at one time.

Verb + Infinitive

forget
learn
need
plan   + infinitive (*to* + base form)
promise
remember
want
would like

Examples

Twenty or thirty years ago, most women only **wanted to be** housewives and mothers. Today many women **want to have** a career and a family too. Many women don't **want to get married** at an early age. They believe that they **need to work** and be independent before marriage. This is why many women **plan to wait** until the age of thirty to get married. Many women **plan to keep** their careers after marriage.

ACTIVITY 13A

Listening Comprehension

☐ Before you read this exercise and fill in the blanks, your instructor may want to use it for a listening comprehension exercise. Listen to your instructor, and then try to describe the difference between Joe's and Diane's personalities.

Grammar Fill-in

☐ There are two verbs below each blank. Choose the correct tense for the first verb, and put the second verb in the infinitive form.

Joe and Diane are two very different people. Their personalities are almost completely different. For example, Joe never forgets anything, but Diane is very forgetful. She frequently *forgets to take* her keys in
(forget, take)
the morning and can't get back into her apartment in the evening. She often _____ for the superintendent of her building
(need, look)
and have him come and open her door. A few months ago, she

_____ her door, and her stereo was gone when
(forget, lock)
she came home. She always _____ her door now.
(remember, lock)
She also _____ her bills. Her landlord sometimes
(forget, pay)
_____ her an angry letter to get the rent. Diane doesn't
(need, send)
_____ forgetful, but she can't _____
(want, be) (learn, remember)
things. She always _____ a string around her finger when
(plan, tie)
she _____ something important, but she usually
(want, remember)
_____ this too. Sometimes Diane drives Joe crazy.[1] For
(forget, do)
example, last week she _____ him in front of a
(promise, meet)
movie theater after work, but she forgot and went home. Joe was very angry with her. He's completely different from Diane. He always

_____ everything.
(remember, do)

[1] *Drive someone crazy* means "do things that make someone crazy."

❏ Answer these questions.

1. Are you forgetful? Tell some things that you sometimes forget to do. Do you ever forget to pay your bills? Do your homework? Lock your door? Send a card on a friend's birthday?
2. Talk about some things that are very important to you. Use "I always remember to ..." or "I never forget to ..."
3. What do you plan to study or do after this course? How much English do you need to know for this?
4. Can you cook? When did you learn to cook? Can you drive? When did you learn to drive?
5. In the United States, many little boys want to be firemen when they grow up. When you were a child, what did you want to be?
6. What countries would you like to visit someday? What cities in the United States would you like to visit?
7. Imagine that your class is planning a party. What do you need to buy for the party? What else do you need to do?

ROLE PLAYING

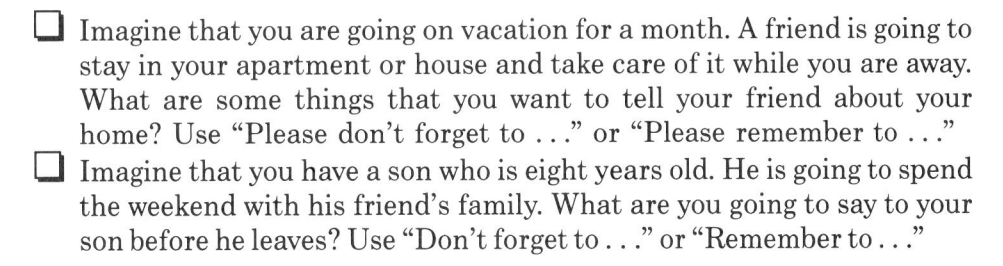

❏ Imagine that you are going on vacation for a month. A friend is going to stay in your apartment or house and take care of it while you are away. What are some things that you want to tell your friend about your home? Use "Please don't forget to ..." or "Please remember to ..."

❏ Imagine that you have a son who is eight years old. He is going to spend the weekend with his friend's family. What are you going to say to your son before he leaves? Use "Don't forget to ..." or "Remember to ..."

Verb + Gerund

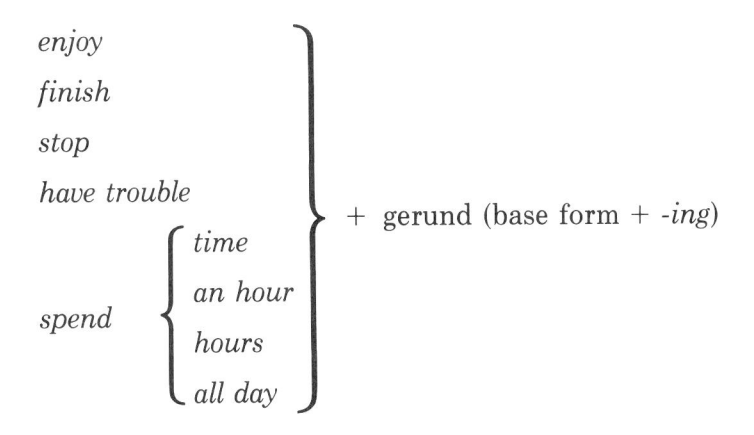

enjoy
finish
stop
have trouble
spend { *time* / *an hour* / *hours* / *all day* }

+ gerund (base form + *-ing*)

Examples

Ruth is very busy. She has a job, she takes courses, and she has a son. She **has trouble finding** time for everything. She **enjoys taking** courses, but she **spends a lot of time studying.** Sometimes she doesn't **finish doing** the housework and her school work until midnight. She enjoys her life, but sometimes she doesn't **stop working** from early morning to late at night.

$$Be + \begin{Bmatrix} afraid\ of \\ worried\ about \\ tired\ of \\ interested\ in \end{Bmatrix} + base\ form + \text{-}ing$$

A verb that follows a preposition (*of, about, in*) takes the gerund form.

Examples

Ruth enjoys spending time with her son. She would like to have more time with him. She **is worried about leaving** her son with a baby-sitter every afternoon. She**'s afraid of being** a bad mother. But Ruth works for two important reasons. First, she and Bill need the money from her salary. Food, clothing, and rent are very expensive, and Bill and Ruth **are** always **worried about paying** the bills. Also, Ruth likes her job. She's **interested in meeting** new people, **helping** people, and **learning** new things.

■ ACTIVITY 13B

❑ Choose the correct tense for the first verb, and put the second verb in the gerund form. For some of the blanks, you need to choose the correct preposition and then put the verb in the gerund form.

Joe and Diane have different personalities, and their interests are different too. Joe loves all sports, and he _enjoys watching_ them on
(enjoy, watch)
TV. He _____ a lot of time _____ and _____
(spend) (read) (talk)
about sports. Diane isn't interested _____ sports on
(of/in/about) (watch)
TV. She doesn't _____ a whole Sunday in front of TV
(enjoy, spend)
watching a baseball game. She always says to Joe, "Aren't you tired

Verb + Infinite, Verb + Gerund _____ *167*

_____ that baseball game? Let's go out and do
(of/if/about)   (watch)

something."

Diane is an excellent dancer. When she and Joe go to a party, she

never _____. Joe doesn't _____ very
        (stop, dance)   (enjoy, dance)

much. He _____ the beat of the music, and he
          (have, trouble)   (follow)

is always worried _____ on Diane's feet.
                  (of/in/about)   (step)

☐ Answer these questions.

1. Do you enjoy watching sports on TV? Which sports do you especially enjoy watching? Which sports do you enjoy participating in?
2. Do you enjoy dancing?
3. Name some things that you enjoy doing when you have free time. Name some things that you don't enjoy doing.
4. Talk about your English class. Do you enjoy practicing dialogs? Do you enjoy going to the language laboratory? Do you enjoy doing homework? Tell some things that you enjoy or don't enjoy doing in your English class.
5. What parts of English grammar do you have trouble understanding? How is your comprehension in English? Do you have trouble understanding Americans when they speak to you? Do people have trouble understanding you when you speak English? Do you have trouble understanding movies and TV programs?
6. What are some things that you're interested in reading about? Are you interested in reading about history? What special period of history? Are you interested in reading about science? Famous people?
7. Tell some things that you are interested in talking about for classroom discussions.
8. How much time do you spend on these different things?
    doing your homework
    studying
    exercising
    cooking
    talking on the telephone
    traveling to and from school
    daydreaming
9. What are some things that you are afraid of doing? Are you afraid of riding public transportation (the bus or the subway)? Are you afraid of staying in a house alone at night? Are you afraid of walking near a cemetery at night? Are you afraid of making mistakes when you speak English? What else are you afraid of?
10. What time did you finish studying last night?

Verb + Infinitive or Gerund

$\left.\begin{array}{l}\textit{hate}\\ \textit{like}\\ \textit{begin}\\ \textit{start}\end{array}\right\}$ + infinitive (*to* + base form)

or

$\left.\begin{array}{l}\textit{hate}\\ \textit{like}\\ \textit{begin}\\ \textit{start}\end{array}\right\}$ + gerund (base form + *-ing*)

A verb that follows these four verbs can be in the infinitive form or the gerund form. Both are correct, and the meaning is the same.

Diane likes to dance   or   Diane **likes dancing.**

ACTIVITY 13C

Choose the correct tense for the first verb, and put the second verb in the infinitive or the gerund form.

Joe's and Diane's personalities are different in other ways too. Diane is a very quiet person, but Joe is very talkative. He _likes to talk_ (like, talk) all the time. He especially _enjoys discussing_ (enjoy, discuss) politics. Diane _____ (hate, discuss) politics. Also, when she is tired, she doesn't _____ (want, talk) about anything; she _____ (need, have) peace and quiet. Joe doesn't understand. When Diane is quiet, he thinks she's unhappy. Sometimes when Joe talks a lot, it drives Diane crazy. Then she jokes and says, "Joe, you never _____ (stop, talk)."

However, Joe and Diane are not completely different. They share some interests, and they _____ (enjoy, do) many things together. For

example, both Joe and Diane are interested _____.
                                              (of/in/about)   (cook)

On Saturdays, they _____ all day _____, but they
                     (like, spend)   (cook)

both _____ dishes. They also _____
       (hate, wash)   (like, go)

to old movies from the thirties and forties together, and they

_____ to the theater. They have some problems in their
  (like, go)

relationship, but in general they _____ together.
                                    (enjoy, be)

▰ ACTIVITY 13D

Go back and read the fill-in selections about Joe and Diane again. Use them as examples. Talk about someone you know well (boyfriend, girlfriend, wife, husband, or someone in your family). How is this person different from you? Try to use the verbs from this chapter with a second verb: *forget, remember, need, plan, learn, want, promise, would like, enjoy, finish, stop, spend time, have trouble, (be) afraid of, (be) worried about, (be) tired of, (be) interested in, begin, start, like, hate.*

Verb + Object + Infinitive

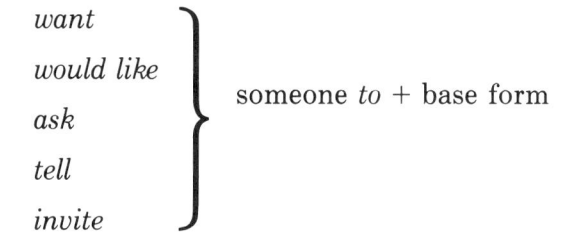

want
would like
ask   } someone *to* + base form
tell
invite

Examples

Bill is worried about Ruth because she's frequently very tired. He **wants Ruth to spend** more time with him and their son. Sometimes their friends **invite them to come for dinner** on the weekends, but they can't because Ruth has to study for her courses. Bill **would like her to quit** school. He **asked her to quit** last year, but she said no. Her family life is very important to her, but her career and her education are important too.

Activity 13E

Write questions and answers. Use *want someone to* + base form.

1.

2.

Example

1. *What does Ruth want Billy to do*?
   She wants him to eat his spinach.

2. _____?
   _____.

3.

4.

Verb + Infinite, Verb + Gerund _____ 171

3. _____?

   _____.

4. _____?

   _____.

5.   6.

5. _____?

   _____.

6. _____?

   _____.

■ Activity 13F

Look at the pictures in Activity 13E again. Make a sentence with *ask/tell someone to* + base form. *Ask* is used for polite requests; *tell* is used for orders.

Example

Picture 1: Ruth is going to ask Billy to eat his spinach.

Picture 2: _____

Picture 3: _____

Picture 4: _____

Picture 5: _____

Picture 6: _____

■ ACTIVITY 13G

❑ Make sentences with *I would like you to* + base form or questions with *Would you like me to* + base form?

Ruth's friend, Susan, has a job and four young children. Susan's husband, John, never helps her with the children or housework. Susan is talking to him about this problem. She's very annoyed.

SUSAN: You know, John, I'm really tired. I can't do all the housework, take care of the children and work too. I *would like you to help* (help) with the housework sometimes.

JOHN: Housework? That's women's work. What do you mean? What _____ (do), for example?

SUSAN: Well, if I cook dinner, I _____ (wash) the dishes. I _____ (help) with the children too.

JOHN: What _____ (do)?

SUSAN: I _____ (give) the children their bath and put them to bed at night.

JOHN: Wash the dishes, give the children a bath—what else?

SUSAN: Well, I _____ (go) to the supermarket to do the shopping sometimes.

JOHN: The shopping? I hate to go to the supermarket. Wait. I have an idea! _____ (find) a new husband for you?

SUSAN: Yes, I think I would. Maybe that's not a bad idea.

JOHN: You know I'm only joking. Okay, okay. I'll help you with the children, and I'll wash the dishes, but I won't go to the supermarket.

❑ After you correct the exercise with your instructor, study it. Then role play in class using the situation.

Note: When you speak directly to a person and say, "I want you to . . ." or "I'd like you to . . . ," it sounds too strong in certain situations. When you want to ask someone politely to do something, use the expressions in the chapter on requests and favors (Chapter 29).

❑ Read the following examples.

1. Developing countries want the rich industrial countries to give them more economic aid.
2. The price of oil is very high. Countries such as the United States, Japan, and England want the oil-producing countries to lower the price of oil.

Think of some other examples from world politics. Is there something that your country wants, or does not want, another country to do?

Role Playing

You are the father or mother of a fifteen-year-old boy or girl. You are unhappy with your child for many reasons. For example, he or she does not study and gets bad marks in school, frequently does not come home on time for dinner and does not telephone to tell you where he or she is, comes home from parties at 1:00 or 2:00 in the morning, has a very messy bedroom, and does nothing to help you around the house.

FATHER
OR MOTHER: (Tell your child what you want him or her to do about these problems.)

CHILD: (Make excuses to say why you can't or don't want to do the things that your father or mother wants you to do.)

14 COMPARATIVE FORMS OF ADJECTIVES AND ADVERBS

Cardiss Collins, U.S. representative from Illinois.

Content Focus

STEREOTYPES ABOUT MEN AND WOMEN

Vocabulary

- smart: intelligent
- logical: using correct reasoning. You must think logically to solve a problem in algebra.
- emotional: easily moved by feelings. An emotional person laughs, cries, gets angry, and becomes very happy easily.
- brave: full of courage. A brave person is not afraid during a time of danger.
- honest: truthful, fair, and sincere
- tender: gentle and affectionate
- patient: able to wait calmly
- equal: the same in size, quantity, or value
- equality: sameness in size, quantity, or value; being equal
- lift: to pick up
- soldier: a person in the army
- athlete: a person who participates in sports or physical activities such as running

ARE MEN AND WOMEN EQUAL?

In the United States today, and in many countries around the world, women are asking for equal rights with men. Many people believe that women can think, create, and lead just **as well as** men. But many men, and even some women, do not believe that women can be completely equal to men. Here are some statements that some people make when they compare men and women. When you read these statements, think about your opinion. Do you agree or disagree?

1. Men are **smarter than** women.
2. Women are **more emotional than** men.
3. Men are **stronger than** women; they can lift **heavier** things and can carry them **longer.**
4. Men are **braver than** women. This is why men are **better** soldiers **than** women.
5. Men are **more honest than** women.
6. Men think **more logically than** women.
7. Men are **better** leaders **than** women.
8. A woman's place is in the home. Women are **better** parents **than** men because they are **more tender** and **more patient** with children.

9. Men are **better** athletes **than** women. They can play most sports **better than** women because women are not **as strong as** men.

10. Women drivers are **worse than** men drivers.

What do you think of these statements? Do some of them make you angry because they are too general or because they are wrong? Are they true for all men and women? People often make statements that are very general and that often are not true. These generalized statements are called stereotypes. Here are some other examples of stereotypes.

1. Most fat people are happy.
2. Most athletes aren't very intelligent.
3. All black people love music and are good dancers.
4. People who have red hair become angry very easily.

Now go back and look again at the statements about men and women. Which ones do you think are stereotypes? Which ones do you think are true? Explain your answers and give examples.

COMPARATIVE FORMS OF ADJECTIVES AND ADVERBS

The Comparative Forms of Adjectives

An adjective gives information about a noun. When we want to use an adjective to compare two things, we frequently use these two different forms.

---

adjective + **-er** + **than**

Men are smarter than women.

or

more + adjective + **than**

Men are more honest than women.

Short Ajectives

When an adjective has only one syllable, add *-er* to form the comparative.

> *Examples*
> Men are **smarter than** women.
> Men are **braver than** women.

Note: In spelling, double the consonant before you add *-er* when a one-syllable word has this pattern: consonant, vowel, consonant.

> *Examples*
> big   b   i   g
>   (consonant) (vowel) (consonant)
> big → bigger   thin → thinner
> hot → hotter   fat → fatter

Long Adjectives

When an adjective has three or more syllables, put *more* in front of the adjective to form the comparative.

> *Examples*
> Men are **more logical than** women.
> Women are **more emotional than** men.

Two-syllable Adjectives

With most two-syllable adjectives, put *more* in front of the adjective to form the comparative.

> *Examples*
> Men are **more honest than** women.
> Women are **more tender than** men.

When a two-syllable adjective ends with *y*, change *y* to *i* and add *-er* to form the comparative.

> *Examples*
>
> Men can lift **heavier** things **than** women.
>
> heavy → heav**ier** pretty → prett**ier**
> dirty → dirt**ier** happy → happ**ier**

IRREGULAR COMPARATIVE

Good: the comparative form of *good* is *better*.

> *Examples*
>
> Men are **better** leaders **than** women.
>
> Women are **better** parents **than** men.

Bad: the comparative form of *bad* is *worse*.

> *Example*
>
> Women drivers are **worse than** men.

Note: Sometimes we put a noun after the adjective.

> *Examples*
>
> A man is a **better leader than** a woman.
>
> Women are **better parents than** men.

ACTIVITY 14A

Fill in the correct comparative form: *-er* or *more* + *than*.

Here is a comparison of Joe and Diane.

Comparative Forms of Adjectives and Adverbs   179

> **Example**
> Joe is twenty-five years old. Diane is twenty-six.
> Diane is _older than_ Joe by one year.
>   **(old)**

1. Joe is 5 feet 10½ inches (1 meter 78 cm) tall. Diane is unusually tall for a woman. She's five feet, eleven inches (one meter eighty centimeters). Diane is half an inch _____ Joe.
                                                        (tall)

2. Diane's and Joe's apartments look very different. Diane's apartment is _more expensive than_ Joe's apartment. Her apartment is also
   (expensive)
   _____ Joe's, but his place is _____
      (big)   **(attractive)**
   hers in many ways. Diane is _____ Joe. She can't find
                                    (busy)
   much time to clean her apartment or to keep it in order. She is also
   _____ Joe about housework. She doesn't care if her place is
      (lazy)
   a little dirty or messy. Joe is a very neat person. His place is always
   _____ and _____ Diane's apartment.
   (neat)   **(clean)**

3. Both Diane and Joe are good cooks. Joe always says that Diane's desserts are _____ his, but Diane says that Joe's soups and
                         (good)
   sauces are _____ hers.
                  (good)

4. Both Joe and Diane are very good in sports. Joe can beat Diane in many sports, such as baseball and basketball, but she is
   _____ tennis player _____ he is. She's a
      (good)
   _____ dancer _____ he is too.
      (good)

5. Their personalities are different. Joe likes to be the center of attention. He likes to meet new people, but Diane becomes shy and quiet when she doesn't know people. Joe is _____ and
                                              (talkative)
   _____ Diane.
      (sociable)

The Comparative Forms of Adverbs

An adverb gives information about a verb. Look at these two sentences.

Men are more **logical** than women.

Men think more **logically** than women.

In the first sentence, the adjective *logical* gives information about the noun *men*. In the second sentence, the adverb *logically* gives information about the verb *think*; *logically* tells how men think.

ADVERBS WITH -LY

We form most adverbs by adding *-ly* to an adjective. Put *more* in front of these adverbs to form the comparative.

ADVERBS WITHOUT -LY

Some common adverbs do not have *-ly* at the end—for example, *fast, hard,* and *long*. Add *-er* to these adverbs to form the comparative.

> *Examples*
> Men can run and swim **faster** and hit a ball **harder than** women.

IRREGULAR COMPARATIVE

The comparative form of the adverb *well* is *better*.

The comparative form of *badly* is *worse*.

> *Examples*
> Men do **better than** women in most sports.
> Women drive **worse than** men.

ACTIVITY 14B

Joe's father is very old-fashioned and conservative. He believes strongly that men are superior to women. Imagine that you are Joe's father, and make statements comparing men and women.

Vocabulary

- **serious:** not fooling; showing purpose. If someone is serious about his or her work, it means that he or she considers the work very important.
- **creative:** able to think of new and different ideas. An artist or a writer has to be creative.
- **executive:** a person with a job in management in a company
- **organized:** arranged in working order. An organized person can take many pieces of work that must be done and get them all done on time. If a lesson is well organized, every part of the lesson is in the right place so that everything is clear.
- **male:** a boy or a man
- **female:** a girl or a woman
- **chef:** someone who cooks for a restaurant
- **jealous:** envious; resentful. Most people feel jealous when they see someone else on a date with the person they love.

Example

(strong) *Men are stronger than women.*

1. (tall) _____
2. (athletic) _____
3. (well) _____ can do better in most sports _____
4. (fast) _____ can run and swim _____
5. (old) A _____ who is forty years old usually looks
        (man/woman)
   _____ a _____ of the same age.
                 (man/woman)
6. (smart) _____
7. (logically) _____ think _____
8. (emotional) _____
9. (serious) _____ about their jobs _____
10. (hard) _____ work _____

11. (*creative*) _____

12. (*good*) _____ business executives _____

13. (*good*) _____ political leaders _____

14. (*afraid*) _____ in times of danger.

15. (*good*) _____ soldiers _____

16. (*lazy*) _____

17. (*organized*) _____

18. (*careful*) _____ with money _____

19. (*good*) _____ chefs _____
    (male/female)   (male/female)
    chefs.

20. (*jealous*) _____

21. (*easy*) A woman's life _____ a man's life.

Expressing Equality

When we want to say that two things are equal, we can use this pattern.

$$as \begin{Bmatrix} \text{adjective} \\ \text{adverb} \end{Bmatrix} as$$

> ### *Examples*
> Many men and women disagree with stereotypes that say men are better than women. They believe men and women are equal in almost every way. They believe women are just **as intelligent as** men. They also believe that in business women are **as logical** and **creative as** men. They don't believe that women are better parents than men. They feel that men can be just **as good** with children **as** women.

Notice that we often use *just* in front of *as*. When we use *just*, we emphasize the equality.

Activity 14C

❑ Fill in the blanks with *as . . . as*.

(Some little boys are playing baseball. A little girl wants to play too.)

GIRL: Hi, everybody. Can I play?

BOY: No, girls can't play baseball.

GIRL: Why not? Girls are just _as good as_ boys.
(good)

I can play baseball _____ you.
(well)

BOY: You can't hit a ball.

GIRL: Yes, I can. I'm _____ you. I can hit the ball just
(strong)

_____ you. And I can run just _____ you too.
(hard)   (fast)

BOY: You're a baby. You're only seven years old.

GIRL: Billy's playing with you, and he's only two months older than I am.

I'm almost _____ he is.
(old)

BOY: Oh, all right. Come on. You can play.

❑ Imagine that you are the little girl. Explain why you think you can play baseball with the boys using *as . . . as* with these adjectives and adverbs: *good, well, strong, hard,* and *fast.* Don't look at the above fill-in exercise when you do this.

What Do You Think?

Can little girls play baseball as well as little boys? Do boys and girls usually play sports together in your country? Is it good for boys and girls to play sports together? Why or why not?

Activity 14D

❑ Fill in the blanks with *as . . . as*.

(RUTH came home from work a few minutes ago.)

BILL: Hi, honey. Did you get the promotion[1]?

RUTH: No, I didn't. Bob Smith got it, and I'm angry about it.

BILL: That's bad news. I'm sorry, Ruth.

RUTH: I think the only reason Bob got the promotion is because he's a man. I'm just _____ Bob, and my work is
(intelligent)
_____ his work. And I think my ideas are
(good)
just _____ his.
(creative)

BILL: Well, I don't understand. Did he start working there before you?

RUTH: He only started working there two week before I did. I can't understand it. I'm going to speak to the boss about it tomorrow.

BILL: I think that's a good idea.

What Do You Think?

1. Is it more difficult for a woman to get a promotion than for a man?
2. Do men usually make more money than women with the same job? Why?
3. What do you think of this statement: *Women often go out with men only because they have a beautiful car or a lot of money.* Is this really true, or is it only a stereotype?

> ☐ In Activity 14B, you are asked to imagine Joe's father's statements comparing men and women. Ruth believes strongly that men and women are equal in most ways. She gets angry when she hears conservative opinions about women. What do you think she believes about the following? Make statements with *as . . . as*.
>
> 1. (*well*) _____ can play most sports _____
>
> 2. (*smart*) _____
>
> 3. (*logically*) _____ think _____
>
> 4. (*serious*) _____ about their jobs _____
>
> 5. (*hard*) _____ work _____
>
> 6. (*organized*) _____

[1]*Get a promotion* means "move up to a better position at your job."

Comparative Forms of Adjectives and Adverbs

7. (*careful*) _____ with money _____

8. (*good*) _____ chefs _____ chefs.
   (male/female)   (male/female)

9. (*jealous*) _____

10. (*hard*) A woman's life _____ a man's life.

Expressing Inequality

When we want to say that something is not equal to another thing, we can use this pattern.

$$\text{not as} \left\{ \begin{array}{c} \text{adjective} \\ \text{adverb} \end{array} \right\} \text{as}$$

Examples

Most people agree that there are some real physical differences between men and women. In general, most women are **not as strong as** men. Most women are **not as tall as** men. In general, women **cannot** run or march **as fast as** men.

■ ACTIVITY 14E

❑ Fill in the blanks with *as . . . as*.

Vocabulary

armed forces: the army, the navy, the marines, and the air force
increase: to become larger
air force: the division of the armed forces that uses airplanes
training: instruction
push-up: an exercise to make the arms stronger. A person must lie down on the floor and push up with his or her arms.
rifle: a gun with a long barrel
uniform: special clothing to make all of the members of a group look the same. The police and people in the armed forces wear uniforms.

Today women play an important role in the armed forces of the United States. The number of women in the armed forces is increasing every year.

Sometimes the physical differences between men and women create problems for the armed forces when they make decisions about training.

Military studies show that the upper parts of women's bodies are only fifty-five percent as strong as men's, so the physical exercises for women cannot be _as difficult as_ the exercises for men.
(difficult)

In basic army training at the U.S. Military Academy at West Point, men do forty-two push-ups in two minutes; women do only eighteen push-ups. Men do fifty-two sit-ups in two minutes; women do fifty. In their first year at West Point, men study boxing; women study self-defense. Women cannot run or march _____ men because their legs are not
(fast)
_____ men's legs, so the army gives women three extra minutes to
(long)
run two miles (3.2 kilometers): Men have fifteen minutes, fifty-four seconds, and women have eighteen minutes, fifty-four seconds.

The army designed new uniforms for women. A small size of a man's uniform does not fit a woman. Women's shoulders are not _____
(wide)
men's, and men's hips are not _____ women's. The legs on
(wide)
women's pants cannot be _____ the legs on men's pants.
(long)

The army is also studying the inside of airplanes. Because women's arms are not _____ men's, many women pilots cannot reach the
(long)
controls.

❑ Do not look at the preceding fill-in exercise when you answer these questions. Use the pattern *not as . . . as* in your answer.

Example
(difficult)
Are the physical exercises for the military the same for men and women?

No, the exercises for women are not as difficult as the exercises for men.

Comparative Forms of Adjectives and Adverbs _____ 187

1. (*strong*)
   In basic army training, men do forty-two push-ups, but women do only eighteen. Why is this?

   _____

   _____

2. (*fast*) (*long*)
   The army gives women three extra minutes to run two miles. Why?

   _____

   _____

3. (*wide*) (*long*)
   The army designed new uniforms for women. Why can't women wear a small size of a man's uniform? Tell about shoulders, hips, and legs.

   _____

   _____

4. (*long*)
   Many women pilots can't reach the controls in army airplanes. Why not?

   _____

   _____

❑ Discuss these questions.

1. Are there women in the military in your country? Do women attend the military academies?
2. If there are women in the military in your country, do they do the same physical exercises as men? If you know about any differences in the training or exercises, tell about them.
3. Which countries have a lot of women in their armed forces?
4. Do you think it is right to have women in the armed forces? Why or why not? What possible problems are there when women are in the armed forces?

Questions with Comparative Adjectives and Adverbs

Here are some ways to ask questions when you compare things.

WHO, WHICH, WHOSE

Examples

Who are better drivers—men or women?

Women are. Men have more accidents than women.

In physical tests for the armed forces, which exercises are easier for women—sit-ups or push-ups?

Sit-ups. Women's shoulders and arms are not as strong as men's.

YES/NO QUESTIONS

Examples

Many working women in the United States say that they want "equal pay for equal work."

Do men earn higher salaries than women for the same work?

Yes. In many offices men earn higher salaries than women who have the same job.

Do women live as long as men?

Yes. In fact, they generally live several years longer than men.

ACTIVITY 14F

In Activity 13A, you read about some of the differences between Joe and Diane. Interview a classmate about the differences between him or her and his or her wife, husband, girlfriend or boyfriend. If your classmate is not married or doesn't have a boyfriend or girlfriend, ask questions about the differences between his or her mother and father.

☐ Ask questions beginning with *who*.

Example

(neat)

Who's neater—you or your wife?

Comparative Forms of Adjectives and Adverbs   189

1. (*interesting*)
   _____

2. (*busy*)
   _____

3. (*intelligent*)
   _____

4. (*a good driver*)
   _____

   ❑ Ask yes/no questions.

   > **Example**
   > (*lazy*)
   > *Are you lazier than your wife about the housework?*

1. (*athletic*)
   _____

2. (*sociable*)
   _____

3. (*talkative*)
   _____

   ❑ Ask yes/no questions using *as . . . as*.

   > **Example**
   > (*cook well*)
   > *Can you cook as well as your wife?*

1. (*dance well*)
   _____

2. (*good-looking*)

_____

3. (*old*)

_____

4. (*tall*)

_____

☐ Make up some questions of your own, and ask a classmate.

READING—STEREOTYPES ABOUT DIFFERENT NATIONALITIES

Vocabulary

view: a way of thinking
be in a hurry: to move fast because you have many things to finish by a certain time
appointment: an agreement to meet at a certain time
chew: to bite with the teeth. It is important to chew your food carefully.
junk food: food that is bad for you because it has very little value other than calories
overweight: fat
dominate: to control; to be stronger
brat: a child who behaves very badly
elders: people who are older than you
teenagers: children from the age of thirteen to nineteen
marijuana: a plant whose leaves are smoked as a drug

People often have very generalized views or opinions about people from other cultures. These generalized views are called stereotypes. Sometimes there is some truth in them, and sometimes there is almost no truth in them at all. Movies often create stereotypes. What is the image of Americans that American movies have created? Are stereotypes dangerous? Think about this question as you read the following stereotypes about some different nationalities.

Stereotypes about Americans

Money is more important to Americans than anything else in the world. They think only about making money.

Americans are always in a hurry. They are more worried about time than other nationalities are. Americans always arrive early or on time for an appointment or for a dinner invitation.

American tourists are very impolite and loud. They wear shorts everywhere, even when they visit a church.

Americans chew gum all the time.

American women dominate their men. American wives control their husbands completely.

Americans eat mostly hamburgers, hot dogs, pizza, and Coca-Cola. Americans eat a lot of junk food, such as potato chips, crackers, and sweets. That's why you see so many Americans who are overweight.

American children are brats; they have very bad manners, and they have no respect for their elders. Almost all American teenagers smoke marijuana.

Vocabulary

extremely:	very
efficient:	able to do a job quickly and well; productive
competitive:	wanting to win. Someone who works hard to be in first place is competitive.
express an opinion:	to say what you think
controversial subjects:	something that many people may disagree on
raw:	not cooked
seaweed:	plants that grow in the ocean
neat:	opposite of messy. If you are a neat person, you like to have things in order.
orderly:	opposite of messy; neat

Stereotypes about the Japanese

The Japanese are very hard-working. They are extremely efficient and are excellent in business. They are also very competitive in business.

Japanese tourists always travel in big groups. They carry cameras everywhere they go. They spend a lot of money on expensive things when they travel.

Japanese people are extremely polite, but you never know what they are really thinking. They don't like to express their real opinions about controversial subjects.

The Japanese eat strange but very healthy foods, such as raw fish, seaweed, and rice. They don't eat much junk food (as Americans do). That's why you don't often see a Japanese person who is overweight.

The Japanese are very clean, neat, and orderly.

Japanese men do not respect their women. Husbands treat their wives as servants. Japanese women must walk behind their husbands.

Japanese young people of today love everything that is American: hamburgers, hot dogs, clothing, music, dances. They are becoming Americanized; they are lazier about work than their parents are, and they don't respect their elders in the same way that they did in the past. They are not as polite as their parents.

Vocabulary

unstable: changing often
faithful: staying with one person. If you are faithful to your wife, you don't have a relationship with any other woman. If you are married but have girlfriends, you are unfaithful to your wife.

Stereotypes about Italians

Italians are lazy. They don't do anything except sit around and eat spaghetti and garlic.

Italians talk a lot and very loudly. They always use their hands when they talk.

Italians are very happy, warm, and friendly people. They love children. They are also extremely emotional people. This is why their governments are always very unstable.

Italian men are great lovers. They never think of anything except sex and women, and they chase every woman they see. They are very unfaithful to their wives, but they want their wives to be good Catholics and to be faithful to them.

Vocabulary

siesta: nap; a time to sleep during the day
hospitable: happy to welcome and entertain guests
admire: to think well of. If you admire someone, you think that person is great. Perhaps you think you would like to be like that person.
macho: very masculine. A macho man thinks it is very important to show everyone that he is a real man.

Stereotypes about Latin Americans

Latin Americans are always late for everything.

Time is not important to them. They are not good in business because they don't like to work very hard. They take long siestas every afternoon, and every other day is a holiday.

Latin Americans are warm, friendly, and hospitable.

Latin Americans eat rice and beans at every meal.

Latin-American families are very large. Almost every family has six or more children.

Latin-American men are very macho. They think they are completely superior to women and that women exist only to serve and admire them.

Latin Americans are wonderful natural dancers.

Discussion

1. What do you think of the statements about these different nationalities? Do you think any of these stereotypes are really true? Which ones? Are any of these statements completely false? Which ones? Which ones are partly true?
2. Which of these stereotypes are especially insulting?
3. Work together with a classmate. First, make a list of stereotypes about your partner's culture or nationality. Then your partner will give you a list of stereotypes about yours. When you finish, share this information with the rest of the class, and add it to the list of stereotypes.
   How does it make you feel when you hear stereotypes like these about people from your country?
   If there are any other countries or cultures that you have not discussed in your class, tell some stereotypes that people have about them.
4. Movies often create stereotypes. What is the image of Americans that American movies have created?
5. Besides movies, how do people form stereotypes of people from other countries.
6. Are stereotypes dangerous? Why?
7. In a country, different groups often form stereotypes about each other. For example, in the United States, white people have stereotypes about black people, and vice versa; people from the northern part of the country have stereotypes about southerners, and vice versa. Is this also true in your country? Give some examples of the different groups and the stereotypes they form about each other.

15 SUPERLATIVE FORMS OF ADJECTIVES

Mother Teresa, winner of the Nobel Peace prize.

Content Focus — **FAMOUS PEOPLE**

READING—ABRAHAM LINCOLN

The most difficult job in the United States is the job of the president. Abraham Lincoln was **one of the most important** presidents of this country. Some people believe that he was **the greatest** president in our history. He was president from 1861 to 1865, during the American Civil War. This was **the saddest** period in American history because Americans from the North fought against Americans from the South. After one of the battles of the Civil War, he made a famous speech. The Gettysburg Address is probably **the best** presidential speech in American history. American schoolchildren have to study this speech in history class.

Abraham Lincoln was born in Kentucky in a house with only one room. His family was **one of the poorest** families in the area. He had to work hard all his life. When he was a young man, he worked in a store. One day he gave a customer the wrong change. When he found his mistake, he walked many miles to the customer's house to give him the extra change. People began to call him Honest Abe. This is why many Americans remember him as **the most honest** of all American presidents.

He was also **one of the tallest** presidents. He was 6 feet 4 inches (190 centimeters) tall. He was not a handsome man. In fact, some people said he was **one of the ugliest** presidents of the United States. When he became president, a little girl wrote a letter to him. She wrote, "Because you are not a handsome man, I think you will look better if you grow a beard." Lincoln followed her advice and grew a beard.

Lincoln died when he was only fifty-six years old. John Wilkes Booth shot him when he was in a theater. It was **one of the greatest** tragedies in American history.

☐ Finish these sentences from the reading about Abraham Lincoln. Use the superlative form of the adjective in parentheses.

Example
(difficult)
The job of the president _is the most difficult job in the United States_.

1. (*important*)

   Lincoln _____.

2. (*great*)

   Some people believe _____.

3. (*sad*)

   The Civil War _____.

4. (*good*)

   Lincoln's famous speech _____.

5. (*poor*)

   Lincoln's family _____.

6. (*honest*)

   Americans remember Lincoln as _____.

7. (*tall*)

   Lincoln _____.

8. (*ugly*)

   Some people said _____.

❑ How much can you remember from the reading about Lincoln? Describe him, his family background, and some interesting facts about his life. Don't look back at the reading.

SUPERLATIVE FORMS OF ADJECTIVES

Use the superlative form of an adjective when you compare more than two things and you want to say that one of these things is "the best" or "the most." Use these two forms.

the + short adjective + *-est*

the most + long adjective

Short Adjectives

When an adjective is only one syllable, add *-est* to form the superlative. Use *the* before the adjective.

> *Example*
>
> Some people believe that Lincoln was **the greatest** president in the history of the United States.

Long Adjectives

- For most adjectives with two syllables and all adjectives with three or more syllables, put *the most* before the adjective to form the superlative.

> *Examples*
>
> **The most difficult** job in the United States is the job of the president.
>
> Americans remember Lincoln as **the most honest** of all American presidents.

- When a two-syllable adjective ends with *y*, change *y* to *i* and add *-est* to form the superlative. Also use *the*.

> *Example*
>
> Some people said Lincoln was **the ugliest** president in the history of the United States.

Irregular Superlatives

- *Good:* the superlative form of *good* is *the best*.

> *Example*
>
> Lincoln's speech is probably **the best** presidential speech in American history.

❏ *Bad:* the superlative form of *bad* is *the worst.*

> ***Example***
> Lincoln was president during **the worst** period in American history.

■ **ACTIVITY 15A**

Here is some information about other famous leaders. Fill in the superlative form of the adjective in parentheses.

1. Some people say that Mao Tse-tung was *the greatest* leader in the
   (great)
   history of the People's Republic of China. For more than forty years,

   he was _____ man in his country. China is one of
            (powerful)

   _____ countries, and Mao did many things to
        (big)

   make it one of _____ countries in the world. Mao died
                       (strong)

   in 1976. After his death, the Chinese people began to criticize him.

   They said that the period of Mao's Cultural Revolution was

   _____ period in the history of modern China.
        (bad)

2. Alexander the Great (356–323 B.C.) was one of _____
                                                          (great)
   leaders of all time. He was one of _____ generals in
                                            (young)
   history. When he was only twenty-two years old, he began his war on

   Persia. He became the king of _____ empire in the
                                        (large)
   world at that time. He married a Persian princess, Roxana. People

   said that she was _____ woman in all of Persia.
                          (beautiful)
   Alexander died of a fever when he was only thirty-three. Today one of

   _____ cities in Egypt, Alexandria, still has his name.
        (important)

3. Queen Victoria (1819–1901) was the queen of England during the time when her country was _____ (powerful) country in the world. She was not one of _____ (intelligent) rulers in the history of England, but she was one of _____ (popular). Her people loved her. She was the queen of England for sixty-four years. This was _____ (long) period for any British ruler. _____ (important) person in her life was her husband, Albert. She loved him very much and always listened to his advice. When he died in 1861, Queen Victoria was heartbroken. She didn't go out in public for three years. Victoria died forty years after her husband at the age of eighty-two. She was one of _____ (old) rulers in English history.

One of the

You often see this pattern with the superlative.

one of the + superlative adjective + plural noun

> ### Example
> Lincoln was **one of the most important** presidents of the United States.

In this sentence, we don't say that Lincoln was *the most important* president, because not all people agree on this. Perhaps some people think George Washington was the most important president. Perhaps some people think John Adams was the most important. But most Americans agree that Lincoln was *one of the most important* presidents.

Activity 15B

Ask a question using the superlative. Then answer using *one of the* and the superlative.

> ***Example***
> (*Caruso, great*)
> Was Caruso the greatest _____ opera singer of all time?
> Some people say that he was. Certainly _he was one of the greatest opera singers_ _____ of all time.

1. (*Confucius, wise*)

   _____ man of all time? That's difficult to say. Certainly _____ of all time.

2. (*Cleopatra, beautiful*)

   _____ woman in the world in her time? Some people say that she was. Certainly _____ _____ in the world in her time.

3. (*Shakespeare, good*)

   _____ writer of all time? Many people believe that he was. Certainly _____ of all time.

4. (*Pavlova, great*)

   _____ ballerina in the history of ballet? Many people think she was. Certainly _____ of all time.

Superlative Forms of Adjectives

5. (*Pele, good*)

_____ soccer player of all time? Many people

say that he is. Certainly _____ of all time.

5. (*Nadia Comaneci, good*)

_____ gymnast of all time? Some people

think she is. Certainly _____ of all time.

ACTIVITY 15C

☐ Read the following example. Notice when the comparative and the superlative forms are used.

> ### Example
> Every person from an Arabic country knows the name of Oum-Kaltoum. Arabic people think she was **the best** singer in the world. They say that she had **the sweetest** voice in the world. They say that her voice was **sweeter than** the voice of an angel. Most of her songs were a lot **longer than** songs from the Western countries. When she gave a concert, sometimes one song lasted for an hour. She was **the most popular** singer in the Arab world for many years. When she died, thousands of people went to her funeral.

☐ Fill in the comparative or the superlative form of the adjective in parentheses.

1. Mother Teresa received the Nobel prize for Peace in 1979. She is a

   Roman Catholic nun who went to India many years ago to help poor

   people. She helps sick and dying people in one _____
   (poor)

   places in the world. People there say that no one in the world is

   _____ or _____ than Mother Teresa.
   (kind)   (generous)

2. King Solomon was one of _____ kings of ancient
   (famous)

   Israel. He was one of _____ kings of his time. Before King
   (rich)

Solomon became the ruler of Israel, several other cities were

_____ and _____ than Jerusalem. Solomon
  (big)   (important)

made Jerusalem into _____ city in Israel.
                             (important)

King Solomon was a wise man. His people brought all of their problems

to him and asked for his opinion. People said, "No man is

_____ than Solomon. We will listen to his opinion."
  (wise)

3. Picasso (1881–1973) is one of _____ persons in the
                                    (famous)

world of art today. He is probably _____ than any other
                                 (famous)

modern painter. *Guernica,* a painting of the Spanish Civil War, is

one of his _____ paintings.
            (good)

Picasso showed his special artistic talent when he was very young. When

he began to study at the Royal Academy of Art in Barcelona, he was

_____ than all of his classmates; he was only fifteen. He
  (young)

continued to produce wonderful works of art until his death at the age of

ninety-one.

■ Activity 15D

Who is one of the most famous people in your country today or in the history of your country? Tell your class about this person. Try to use some superlative adjectives in your talk.

■ Activity 15E

Interview a classmate. Ask questions about famous places or people in his or her country. Use the words in parentheses.

Example
(long, river)

What's the longest river in your country?

1. (*tall, mountain*)

2. (*big, city*)

3. (*beautiful, place*)

4. (*expensive, city*)

5. (*old, building/church/mosque*)

6. (*popular, TV show*)

7. (*good, singer*)

8. (*famous, tourist attraction*)

9. (*bad, period in your country's history*)

10. (*powerful, person*)

11. (*rich, person*)

16 SIMPLE PRESENT TENSE TIME CLAUSES

A bride and groom.

Content Focus: **CUSTOMS AND MANNERS IN THE UNITED STATES**

SOME AMERICAN WEDDING CUSTOMS

Here are customs that some Americans follow when a man and a woman get married.

1. **The night before a man gets married,** his friends give a party for him. This party is only for men.
2. **When a bride gets dressed for her wedding,** she puts on "something old, something new, something borrowed, and something blue."
3. Everyone stands up **when the bride enters the church.**
4. **After the groom puts the ring on his bride's finger,** the clergyperson says, "I now pronounce you husband and wife," and the couple kisses.
5. **When the bride and groom leave the church,** the guests throw rice at them.
6. **Before the bride dances with her new husband at the wedding reception,** she dances with her father.
7. Friends and family decorate the groom's car with empty cans and colored paper **before he and his bride leave the party** to begin their honeymoon.

What are the customs in your country? Do the groom's friends give a party for him the night **before he gets married?**
When a bride gets dressed for her wedding, does she put on "something old, something new, something borrowed, and something blue"?
Find out if your classmates follow the same wedding customs in their countries. Ask questions similar to the ones just given.

SIMPLE PRESENT TENSE TIME CLAUSES

Statements

Some sentences have two parts: a main clause and a time clause. A time clause can begin with *when, before,* or *after.*

When the bride and groom leave the church, the guests throw rice at them.

                time clause   main clause

The time clause can also come at the end of the sentence:

The guests throw rice at the bride and groom **when they leave the church.**

Questions

Use the question word order only in the main clause.

$\underbrace{\text{The guests throw rice}}_{\text{main clause}}$ when the bride and groom leave the church.

> ### *Examples*
>
> **What do the guests do** when the bride and groom leave the church?
> They throw rice.
>
> **Do people in your country throw rice** when the bride and groom leave?

ACTIVITY 16A

Look at the following common expressions.

1. "I beg your pardon."
2. "Get well soon."
3. "God bless you."
4. "Congratulations."
5. "You're welcome."
6. "I'm sorry. Please excuse me."
7. "Excuse me." or "Pardon me."
8. "Thank you."
9. "I'm sorry to hear about your father. Tell me if I can do anything to help."
10. "Don't mention it."

Now choose the correct expression to answer these questions.

Simple Present Tense Time Clauses

Example

What do you say when someone ...
graduates from school

When someone graduates from school, you say, "Congratulations!"

1. sneezes
2. says "Thank you" to you
3. says "I like your new suit"
4. is sick

What do you say when you ...

5. hear that a friend's father died
6. didn't hear a friend's question
7. push someone by accident
8. want to leave the dinner table

■ Activity 16B

☐ Ask your instructor questions about customs in the United States, or ask your classmates about customs in their countries.

1. In most countries, parents give their children a present when the child graduates from high school.

   In the United States what do parents give their children when they graduate from high school?

2. In some countries, when a woman has a baby, her husband gives a small gift to his friends.

3. In some countries, you usually take a gift when you visit a sick friend in a hospital.

4. In some countries, you usually take a gift when you go to a friend's house for dinner.

5. In most countries, you say something when a friend introduces you to another person.

☐ Ask yes/no questions.

1. In some countries, a man speaks to his girlfriend's father before he asks his girlfriend to marry him.

    In the United States, does a man speak to his girlfriend's father before he asks his girlfriend to marry him?

2. In some countries, university students stand up when their instructor enters the classroom.

3. In some countries, when a person invites friends to come to dinner at his or her house, the friends usually come half an hour or an hour late.

4. In some countries, you snap your fingers when you want to call a waiter.

Simple Present Tense Time Clauses

5. In some countries, men stand up when a woman enters the room.

6. In some countries, men always whistle or say something when they pass a beautiful woman on the street.

7. In some countries, when a person offers you food or something to drink, you always take it.

8. In some countries, people take off their shoes before they enter a house.

■ Activity 16C

- ☐ Prepare a short talk for your class. Be sure to include some sentences with time clauses (*when, before,* or *after*) in your talk.
- ☐ Talk about wedding customs in your country.
- ☐ Talk about some other interesting customs in your country.

17 SIMPLE PAST TENSE TIME CLAUSES

A statue of Buddha in South Korea.

Content Focus

STORIES FROM THE MAJOR RELIGIONS OF THE WORLD

READING— THE STORY OF ADAM AND EVE

Vocabulary

- religion: a system of belief in a god
- belief: what someone believes in (the noun form of *believe*)
- share: to have or to use together
- peace: quietness; no war
- eternal: existing forever; without beginning or end
- lonely: sad because you are alone (without companions or friends)
- ashamed: embarrassed; feeling guilty about something wrong you have done
- rib: one of the curved bones that enclose the chest
- knowledge: all of the facts that a person knows
- Satan: the Devil
- pain: a very uncomfortable feeling. If you have pain in your stomach, your stomach hurts.
- serpent: snake
- naked: without clothing

    The three major religions of the Western and Middle Eastern countries are Christianity, Judaism, and Islam. These three religions share some of the same beliefs and stories. All three of these religions tell the story of the first man and first woman, Adam and Eve.

    When God made the first man, He put him in a beautiful garden, the Garden of Eden. Here Adam lived in peace with all of the animals. God gave Adam eternal life. **But before God made the first woman,** Adam was lonely in the garden. **When God saw that Adam was lonely,** He made Eve. God took a rib from Adam **when he was asleep one night.** From Adam's rib, God made Eve. Adam was happy **when he woke up the next morning** and found Eve next to him. God said to Adam and Eve, "Here in the garden you have everything. But you cannot have one thing: You cannot eat the apples from the Tree of Knowledge."

    One day Satan came to the Garden of Eden. He changed into a serpent and went to live in the Tree of Knowledge. **When Eve came near the tree one day,** the serpent called her. He gave her an apple and said, "Here. Take this apple and eat it. Don't listen to God. Eat it." **After Eve took a bite,** she took the apple to Adam. He was afraid, but Eve repeated again and again, "It's good. Here. Eat it. Why not?" So he finally ate the apple. Before they ate the apple, Adam and Eve did not know that they were naked. But **after they ate the apple,** they were ashamed and covered their bodies with leaves. God was angry with them. He said, "Leave the garden. You cannot stay here." **When Adam**

and Eve left Eden, they had their first experience with pain and hard work in the cold, hard world outside.

SIMPLE PAST TENSE TIME CLAUSES

Statements

Some sentences have two parts: a main clause and a time clause. A time clause can begin with *when, before,* or *after.*

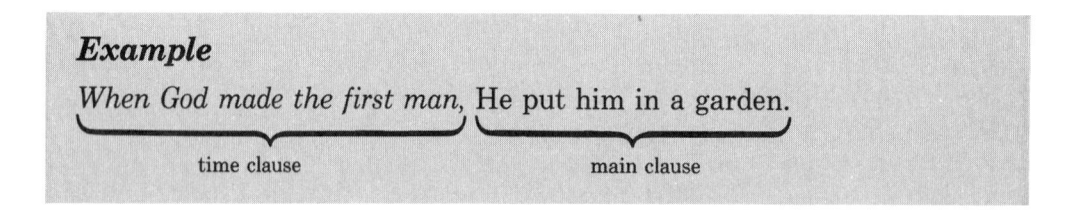

> *Example*
> *When God made the first man,* He put him in a garden.
>   time clause   main clause

A time clause can also come at the end of the sentence.

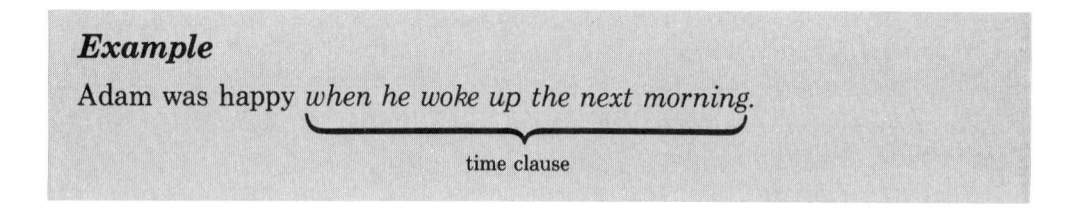

> *Example*
> Adam was happy *when he woke up the next morning.*
>   time clause

Questions

Use the question order only in the main clause.
When Eve came near the tree, the serpent called her.
                              main clause

> *Example*
> When Eve came near the tree, **what did the serpent do?**
> He called her.

Simple Past Tense Time Clauses 213

■ ACTIVITY 17A

☐ Answer these questions about the story of Adam and Eve. For practice, include a time clause in your answer.

1. When God created the first man, where did He put him?

2. Was Adam completely happy in the garden before God made the first woman?

3. What did Satan do when Eve came near the Tree of Knowledge one day?

4. What did Eve do after she took a bite of the apple?

5. Did Adam and Eve know that they were naked before they ate the apple?

6. Why did they cover their bodies with leaves after they ate the apple?

7. Was their life easy after they left the garden?

❏ Complete these sentences from the story of Adam and Eve.

1. When God _____ the first man, _____ in a beautiful garden.

2. Before God _____ the first woman, Adam _____.

3. When God _____ that Adam was lonely, He _____.

4. Adam _____ when _____ Eve next to him.

5. When Eve _____ one day, the serpent _____.

6. He gave her an apple. After she _____, she _____.

7. Before they ate the apple, Adam and Eve did not know that they were naked. After they _____ the apple, _____
_____.

READING—THE LIFE OF BUDDHA

Vocabulary

luxury: something that is enjoyable but not necessary—for example, expensive clothing, jewelry, satin sheets, and servants
palace: the home of a king or queen
monk: a religious man who separates himself from the world to devote his life to God
unhappiness: the opposite of happiness. When someone is not happy, that person has a feeling of unhappiness.

Buddha was an important teacher in the Buddhist religion. He was born in 563 B.C. in Nepal. His father was a king, so when Buddha was a child, he had a life of luxury. When Buddha was twenty-nine, he left the palace to see the world outside. That's when he saw death and unhappiness for the first time. He saw an old man, a sick man, a dead man, and a monk. After he saw these people, he thought for a long time about the meaning of life and death. Then he left his wife and child and his life of luxury. He said good-bye to everything from his old way of life and became a religious man. One night when the moon was full, he sat down under a tree. On this night, he found a complete understanding of the meaning of life and death. He was thirty-five years old when this happened. He became a great teacher. When he talked, hundreds of people came to listen to his teachings.

■ Activity 17B

Complete these questions about the life of Buddha. Then ask a classmate the questions.

> *Example*
>
> When <u>*Buddha was*</u> a child, <u>*did he have*</u> a hard life?

1. How old _____ when _____ death and unhappiness for the first time?
2. What _____ when _____ to see the world outside?
3. What _____ after _____ an old man, a sick man, a dead man, and a monk?
4. How old _____ when _____ a complete understanding of the meaning of life and death?

READING—THE LIFE OF MUHAMMAD

Vocabulary

prophet: a person who delivers the words of his or her god to the people; someone who predicts what will happen in the future
leader: someone who shows people what to do or how to do it. Presidents, prime ministers, and kings are leaders.
wealthy: rich
merchant: someone who buys and sells things
victory: the winning of a contest, a battle, or a war

Muhammad is the great prophet and leader of the Muslim religion. He was born around 570 A.D. in Mecca, Arabia. When he was a young man, he was a wealthy merchant. When he was forty years old, he went up on a mountain and God spoke to him. God told him to become a prophet and tell his people about the one true God. When Muhammad went to the people of Mecca and told them about the one true God, the people were angry. They didn't want to listen to Muhammad because they believed in many gods. In 622, some people in Mecca made a plan to kill Muhammad. When Muhammad heard about this plan, he left Mecca at night and went to the city of Medina. In Medina, many people followed Muhammad and believed in his teachings. In 630, he took an army to Mecca and won a great victory for Islam. After Muhammad won this victory, Islam became the important religion throughout Arabia. Today, Islam is the religion of many countries throughout the world.

▌ ACTIVITY 17C

Complete these sentences about the life of Muhammad.

1. When _____, _____ a wealthy merchant.

2. When _____ forty years old, _____ _____.

3. When Muhammad _____ the people of Mecca _____, _____ angry.

4. Some people made a plan to kill Muhammad. When Muhammad _____, _____ to the city of Medina.

5. After Muhammad _____, Islam _____ _____ throughout Arabia.

FREE ASSIGNMENT

Do you know other stories from the lives of Jesus, Buddha, Muhammad? For example, do you know the story of Jesus's birth? Do you know the story of Muhammad's death?

If you follow a religion other than Buddhism, Christianity, or Islam, can you tell any stories from that religion? At home, prepare a story to tell the class. Don't write the story. Just use your dictionary to find words that you don't know and write them on a piece of paper. Be sure to include some sentences with examples of time clauses (*when, before,* and *after*). Practice telling the story at home, or your teacher can help you before you tell it to the class.

18 INTEGRATION OF VERB FORMS FOR CHAPTERS 1–17

Content Focus: PARENTS AND TEENAGERS

In this chapter, you will practice using all of the verb forms that you learned in the preceding chapters.

Activity 18

Fill in each blank with the correct tense of the verb given below it. Choose from the present continuous, simple present, simple past, and future (with *going to* or *will*) tenses, and the base form, infinitive form, or gerund form. When you see *modal*, choose from *can, could, have to, had to,* and *should*.

(Because Ruth Johnson is a social worker, she spends a lot of time advising parents about their problems with their children. Mrs. Mason is a client of Ruth's.)

RECEPTIONIST: Excuse me, Mrs. Johnson. Mrs. Mason is here to see you. She _____ (negative for **have**) an appointment, but she would like _____ (speak) with you.

RUTH: Please tell her that I _____ (work) on an important report right now, but I _____ (be) finished in about five or ten minutes. Ask her _____ (take) a seat over there.

RECEPTIONIST: All right.

(About five minutes later. Ruth has finished her report.)

RUTH: Hello, Mrs. Mason, How are you? Sorry I _____ (negative modal) _____ (see) you right away, but I _____ (modal) _____ (finish) an important report for my boss.

MRS. MASON: That's okay. I'm sorry to come without an appointment, but I really _____ (need) _____ (talk) with you.

Integration of Verb Forms for Chapters 1–17 219

RUTH: Is it about your son? When you _____ (be) here last week, we _____ (talk) about his friends. I know you are worried that he _____ (modal) (get) into trouble someday because of his friends.

MRS. MASON: Yes, I _____ (negative for **like**) some of his friends at all. I _____ (speak) to him about Dave and Rick a few weeks ago. He _____ (promise) _____ (stop) _____ (spend) so much time with Dave and Rick, but I _____ (see) him with those two the other day. I'm very worried about it. You know, those two boys _____ (throw) rocks and _____ (break) some windows at the school last week.

RUTH: _____ (be) Bobby with them when they _____ (do) that?

MRS. MASON: Fortunately, no. He _____ (modal) _____ (study) for a test that evening, so he _____ (negative modal) _____ (go) out. Besides, I almost never _____ (allow) him _____ (go) out on a school night.

RUTH: How are his grades in school? I remember that his report card _____ (be) pretty good last semester.

MRS. MASON: Yes, he usually _____ (do) well at school. His teacher always _____ (say) that he _____ (be) a very intelligent boy. He _____ (negative for **have**) trouble _____ (learn).

RUTH: Well, what's the problem? Let's talk about it.

MRS. MASON: I'm so worried. I'm almost sure that when he _____
(go)
out with his friends on weekends, he _____ beer.
(drink)

RUTH: Why _____ you _____ that?
(think)

MRS. MASON: Well, every Sunday, he _____ the whole morning
(spend)
_____. He _____ until noon. And
(sleep) (sleep)
when he _____ up, he always _____ a
(get) (have)
headache. When I _____ _____ him
(offer) (make)
breakfast, he never _____ _____. I think
(want) (eat)
he has a hangover.[1] I'm so worried. What _____
(modal)
I _____? My son is a good boy. He
(do)
_____ to college next year. He's smart. He
(apply)
can be anything that he _____ _____.
(want) (be)

RUTH: Let's think about this a minute. Here's my advice. You
_____ _____ at him. You
(negative modal) (yell)
_____ _____ down and _____ him
(modal) (sit) (ask)
a direct question: _____ you _____ when
(drink)
you _____ out with your friends on the weekend?
(go)

MRS. MASON: Okay, but _____ he _____ me the truth?
(tell)

RUTH: I don't know. But, even if he says no, you should talk to him
about the dangers of drinking. Listen, I _____ an
(have)
idea. There _____ a good movie about teenagers
(be)
and drinking. Why don't you ask him _____ and see
(come)
me? I _____ him the movie and _____
(show) (talk)
with him about it.

[1] *Have a hangover* means "to have a headache and stomachache the day after you drink too much."

Mrs. Mason: Good idea. Maybe he _____ to his mother,
(negative for **listen**)

but I think he _____ to you. You're great
(**listen**)

at talking with kids.

Ruth: Well, thanks. That's nice to hear. I _____
(**enjoy**)

_____ kids with their problems.
(**help**)

What Do You Think?

1. Are the teenage years an especially difficult period in someone's life? Why or why not?
2. (This question is for those who are over the age of twenty-one.) Do you remember your teenage years as a happy period in your life? Did you do a lot of crazy things? Can you tell the class about some of them?
3. (This question is for parents of teenagers.) Do you think that most parents have problems talking with their teenagers? Do you think that you have good communication and a good relationship with your teenager?
4. What do you think about teenagers and drinking? Why do a lot of teenagers drink? What should their parents do about this problem? At what age should parents allow their children to have their first alcoholic drink? If your religion does not allow you to drink, explain why you believe your religion has this rule.
5. What should parents do if they don't like the friends that their teenager has chosen?

19 THE PAST CONTINUOUS TENSE

Content Focus: POLTERGEISTS AND GHOSTS

Dialog

(JOE is talking to BILL on the telephone.)

BILL: Hello?

JOE: Hi. This is Joe. What's happening?[1]

BILL: Nothing much. What about you?

JOE: Something really weird happened last night. I want to talk to you about it. I called you about half an hour ago, but there was no answer.

BILL: Oh, that was you? I couldn't get to the phone before it stopped ringing.

JOE: Oh, yeah? What **were** you **doing** when I called?

BILL: **I was painting** the bedroom, so my hands were covered with paint. But I'm finished now, so go ahead and tell me what happened.

JOE: Okay, but you'll never believe it. Last night, while I **was sleeping,** something woke me up. The bed **was moving** from side to side. After I turned on the light, it stopped.

BILL: Aw, come on. You **were** probably **dreaming.**

JOE: No, I **wasn't.** I was completely awake. I know I **wasn't dreaming.** I'm sure the bed **was moving** when I woke up.

BILL: Maybe it was ... I don't know ... a small earthquake, or maybe your neighbors **were moving** furniture.

JOE: Moving furniture at 3:00 in the morning? And you know we don't have earthquakes here in New York.

BILL: Well, I don't know then. Who knows? Maybe it was a poltergeist.

JOE: A what?

BILL: A poltergeist. It's an invisible ghost. Poltergeists like to move furniture or throw things at people, but you can't see them, and they don't usually speak.

JOE: Are you serious? Nobody believes in ghosts. Are you saying that you believe in them?

BILL: I don't know. There are a lot of things we don't understand. I think anything is possible.

JOE: Well, maybe I have a poltergeist in my apartment. I hope it likes me.

Comprehension Questions

1. Why didn't Bill answer the telephone when Joe called the first time?
2. Did Joe sleep well last night?

---

[1] *What's happening?* means "What's new?"

3. Why was Joe's bed moving when he woke up last night? Give three or four possible explanations that Bill mentioned.
4. Can people see poltergeists?
5. What do poltergeists like to do?
6. Does Bill believe in poltergeists?

What Do You Think?

1. Do you believe that there are ghosts or poltergeists? Explain why or why not. If you have any information about ghosts from newspapers, books, or personal experience, share it with the class.
2. Why do so many people from all countries around the world believe in ghosts?

Grammar Fill-in

Read the dialog again, beginning where Bill says, "Oh, that was you?" and ending where Joe says, "Moving furniture...?" Pay careful attention to the words in boldface type. Then fill in as many blanks as possible without looking back at the dialog.

BILL: Oh, that was you? I couldn't get to the phone before it stopped ringing.

JOE: Oh, yeah? What _____ when I _____?

BILL: _____ the bedroom, so my hands were covered with paint. But I'm finished now, so go ahead and tell me what happened.

JOE: Okay, but you'll never believe it. Last night while I _____, something _____. The bed _____ from side to side. After I turned on the light, it stopped.

BILL: Aw, come on. You _____.

JOE: No, I _____. I was completely awake. I know I _____. I'm sure the bed _____ when I _____ up.

BILL: Maybe it was ... I don't know ... a small earthquake, or maybe your neighbors _____ furniture.

THE PAST CONTINUOUS TENSE

The Past Continuous Tense with Interrupted Action

WHEN

Look at these sentences.

Bill was painting the bedroom when the phone rang.

Bill started to paint at 7:00. The phone rang at 7:30. Bill was in the middle of painting when the telephone rang.

When one action interrupts another action, use the following pattern.

---
subject + {was / were} (not) + base form + -ing + when + subject + simple past

The bed was moving when Joe woke up.

You can also put *when* at the beginning of the sentence.

When Joe woke up, the bed was moving.

> **Examples**
>
> In 1937, a newspaper in Cape Town, South Africa, reported a strange story about a poltergeist. One evening, Mrs. Olive Strong **was walking** by a bedroom in her house **when** she **heard** a strange noise in the room. No one was in the room. **When** she **opened** the door and looked inside, the blankets and pillows **were flying** through the air. Mrs. Strong was terrified and ran downstairs to the living room. A few minutes later, she **was telling** her family about the strange event in the bedroom **when** the sofa suddenly **moved** across the room. Next, the family heard a loud noise in the kitchen.[2]

---

[2]*Source:* I.D. DuPlessis, *Poltergeists of the South* (Cape Town: Howard Timmins). 1966.

While

You can also use the following pattern to talk about one action that interrupts another action.

While + subject + {**was** / **were**} (**not**) + base form + **-ing**, subject + simple past

While Joe was sleeping, something woke him up.

You can also put *while* at the end of the sentence.

Something woke Joe up *while he was sleeping.*

> ### *Examples*
> When the Strong family heard this loud noise, they ran into the kitchen and saw broken plates all over the floor. **While** they **were cleaning** up the broken plates, the teapot **rose** into the air from the table. Then it fell to the floor and broke.
>
> Later that night, Mrs. Strong **saw** a ghost **while** she **was sitting** in the kitchen. It was a ghost of a woman with an invisible head.

You will often see *when* used in place of *while*.

Mrs. Strong saw a ghost *while/when* she was sitting in the kitchen.

Questions with *When* Clauses

(Question word) + {**was** / **were**} + subject + base form + **-ing** + **when** + subject + simple past?

What were you doing when I called?

Examples

In 1850, a New York newspaper reported a story of a poltergeist in the house of a Dr. Phelps in Stratford, Connecticut. Many strange things happened in the Phelpses' house. Furniture rose into the air. Several windows broke, and no one knew why or how. One day a lamp moved across a room toward some papers and started a fire.[3]

Were people **watching when** these strange things **happened?**

Yes, they **were.** People in Dr. Phelps's family were watching. Frequently, other people were watching too.

A newspaper reporter visited the house. He was in a room with Mrs. Phelps and her daughter when the daughter screamed, "Ow! Something hit me!" The reporter looked and found a red mark on her arm.

Was the reporter **watching** the girl carefully **when** this **happened?**

Yes, he **was,** but he didn't see anyone hit her arm.

What **was** Mrs. Phelps **doing when** this **happened?**

She was sitting in a chair, reading a book.

Was she **sitting** near her daughter?

No, she **wasn't.** She was sitting across the room when it happened.

■ Activity 19A

Vocabulary

amazing: surprising; hard to believe
coincidence: the happening by chance or accident of two things at the same time
incredible: unbelievable; very hard to believe
come true: to actually happen. When you dream that something happens and then it actually does happen, your dream has come true.
dance cheek to cheek: to dance with your face very close to your partner's face
guy: a man
stare: to look at someone or something for a long time

---

[3]*Source:* Hereward Carrington and Nandor Fodor, *Haunted People: Stories of the Poltergeist Down the Centuries* (New York: E.P. Dutton and Co., Inc.). 1951.

Practice this pattern.

subject + past continuous + *when* + subject + simple past

> ❏ Fill in each blank with the past continuous or simple past form of the verb below the blank.

BILL: Listen to this. This is really strange. Last night I dreamed about my best friend from high school. The last time I saw him was about ten years ago, when he moved to California. Then this morning I *was waiting* (wait) at the bus stop when someone *came* (come) up to me and *asked* (asked) for the time.[4] Guess who it was?

RUTH: Your best friend from high school?

BILL: Yes. It was amazing. He just moved back here a few weeks ago.

RUTH: Something similar happened to me a few months ago. Diane was here one evening. We _____ (look) at some old photographs of me and my best friend in elementary school when the phone _____ (ring). It was my friend!

BILL: You mean your friend in the photograph?

RUTH: Yes. I couldn't believe it. I can't remember the last time I talked to her. She lives in Texas now.

JOE: That's really a coincidence. My story isn't so interesting, but the other night I _____ (read) an interview of Henry Kissinger in a magazine when Hiro _____ (turn) on the TV. Who do you think was on TV?

RUTH: Kissinger?

[4]*Asked for the time* means "asked, 'What time is it?'"

The Past Continuous Tense _____ 229

JOE: Right. I was really surprised. What a coincidence!

RUTH: You know, Bill, you told us about your dream. Dreams are really strange. A friend of mine told me about a dream she had. In her dream, her brother _____ (drive) along a street when another car _____ (go) through a red light and _____ (run) into her brother's car. At that moment, my friend woke up. The next day, she felt very nervous and worried all day. That evening she _____ (think) about her dream again when the telephone _____ (ring). It was her parents. They told her that her brother was in the hospital because of a car accident. The accident happened almost exactly the way the accident in her dream occurred. Fortunately, her brother had only a broken leg.

DIANE: That's incredible! I once had a dream that came true. In my dream, I met a very handsome man. It was a wonderful dream. We _____ (dance) cheek to cheek when the alarm clock _____ (ring) and ended my beautiful dream.

JOE: Hey, you never told me about this dream before! Who was this handsome guy in your dream? Was it me?

DIANE: No, Joe, it wasn't you. But don't get jealous. I had this dream before I met you.

JOE: That's different. Go on. Finish telling us about your dream. Did you ever really meet this guy?

DIANE: Well, I didn't really meet him. Listen. The next day I _____ (sit) on the train when a man _____ (sit) down directly across from me.

RUTH: And it was the handsome man from your dream?

DIANE: Yes. I'm almost sure that he had the same face. I stared and stared at him. He probably thought I was crazy.

JOE: And then what? Did you say anything to him?

DIANE: No, I _____ to think of something to say when
(try)
the train _____ and he got off. I never saw him again.
(stop)

JOE: That's good. He was probably a nerd[5] anyway.

❏ Do you know any stories about strange coincidences? Tell them.

Activity 19B

Vocabulary

scare: to frighten; to make someone feel afraid
palace: the home of a king or queen
furious: very angry
pat: to touch gently. When you pat a cat or a dog, you put your hand on the animal's head or back and move it up and down softly and gently.
cemetery: the place where you bury people after they have died. There are many graves in a cemetery.
scratch: to use your nails to hurt someone. Cats usually scratch someone when they are angry.

Practice this pattern.

While + subject + past continuous + subject + simple past

Fill in the past continuous or simple past form of the verb below each blank.

Some people believe in ghosts; others don't. Ghosts are the spirits of dead people. They are different from poltergeists, because frequently people can see ghosts and sometimes have conversations with them. In this imaginary dialog, two ghosts are talking to each other.

[5] *A nerd* means "a foolish person" or "someone you might not want to know socially." (slang).

The Past Continuous Tense

GHOST 1: Hello. Did you have a good night? How many people did you scare?

GHOST 2: Oh, I had a great night. I scared about twenty or thirty people. How about you?

GHOST 1: I didn't have much luck at first. There weren't many people out tonight. Where did you go?

GHOST 2: I went to the palace to visit the king and queen. First, I went to the dining room. While the servant *was serving* (serve) the king's dinner, I *came* (come) up behind him and *pushed* (push) him. The food fell all over the king. He was furious with the servant. Of course I was invisible, so they didn't know I was there. I couldn't stop laughing. Then I went to the queen's room.

GHOST 1: What _____ she _____ (do) when you _____ (come) into her room? _____ she _____ (sleep)?

GHOST 2: No, she _____. She _____ (sit) in front of her mirror. While she _____ (brush) her hair, I _____ (take) the brush right out of her hand and _____ (throw) it across the room. The poor queen looked so surprised. She couldn't see me, of course. Then, a few minutes later, while she _____ (pat) her cat, I _____ (pull) its tail, and it scratched her. But what about you? Tell me about your night.

GHOST 1: Well, I waited near the cemetery for a long time, but nobody passed by, so I finally went to a party. I had a great time.

GHOST 2: _____ all the guests _____ (have) a good time when you _____ (arrive)?

GHOST 1:   Oh, sure. Listen to what I did. While the guests _____ (dance) and _____ (enjoy) themselves, I suddenly _____ (appear) in the middle of them. I had my head under my arm. They all took one look at me, screamed, and ran out. I stayed and finished the champagne.

GHOST 2:   Not a bad night.

■ ACTIVITY 19C

Joe and Diane's first date was a disaster. The first time they went out together, everything went wrong. Use your imagination to describe their first date.

1. On the night of their first date, Joe planned to pick Diane up at her apartment at 8:00. Diane had an emergency at the hospital and couldn't get home until 7:45. What was she doing when Joe arrived at her apartment?

   _____
   _____

2. While Joe was waiting for Diane in the living room, he knocked over a vase, and it broke. What was he doing when Diane came into the living room to say that she was finally ready?

   _____
   _____

3. It was very cold that night, and the sidewalks were very icy. What happened while they were walking along the street?

   _____
   _____

4. After they entered the restaurant, Joe helped Diane take off her coat. He was a little nervous, so he was clumsy.

   _____
   _____

5. Unfortunately, their waiter was clumsy too.

   _____

   _____

   Later, _____.

6. After dinner, they went to a nightclub. Joe didn't tell her that he couldn't dance very well.

   _____

   _____

7. If you can imagine a few other embarrassing moments that happened on Joe and Diane's first date, write them.

   _____

   _____

READING—THE GHOSTS OF KING HENRY VIII'S WIVES[6]

Vocabulary

divorce:	to end a marriage legally
give birth to a baby:	to have a baby. The baby is born. The mother gives birth to the baby.
execute:	to kill someone (put someone to death) according to the law
chop off:	to cut off
fall in love with someone:	to begin to love someone. Some people fall in love the first time they meet.
anniversary:	the celebration of the date on which an important event happened
resident:	someone who lives in a place
appear:	to become visible; to come into view
coach:	a carriage with seats inside that is pulled by horses
headless:	without a head

[6]*Source:* Christina Hole, *Haunted England: A Survey of English Ghost-lore* (London: B.T. Batsford, Ltd.). 1940.

tower: a high, slender building
stand guard: to stand near a place to make sure that no one goes in or out without permission
chapel: a small church
pray: to speak to your God
beg: to ask as a favor
change a person's mind: to do or say something to make a person think differently

King Henry VIII of England had six wives. He divorced two of them, he executed two of them, one died while she was giving birth, and the last one lived on after Henry died.

Anne Boleyn was King Henry's second wife. When Henry married Anne, he was deeply in love with her. This soon changed. The king was getting old and wanted a son to become king when he died. Unfortunately, Anne gave birth to a daughter. Henry became angry with her, and soon after he fell in love with another woman. He ordered his soldiers to arrest Anne—and later to chop off her head.

There are many stories about the ghost of poor Anne Boleyn. Every year on the anniversary of her execution, Anne's ghost returns to Blickling Hall, the place were she was born. One resident of this house told this story.

> Last night I saw the ghost of Anne Boleyn again. When she appeared this time, she was sitting in a coach and holding her head on her knees. Four headless horses were pulling the coach, and the driver was also headless.

Anne Boleyn's ghost also returns to the Tower of London, where she was a prisoner before her execution. One night a soldier was standing guard at the tower when he noticed a light in the chapel. He looked through a window and saw a group of men and women walking around inside the chapel. One of them was the ghost of Anne Boleyn. On another night at the tower, a soldier was standing guard when he saw a woman in a white dress. He called to the woman, but she didn't answer. He could not see very well at first because the moon was behind some clouds. When the moon came out from the clouds, the guard saw that the lady had no head. He ran away in terror.

King Henry's fifth wife was Catherine Howard. In 1541, Henry ordered his soldiers to arrest Queen Catherine because he still had no son and by this time was in love with still another woman. The soldiers came to the palace to take poor Catherine away to the Tower of London. On the way to the tower, they passed the chapel where King Henry was praying. Catherine escaped from the soldiers and ran toward the chapel screaming and crying, "Henry, how can you do this to me? Henry, please don't do this to me!" The soldiers stopped her before she could open the door to the chapel, and Henry did not pay any attention to her screams and cries. Later he chopped off Catherine's head too. Some years after her execution, a resident of the palace told this story.

I was sleeping one night when the screams of a woman woke me up. The screams were coming from the hall near the chapel. This happened on several other nights too. Also, one night while I was walking along the hall near the chapel, I saw the ghost of a woman in a white dress. I am sure it was the ghost of Queen Catherine.

Comprehension Questions

1. Did King Henry VIII execute all of his wives?
2. Did Henry and Anne have a son?
3. Why did Henry's love for Anne change?
4. How did Anne Boleyn die?
5. A resident of the house where Anne was born saw her ghost one night. Describe what he saw.
6. What were the two soldiers doing at the Tower of London when they saw Anne's ghost? Describe what they saw.
7. Where was King Henry when his soldiers came to the palace to arrest Queen Catherine? What was he doing?
8. What happened while the guards were taking Catherine away to the Tower of London?
9. Why did Catherine run toward the chapel? Did she have a chance to speak with her husband one last time?
10. What did Henry do when he heard Catherine's screams?
11. How did Catherine die?
12. What did a resident of the palace see and hear years after Catherine's execution?

Telling a Story

If you know any stories about ghosts, prepare a story at home to tell your class the next day. Don't write the story. Go home and use your dictionary to find words that you need but don't know. Then practice telling the story at home before you tell it to your classmates.

20 THE PRESENT PERFECT CONTINUOUS TENSE

PICTURE STORIES

It's 5:30 P.M. in the picture on the preceding page. Diane is sitting in a restaurant with a bottle of soda and a bowl of peanuts. She's waiting for Joe. She spoke to him this morning, and they planned to meet at about 5:30 for a hamburger.

Now it's 7:00. Diane is still waiting for Joe. She's very upset because she **has been waiting** for a long time. She **has been drinking** soda and **eating** peanuts for an hour and a half. The men at the bar **have been bothering** her. They **have been looking** at her and **talking** about her. The man with the beard **has been staring** at her since 6:30. She **has been asking** herself, "Where's Joe? Why is he so late? What **has he been doing** all this time?"

Joe had a class from 4:00 to 5:00. It's 7:00 now, and he's still at school. After the class, one of Joe's classmates asked him a question about the class. They have been talking since 5:00. Joe **hasn't been thinking** about Diane; he **has only been thinking** about his beautiful classmate.

What Do You Think?

1. How does Diane feel?
2. Why did Joe forget his date with Diane?
3. What's going to happen the next time Diane sees Joe?

■ ACTIVITY 20A

Study the stories for the pictures again. Then talk about the pictures without reading the stories.

THE PRESENT PERFECT CONTINUOUS TENSE

Use the present perfect continuous tense to talk about an action that began in the past and is continuing at the present moment.

Statements

$$\left.\begin{array}{l}I \\ you \\ we \\ they\end{array}\right\} \text{have (not) + been +} \dfrac{\text{base}}{\text{form}} + \text{-ing} \quad \left.\begin{array}{l}he \\ she \\ it\end{array}\right\} \text{has (not) + been +} \dfrac{\text{base}}{\text{form}} + \text{-ing}$$

Joe and his classmate have been talking since 5:00

Diane has been waiting for Joe for a long time.

$$\left.\begin{array}{l}I \\ you \\ we \\ they\end{array}\right\} + have = \begin{array}{l}I've \\ you've \\ we've \\ they've\end{array} \qquad \left.\begin{array}{l}he \\ she \\ it\end{array}\right\} + has = \begin{array}{l}he's \\ she's \\ it's\end{array}$$

Questions

> (Question word) $\begin{Bmatrix} \text{have} \\ \text{has} \end{Bmatrix}$ + subject + **been** + base form + **-ing**?
>
> *Has Joe been talking with his classmate all this time?*

SHORT ANSWERS

Yes, subject + $\begin{cases} have. \\ has. \end{cases}$

No, subject + $\begin{cases} haven't. \\ hasn't. \end{cases}$

Examples

(A friend of Diane's walked into the restaurant a minute ago.)

FRIEND: Hi, Diane. What are you doing here?

DIANE: I'm waiting for Joe, and I'm going to kill him when I see him. He's really late.

FRIEND: Wow! Look at all those empty soda bottles! How long **have you been waiting?**

DIANE: **I've been waiting** for an hour and a half. **I've been drinking** soda and **eating** peanuts all the time. Now I feel sick. And look at those men at the bar.

FRIEND: **Have** they **been bothering** you?

DIANE: Yes, they **have.** The guy with the beard **has been staring** at me for half an hour.

FRIEND: Where's Joe? What **has** he **been doing** all this time?

DIANE: Who knows? But I know he **hasn't been thinking** of me.

■ ACTIVITY 20B

Study the dialog in the example. Then use the guide below to practice the dialog with a classmate. Don't look back at the example.

FRIEND: Hi, Diane. What are you doing here?

DIANE: I'm waiting for Joe, and I'm going to kill him when I see him. He's really late.

FRIEND: Wow! Look at all those empty soda bottles! How long _____ _____?

DIANE: I _____ an hour and a half. I _____ soda and _____ peanuts all this time. Now I feel sick. And look at those men at the bar.

FRIEND: _____ you?

DIANE: Yes, _____. The guy with the beard _____ at me for half an hour.

FRIEND: Where's Joe? What _____ all this time?

DIANE: Who knows? But I know he _____ of me.

Time Expressions

for + a period of time   *since* + a specific date or time in the past

$$for + \begin{cases} \text{two days} \\ \text{a week} \\ \text{five years} \\ \text{ten minutes} \\ \text{an hour} \\ \text{a long time} \end{cases} \qquad since + \begin{cases} \text{5:30} \\ \text{1968} \\ \text{last year} \\ \text{last week} \\ \text{July} \\ \text{Monday} \end{cases}$$

$$all + \begin{cases} \text{day} \\ \text{this time} \\ \text{semester} \\ \text{week} \\ \text{year} \end{cases}$$

The Present Perfect Continuous Tense ———————————————————————— 241

> ### *Examples*
> Diane arrived in the restaurant at 5:30. Now it is 7:00.
>
> She has been waiting for Joe **for** an hour and a half.
>
> > or
>
> She has been waiting for Joe **since** 5:30.
>
> She has been drinking soda **all** evening.
>
> > or
>
> She has been drinking soda **all** this time.

ACTIVITY 20C

Use the present perfect continuous tense and the correct word for each time expression—*for, since,* or *all*.

1.

   Bill is jogging in the park. He began at 3:00, and now it's 3:15. Last week, Bill went to the doctor. The doctor said, "Bill, you need to get some exercise." So last week Bill started to jog.

   a. How long has Bill been jogging today?

   _____ fifteen minutes.

   b. Has he been jogging every day for several months?

   No, _____ last week.

Now look only at the picture and tell about it.

2.

Joe is working in a restaurant tonight. He started work at 7:00 P.M., and it's 12:00 midnight now. The restaurant was crowded when Joe started to work, and it's still crowded now.

a. What has Joe been doing _____ night?

_____

b. How long has he been working?

_____ 7:00 P.M.

c. Have he and the other waiters been taking it easy[1] _____ night?

No, _____.

Now look only at the picture and tell about it.

[1]*Taking it easy* means "relaxing; not working hard."

The Present Perfect Continuous Tense

3.

Mr. Rose is in the waiting room of a hospital. His wife is having major surgery. She went into the operating room at 9:00 A.M., and now it's 11:00 A.M.

a. How long has Mr. Rose been waiting?

   _____ two hours.

b. Has he been walking back and forth _____ 9:00 A.M.?

   Yes, _____.

c. What else has he been doing _____ morning?

   _____ cigarettes.

d. Has he been looking at the clock _____ morning?

   Yes, _____.

Now look only at the picture and tell about it.

Simple Present Perfect of *Be, Have,* and *Know*

Be, have, and *know* usually do not have a continuous *-ing* form in the present perfect tense. For these verbs use this pattern.

$$\left.\begin{array}{l}\text{have}\\ \text{has}\end{array}\right\} + \text{past participle}$$

BE

The following are the three forms of the verb *be*.

am, is, are   was, were   been

We call the third form (*been*) the past participle.

> *Examples*
>
> BILL: How long **have** you **been** in the United States?
> HIRO: **I've been** here for four months.

HAVE

The following are the three forms of the verb *have*.

have   had   had

> *Examples*
>
> RUTH: I think you need some new blue jeans. Those jeans are really old. How long **have** you **had** them?
> BILL: I'm not sure. **I've had** them for a long time. I love these jeans. I don't want new ones.

KNOW

The following are the three forms of the verb *know*.

know   knew   known

The Present Perfect Continuous Tense — 245

Examples

ANNE: You and Bill always look so happy together. You look like young lovers. How long **have** you **known** each other?

RUTH: **I've known** him for about five years.

ACTIVITY 20D

☐ Fill in the present perfect form of the verbs and the correct word for the time expression—*for, since,* or *all.*

1. (Ruth and Diane are talking on the telephone.)

    DIANE: Hi. This is Diane. How are you?

    RUTH: I feel terrible. I '*ve been* sick in bed *all* day.
    (be)

    DIANE: That's too bad. What's the matter?

    RUTH: I _____ a cold for three days. Today I decided to stay
    (have)
    home and rest.

    DIANE: Well, feel better soon.

    RUTH: Thanks.

2. (Joe is talking on the telephone to the landlord of his building.)

    LANDLORD: Yes? What can I do for you?

    JOE: We _____ any hot water in our building
    (negative for **have**)
    _____ five days. When are you going to fix it?

    LANDLORD: We'll fix it right away. Why didn't you call me sooner?

    JOE: What do you mean? I called you on Monday and again two days
    ago. You _____ about the problem with the
    (know)
    water _____ Monday.

3. Hiro: How long _____ Diane?
   (know)

   Joe: I _____ her for a year and a half.
   (know)

   Hiro: Were you and she just friends for a while, or _____ you _____ in love since the day you met?
   (be)

   Joe: I think I _____ in love with her since the day we met.
   (be)

☐ Answer these questions. For your answers, you can use *for* (number) *years*, *since* + a date, or *since I was* (number) *years old*.

1. Is there something you own that is really special to you? How long have you had it? Why is it special to you? _____

2. How long have you known your girlfriend/boyfriend? husband/wife? best friend? _____

3. How long have you known how to read? drive? cook? _____

4. Are you in love with someone? How long have you been in love? _____

5. How long have you been in the United States? _____

6. How long have you been in this English course? _____

Activity 20E

Work with a classmate. Write a short dialog for these situations. In your dialog, include one or more examples of the present perfect continuous or simple present perfect tense of *be, have,* or *know.*

1. Joe is waiting for a classmate in front of the library. His classmate is very late. It's a cold day, and Joe is freezing. Hiro is passing by the library and sees Joe.

   HIRO: *Hi, Joe. What are you doing here? Are you waiting for someone?*

   JOE: *Yeah, and I've been waiting for half an hour. I'm freezing. I think I'm going to leave. It's too cold out here.*

2. Joe and Diane are dancing at a party. Joe is tired and wants to sit down. Diane doesn't want to stop dancing.

   JOE: _____

   DIANE: _____

3. Ruth is studying for an important exam. Bill wants to go out to a movie. He wants Ruth to stop studying and go with him.

   BILL: _____

   RUTH: _____

4. Diane is talking to a patient. He came to see her because he has a bad stomachache.

   DIANE: _____

PATIENT: _____
_____

5. It's 3:00 in the morning. Bill and Ruth live in an apartment building. Their neighbors are having a noisy party, and Bill can't sleep. He's standing at his neighbor's door and talking to him about the noise.

BILL: _____
_____

NEIGHBOR: _____
_____

Contrast of Simple Past, Present Continuous, and Present Perfect Continuous Tenses

Look at this information about Maria.

1982–1986—a student at the University of Mexico

1986–1989—a teacher of history in a high school

September 1989—arrived in the United States

1990–now—a graduate student at Columbia University

Now study the following questions and answers.

1. How long did Maria study at the University of Mexico?
   She studied there for four years.

2. What did she do after she graduated?
   She taught history in a high school.

3. How long has she been in the United States?
   She's been in the United States since September 1989.

4. What is she doing now?
   She's studying at Columbia University.

ACTIVITY 20F

❑ Work with a classmate. Look at this information about Joe. Then ask questions and answer them.

1980–1984—a student at Boston University

1984–1986—in the army

1986–1990—a salesman for IBM

September 1990–now—a part-time student at Columbia University and a waiter

1. How long _____ at Boston University?
   (study)

   Answer: _____

2. What _____ after he graduated from the university?
   (do)

   Answer: _____

3. How long _____ in the army?
   (be)

   Answer: _____

4. What _____ after he left the army?
   (do)

   Answer: _____

5. _____ for IBM now?
   (work)

   Answer: _____

6. What _____ now?
   (do)

   Answer: _____

7. How long _____ at Columbia University?
   (study)

   Answer: _____

8. How long _____ a waiter?
   (be)

   Answer: _____

❑ Look at this information about Bill. Then ask questions and answer them.

1981–1985—a student at Howard University

1983—married Susan

1986—got divorced from Susan

1985–now—a manager at the telephone company

1987—met Ruth

1988—married Ruth

21 FUTURE TIME CLAUSES

Content Focus: **A STORY WITH A MORAL; PROVERBS**

READING—"DON'T COUNT YOUR CHICKENS BEFORE THEY HATCH"

Vocabulary

- **foolish:** silly; not intelligent
- **daydream:** to think about other things when you are supposed to be working or studying
- **hatch:** to break out of an egg; to be born from an egg
- **chick:** a baby chicken
- **hen:** a female chicken
- **calf/calves:** a baby cow/baby cows
- **notice:** to see; to realize that something is happening
- **trip over:** to hit your foot on something that is in the way and fall (or almost fall)
- **moral:** a lesson to be learned from a story or an experience

Once upon a time, a foolish young man took all of the money he had in the world (it wasn't much money) and went to the marketplace. He bought twelve beautiful, large eggs, placed them carefully and lovingly in a basket, and then started on the long walk back home. On the way, he began to daydream happily about what he planned to do with these eggs. This is what he said to himself.

These eggs are of the finest quality. **When they hatch, I'll have twelve healthy little chicks.** I'm going to take care of those chicks and feed them the best food, so **when they grow up to be fine fat hens, they'll lay the best eggs in the country.** I'll sell those eggs for the highest possible price, but of course I won't sell all of them. I'm going to keep some and hatch them, and pretty soon I'll have a lot of big fat hens. **When I have one hundred hens, I'm going to sell them.** Then let me see. **After I sell my hens, what am I going to do with all that money?** I know! I'll buy some cows. I can sell the milk for a lot of money, and those cows will have calves, and the calves will grow up and have calves, and pretty soon I'll have one hundred cows. Then I'll sell all of them and be rich. Then I'll ask Eva to marry me. Eva doesn't know I'm alive now. She won't look at me because I'm just a poor man, but **before I ask her to marry me, I'm going to build the biggest and finest house around here.** Then she'll notice me. She'll marry me then. And **when we're married, we'll have twelve children.** We'll ...

In the middle of this pleasant daydream, this foolish young man suddenly tripped over a big rock that was in the road. Splat! He found himself flat on his face in the road, with his twelve beautiful eggs lying broken all around him.

The moral of this story is, don't count your chickens before they hatch.

Comprehension Questions

1. What did the foolish young man buy with his money at the marketplace?
2. What did he daydream about on the long walk back home from the market?
3. What did he plan to do with the twelve eggs—eat them or hatch them?
4. Did he daydream about becoming a rich man?
5. How did he plan to get Eva's attention?
6. Suddenly he fell down and dropped his basket of eggs. Why? What happened to the eggs?
7. Did he ever become a rich man?

FUTURE TIME CLAUSES

When a sentence or a question about the future has a time clause, the verb in the time clause is in the simple present. Only the verb in the main clause is in the future tense (*will* or *going to*).

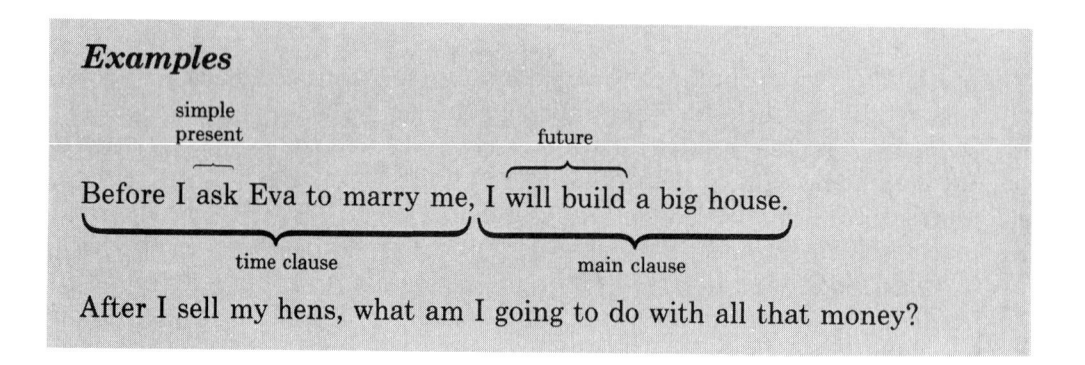

Examples

Before I ask Eva to marry me, I will build a big house.
(time clause — simple present) (main clause — future)

After I sell my hens, what am I going to do with all that money?

Activity 21A

Look back at the story of the foolish young man and his eggs. Read the sentences in boldface type carefully again. Complete these sentences. Use the present tense for the verb in each time clause and the future tense for the verb in each main clause.

1. When these eggs *hatch*, I *'ll have* twelve healthy little chicks.

Future Time Clauses

2. When the chicks _____ to be fine fat hens,

 they _____ the best eggs in the country.

3. I'm going to keep some of the eggs and hatch them. When I

 _____ one hundred hens, I _____ them.

4. After I _____ the hens, I _____ some

 cows.

5. Those cows will have calves. When I _____ one

 hundred cows, I _____ all of them and

 _____ rich.

6. Before I _____ Eva to marry me, I _____

 the biggest and finest house around here.

7. When Eva _____ my beautiful house,

 she _____ me.

8. When we _____ married, we _____ twelve

 children.

▮ ACTIVITY 21B

First use a time clause to answer each question. Then make a complete sentence with a time clause and a main clause.

1.   2.

Come on. Let's go. It's late.

Okay, okay. I just want to finish my soda.

Example

When are these people going to leave the party?

Short Answer: *After the man finishes his soda.*

Complete Sentence: *They're going to leave after the man finishes his soda.*

2. When are these people going to leave for their vacation?

   Short Answer:

   Complete Sentence: _____

3.   4.

3. When are these children going to go outside to play?

   Short Answer:

   Complete Sentence: _____

4. When's this boy going to go outside to play baseball with his friends?

   Short Answer:

   Complete Sentence: _____

   _____

5.   6.

   (The telephone is ringing.)

   (Uh, oh. I can't give Daddy my report card and tell him about my F in science now. He's in a bad mood.)

5. When's the cat going to steal the fish?

   Short Answer:

   Complete Sentence: _____

   _____

6. When's Betty going to show her report card to her father?

   Short Answer:

   Complete Sentence: _____

   _____

Activity 21C

☐ Complete the questions about the pictures. Use your imagination to answer the questions.

1.   2.

1. What *is* the girl's mother *going to do* when she
                                                                       (do)

   sees her favorite vase?
   (see)

   _____

   _____

   _____

2. What _____ when _____ the
          (do)   (find)
   hundred-dollar bill on the sidewalk?

   _____

   _____

Future Time Clauses 257

3.

4.

3. What _____ when the teacher _____ into
         (happen)
the classroom?

_____

_____

4. What _____ the policeman _____ after
                                          (do)
_____ the speeding car?

_____

_____

☐ Now write your own questions and answers.

5.

6.

Mr. Jones, I have extra good news for you.

5. _____

_____?

_____

_____

6. _____

_____?

_____

_____

■ ACTIVITY 21D

Answer these questions. For practice, include both a time clause with *when, before,* or *after* and a main clause in your answer. (Depending on the question, it is perfectly natural to answer with the time clause by itself or the main clause by itself.) You can work as a class here, or you can work in pairs.

1. What are you going to do after you leave school today? _____

_____

2. Are you going to do your homework or study before or after you watch TV this evening? _____

_____

3. What are you going to do after you finish this English course? _____

_____

4. Do you think you will speak English perfectly when you finish this course? _____

5. Are you going to take the next level after this course ends? _____

_____

6. When you have your next chance to take a vacation, where are you going to go? _____

7. (This question is for single people.) Do you think it's important to do certain things with your life or to achieve certain things before you get married? What are you going to do with your life or achieve before you get married? _____

READING—PROVERBS

A proverb is a popular saying that people frequently use in certain situations. Proverbs give people advice. Very often proverbs are the moral of a story, such as the one you read at the beginning of this chapter. The following are some proverbs from the United States.

_____ Don't cry over spilled milk.

_____ Many hands make light work.

_____ You can lead a horse to water, but you can't make him drink.

_____ Beauty is only skin deep.

_____ People who live in glass houses shouldn't throw stones.

_____ You can't tell a book by its cover.

Activity 21E

Match each proverb with one of the following explanations. Write the letter of the explanation next to the proverb.

a. When you have a lot of people who work together and help one another, the work is easier.
b. You shouldn't criticize or laugh at someone if you have the same problem as that person.
c. If you make a mistake or if something bad happens, it doesn't do any good to think and think and worry about it. Learn from your mistake, and then try to forget it.
d. A person who is handsome or beautiful is not always a good person.

e. Just because something looks good, it doesn't mean it is good.

f. You can do many things to try to help someone, but that person has to want your help and has to cooperate. If he or she doesn't want your help, all of your effort will be wasted.

■ Activity 21F

Read the situations and imagine which proverb the second speaker would choose as a response.

1. Rosemary and Joshua are eating dinner in a fancy restaurant.
   ROSEMARY: You know, the food here really isn't very good. I'm surprised. It's really a beautiful restaurant and expensive too. The food looks great, but it's very ordinary.
   JOSHUA: I agree. This place is beautiful, but the food isn't good. _____

2. Lou is moving into a new apartment. Joe and Bill are helping him.
   LOU: I really want to thank you guys for giving me a hand. Moving all of this heavy stuff isn't much fun. I really appreciate it.
   JOE: Hey, that's all right. Don't mention it. _____

3. BILL: What's the matter? You look upset.
   RUTH: I am. I lost fifty dollars this morning. I don't know why I was so stupid. I'm usually so careful with money, but this morning I didn't put the money in my purse. Instead, I just put it in my jacket pocket. When I went to pay for something this afternoon, the money was gone. I guess it fell out of my pocket. Fifty dollars! That's a lot of money to lose because of a careless mistake. I can't stop thinking about it. I'm so angry with myself.
   BILL: Come on. It's only money. Stop thinking about it. There's nothing you can do to get it back. _____

4. DIANE: Hey, Sarah. How was your date with that new guy who works in your office? Did you have a good time? Is he nice?
   SARAH: I didn't enjoy the date at all. I really don't like him. He doesn't have any personality.

Future Time Clauses _____ 261

DIANE: That's too bad, because he sure is good-looking. I guess that old saying is true: _____

_____ .

5. CLIENT: I'm worried about my son. His grades were terrible last semester. I sat down and talked to him about it, and we made up a study schedule for him to follow. I even hired a private tutor to help him with geometry once a week. My son knows he can't get into college if his grades don't improve, but he just refuses to follow the study schedule. He just listens to his records and watches TV after school.

RUTH: Well, teenagers don't like to listen to anyone. _____

_____ .

6. RUTH: Did you see Lillian at the party the other night? She looked terrible in that dress. It was much too tight. Is she getting fat?
BILL: I think so. She needs to lose about ten or fifteen pounds.
RUTH: Hey, what are we talking about? You and I need to lose a few pounds too.
BILL: I guess you're right. _____

_____ .

ACTIVITY 21G

Do you know some proverbs from your country that have a similar meaning to the proverbs on page 259? Tell them to the class. Do you know any other popular proverbs from your country that you can tell the class? (It's not necessary for them to have a similar meaning to the proverbs in the reading.)

22 REAL CONDITIONAL FOR FUTURE EVENTS— *IF, WILL*

Content Focus — Worry

Dialog

(Joe is talking to his mother, Mrs. Haley, on the telephone.)

Joe: Well, Mom, what did you and Dad decide? Are you going to come to New York City for a visit next weekend?

Mrs. Haley: Yes. We're going to stay for three or four days.

Joe: Good. How are you going to come? Are you going to drive?

Mrs. Haley: No. We don't want to bring our car to New York City. **If we park the car on the streets in New York City, someone will steal it. And we'll spend a fortune[1] if we park in a garage.** Parking is so expensive in New York City.

Joe: So how are you going to come?

Mrs. Haley: Your father wants to fly, but you know I'm afraid of flying. **If we fly, I'm sure the plane will crash.**

Joe: Oh, Mom! So you're going to take the train?

Mrs. Haley: Yes. Our train will arrive at 5:00 P.M. on Friday.

Joe: Okay. I'll meet you at the station.

Mrs. Haley: All right, but don't be late. **Your father will be very upset if you are late.** You know he hates to wait.

Joe: Yeah, I know. I'll be on time. Are you planning to stay at my apartment, or do you want to stay at a hotel?

Mrs. Haley: Well, I don't know. Hotels are so expensive. But you have a cat, and you know your father is allergic to cats. **If we stay at your apartment, your father will sneeze all weekend.**

Joe: Diane can take my cat for the weekend. Don't worry about Dad. You can stay at my place.

Mrs. Haley: But what about your roommate? Your apartment is so small. **Will your roommate be annoyed if we stay with you?**

Joe: Don't worry about it. He isn't going to be here next weekend. He's going to visit a friend in New Jersey.

Mrs. Haley: All right.

Comprehension Questions

1. When are Joe's parents going to come to New York City to visit him?
2. How long are they going to stay?
3. How are they going to get to New York City?
4. Why aren't they going to drive?

[1] *A fortune* means "a lot of money."

5. Why aren't they going to fly?
6. Why is Diane going to take Joe's cat for the weekend?
7. Is Hiro going to be at the apartment when Joe's parents are there?
8. Do Joe's parents worry a lot?

What Do You Think?

1. Joe loves his mother, but sometimes she drives him crazy. Why? What does she do all the time?
2. Do you know people who worry about everything? Give examples of the things they worry about.
3. Do you worry a lot? What do you worry about?

Grammar Fill-in

Study the sentences with *if . . . , will. . . .* Then complete these sentences from the dialog.

1. JOE: Good. How are you going to come? Are you going to drive?

   MRS. HALEY: No. We don't want to bring our car to New York City.

   If _____ on the streets in New York City,

   someone _____. And we

   _____ if _____ in a garage.
   Parking is so expensive in New York City.

2. MRS. HALEY: Your father wants to fly, but you know I'm afraid of flying.

   If _____, I'm sure the plane

   _____.

3. JOE: Okay. I'll meet you at the station.

   MRS. HALEY: All right, but don't be late. Your father _____

   _____ if you _____.

   You know he hates to wait.

4. JOE: Yeah, I know. I'll be on time. Are you planning to stay at my apartment, or do you want to stay at a hotel?

   MRS. HALEY: Well, I don't know. Hotels are so expensive. But you have a cat, and you know your father is allergic to cats. If

_____ your apartment, your father

_____.

5. MRS. HALEY: But what about your roommate? Your apartment is so small.

_____ if we

_____ with you?

REAL CONDITIONAL FOR FUTURE EVENTS—*IF, WILL*

There are many different ways to form the real conditional. A real conditional sentence has two parts: an *if* clause and a main clause. When you want to talk about things that are generally true or habits that people have, use the simple present tense for the *if* clause and the main clause.

> *Example*
>
> If Joe's mother **takes** a trip, she **worries** about everything.

Notice that *if* has almost the same meaning as *when* in this sentence. We can say, "When Joe's mother takes a trip, she worries about everything," and the meaning doesn't really change very much.

This chapter focuses on the use of the real conditional to talk about future events because this is where students often make mistakes. They get confused about where to use the future tense. Use the future tense in the main clause only.

Statements

Use the simple present tense in the *if* clause; use the future tense (*will* or *going to*) in the main clause.

If + subject + simple present + subject + *will* + base form

> *Example*
>
> **If we park the car on the streets, someone will steal it.**

The *if* clause can also come at the end of the sentence.

> **Example**
> We'll spend a fortune **if we park in a garage.**

Note: In this chapter, you are asked to practice using *will* in the main clause of a real conditional sentence, but you can also use *going to*.

Questions
Use the question order only in the main clause.

> **Example**
> If we stay at your apartment, **will your roommate be annoyed?**

■ ACTIVITY 22A
Joe's mother and father worry about everything. Use your imagination to make sentences with *if . . . , will. . . .*
Joe's parents are at his apartment in New York City now.

1. JOE: Is it too hot in here? I think I'll open the window.
   MRS. HALEY: Oh, no. Don't open the window. It's cold outside. If you _____ the window, _____ _____.

2. JOE: What would you like to do tonight? Do you want to go to the theater?
   MR. HALEY: Well, I don't know. You have a cold, and I think it's going to rain tonight. You _____ if we _____ tonight.

3. MRS. HALEY: Your father is right. And all the theaters are near Times Square. Times Square is so dangerous. There are a lot of horrible people around there. If _____ there, someone _____.

4. JOE: You can't come to New York City for a visit and stay inside the apartment all weekend. Come on. We're going to the theater.

   MR. HALEY: Okay, but let's take a taxi. I'm afraid of the subways. If _____ the subway, _____ _____.

   MRS. HALEY: But, dear. Taxis are so expensive. We _____ _____ if _____ a taxi.

   MR. HALEY: That's okay. I'm not going to take the subway, and the buses are too slow.

5. MR. HALEY: Let's walk down the stairs. I don't want to take the elevator. Elevators make me nervous. If we _____ the elevator, _____.

   (Now they are outside in front of the apartment building.)

6. MRS. HALEY: Joe, don't walk under that ladder! If _____ _____, _____.

   (Now they are in the taxi.)

7. MRS. HALEY: Why is he driving so fast? Joe, ask him to drive slowly. We _____ if he _____.

   (Joe is smoking.)

8. MR. HALEY: I'm worried about you. You should stop smoking. You _____ if you _____.

   (Now they are waiting to cross the street.)

9. MR. HALEY: Joe, wait! We can't cross now. The light is red. If _____ _____.

   (Now they are in front of the theater.)

10. MRS. HALEY: Oh, no! There's a black cat. Don't let that cat walk in front of you. _____ if it _____ in front of you.

    JOE: Do you really believe that superstition, Mom?

    MRS. HALEY: I certainly do.

    (Now they are at Joe's apartment after the theater.)

11. JOE: Would you like to go to the top of the Empire State Building tomorrow? There's a great view of the city from there.

    MR. HALEY: Well, I don't know. Your mother is afraid of high places. She _____ if _____ to the Empire State Building.

ACTIVITY 22B

Joe's mother is superstitious about black cats. She thinks that if a black cat walks in front of her, she will have bad luck. Do you know some other superstitions that people have about things that bring bad luck or good luck? Tell these superstitions to the class using this pattern: *If* + simple present, . . . *will* + base form. Here are some cues to help you think of some superstitions.

mirror	the palm of your hand
a four-leaf clover	a black butterfly
a penny	an owl
a spider	the crack between two sections of the sidewalk

ACTIVITY 22C

What worries do the following people have? Make a question with *What will happen if . . . ?* Another student can answer the question. Work as a whole class or work with a partner.

1. Joe isn't doing very well in his statistics course. He got a C[2] on the midterm exam. The final exam is tomorrow.

   _____?

   _____.

2. Jeanne Simmons works for the telephone company. Bill is her boss. He had to have a serious talk with her last week because she often comes to work late. Last night she set her alarm clock for 6:30 A.M. Now it's 7:30, and she is just getting out of bed. She overslept.

   _____?

   _____.

[2]*C:* The best grade is A, then B, C, D, and F (Fail). C is not a good grade.

Real Conditional for Future Events—If, Will   269

3. John is eleven years old. He got his report card[3] from school today, and it's not good news. He got two C's and two D's. John's father gets angry very easily. John doesn't want to show his report card to his dad.

    _____?
    _____.

4. Joe is worried about Diane. She works very long hours at the hospital. Some nights she gets only a few hours of sleep. Joe thinks she looks exhausted.

    _____?
    _____.

5. Hiro is planning to take the Test of English as a Foreign Language next month. He needs a score of 600 to get into the American university that he wants to attend. He's very nervous about the test.

    _____?
    _____.

6. One of Hiro's classmates is worried about her English, too, because she lives in a Spanish-speaking neighborhood. She speaks Spanish all the time when she goes home.

    _____?
    _____.

7. Mrs. Mason frequently comes to Ruth to ask for advice about her teenage son, Bobby. Bobby is a good boy, but he has some friends who are a little wild and get into trouble sometimes. She's worried about her son. She doesn't know if she should allow her son to be friends with these boys.

    _____?
    _____.

8. Nintendo is an extremely popular video game that kids (and adults) can play on their TV screens at home. Many American parents are worried because their kids spend many hours playing Nintendo.

    _____?
    _____.

[3]*Report card* means "written information that a school sends home to parents to let them know how their child is doing in his or her courses."

23 PRESENT UNREAL CONDITIONAL

Content Focus: BAD HABITS

Dialog

(It's a cold, gray winter day. DIANE arrived at JOE's apartment a few minutes ago. She came from work at the hospital.)

JOE: Diane, you know something? You look completely bushed.[1] **If I were you, I would slow down.**[2]

DIANE: You know something? I am bushed. I think I'm getting another cold.

JOE: What? Another cold? **If I were a doctor, I'd tell you to take a vacation right away.** You're not a machine. You have to rest some time.

DIANE: Yeah, but I can't go anywhere right now. I have a medical exam the week after next. Besides, I'm broke.[3]

JOE: Me too. **If I had the money, I'd take you on your dream vacation.**

DIANE: My dream vacation! Let's dream for a minute. **Where would we go next week if I didn't have that exam and if we had the money?**

JOE: **We'd go to a Caribbean island. We'd lie around in the sun and do nothing.**

DIANE: That sounds fantastic. These cold, gray winters in New York City really make me feel depressed. **I'd feel a hundred percent better if I could feel some nice warm sun on my back.**

Comprehension Questions

1. How does Diane look—tired or full of energy?
2. If Joe were a doctor, what would he order Diane to do?
3. Can Diane take a vacation now? Why or why not?
4. What would Joe do if he had the money?
5. If Diane and Joe could take a vacation next week, where would they go?
6. Does Diane like winter in New York City?
7. Diane says that she's getting another cold. Complete this sentence: Diane would feel a hundred percent better if _____

How about You?

If you could leave tomorrow for a one-week vacation, where would you go?

---

[1] *Bushed* means "very tired; exhausted."
[2] *Slow down* means "to stop doing so many things; to relax a little."
[3] *Broke* means "to have no money left."

PRESENT UNREAL CONDITIONAL

Here is the pattern for a present unreal conditional statement.

If + subject + past tense, subject + (*would/could*) + base form

> *Example*
> If I had the money, I would take you on your dream vacation.

Use the present unreal conditional to talk about a situation in the present that is the opposite of reality.
Look at this example from the dialog:

If Joe were a doctor, he would tell Diane to take a vacation right away.

Reality: Joe is not a doctor.

Unreal conditional *if* clause

If he were a doctor, ...

Notice that the present tense verb *is* shifts to the past tense *were*. The correct grammar for the present unreal conditional is *were* for all subjects.

If I were a doctor, ...   If we were doctors, ...

If you were a doctor, ...   If they were doctors, ...

If he/she were a doctor, ...

Some Americans use *was* with *he* or *she* for present unreal conditional statements, especially in informal conversation.
When the verb that states the reality is negative (*Joe isn't a doctor*), the verb in the *if* clause is positive (*If Joe were a doctor, ...*). When the verb that states the reality is positive (*Diane has an exam the week after next*), the verb in the *if* clause is negative (*If Diane didn't have an exam, she could take a vacation*).
There is a comma when the *if* clause starts the sentence. When the *if* clause ends the sentence, there is no comma.

If Diane didn't have an exam, she could take a vacation.

Diane could take a vacation if she didn't have an exam.

CONTRACTIONS

When we speak, we often make a contraction of the subject and *would*.

subject + *would* = *I'd, you'd, he'd, she'd, we'd, they'd*

ACTIVITY 23A

We often use the present unreal conditional pattern to give advice.

If I were you, I would(n't) + base form

In the following example, Joe is giving advice to Diane about how to change her bad habits in order to improve her health.

Example

JOE: You work too hard. You work long hours at the hospital. Then you come home and read medical journals. You shouldn't work so hard. If I were you, I wouldn't work so hard.

Finish Joe's advice with a sentence beginning *If I were you, ...*

1. JOE: You can't seem to take your mind off your work when you come home. You always talk about your patients. You don't read novels or watch TV or have a hobby. You need to do something to take your mind off your work.
2. JOE: You don't know how to relax. You're frequently tense and nervous when you come home from the hospital. You need to take a course in relaxation techniques.
3. JOE: You always tell me you have trouble falling asleep. Why don't you stop drinking coffee at night?
4. JOE: You don't eat right. You get up late in the morning, so you don't have time to eat breakfast. Breakfast is the most important meal of the day.
5. JOE: When you feel tired, you eat a candy bar. It's true that sugar gives you quick energy, but it makes you feel even more tired later. You shouldn't eat sugar when you feel tired.
6. JOE: You don't eat a balanced diet.[4] You eat too many fast foods like pizza, hot dogs, and fried chicken.
7. JOE: You drink diet soda all the time. It's full of chemicals. Don't drink that garbage.

[4]*Eat a balanced diet* means "to eat healthy foods from all of the major food groups (cereals and grains; red meat, poultry, and fish; vegetables and fruits; dairy products, such as milk and cheese)

8. JOE: You don't exercise. When you exercise, you have more energy. You say you don't have time, but you need to make time.
9. JOE: You don't take vitamins. That's why you get so many colds.

ACTIVITY 23B

Use the present unreal conditional to tell how things would be different if Diane didn't have habits that are bad for her health.

> *Example*
>
> Diane works too hard, so she is exhausted all the time.
>
> If *she didn't work* so hard, *she wouldn't be* exhausted all of the time.

1. She drinks coffee at night, so she has trouble falling asleep.

   If _____ coffee at night, _____ falling asleep.

2. She gets up late in the morning, so she doesn't have time to eat breakfast.

   If _____ a little earlier, _____ time to eat breakfast.

3. She doesn't east breakfast, so she runs out of energy at around 11:00 every morning.

   If _____ breakfast, _____ energy at 11:00.

4. She doesn't exercise, so she isn't in good shape.

   _____

5. She doesn't eat right or take vitamins, so she gets a lot of colds.

   _____

6. She doesn't have a hobby or interests outside of her work, so she can't take her mind off her job.

   _____

   _____

7. She can't take her mind off her job, so she can't relax when she gets home.

   _____

   _____

Questions

Use this pattern to form questions.

(Question word) + *would/could* + subject + base form + *if* clause?

    Would Diane take a vacation if she weren't broke?

Answer: Yes, she would.

    Where would Joe and Diane go if they had the money?

Answer: They'd go to a Caribbean island.

Notice that the *if* clause can come at the beginning of the question.

If Joe and Diane had the money, where would they go?

ACTIVITY 23C

José, one of Hiro's classmates, is very unhappy with his progress in English. He thinks that he should speak and understand English better by now because he has been in class for almost three months. Hiro doesn't really want to tell his friend this, but he thinks that José has some very bad study habits. Ask a classmate a question using this pattern:

What would you do if you were José?

Your classmate will answer. After you and your partner finish the oral practice, you can write the questions and answers. Give your own opinion for the answer.

> **Example**
> He speaks Spanish with his friends during and after class.
> *What would you do if you were José?*
> *I would speak English during class (and sometimes after class).*

1. He arrives late to class all of the time, so he doesn't understand what's happening most of the time.

2. When he goes into a store, he doesn't try to speak English. He always asks first if the person speaks Spanish.

3. There's a Spanish newspaper in New York City, so he always buys that instead of a newspaper in English.

4. When his teacher gives the class a story to read in English, it always takes him a long time to read it because he looks up every unfamiliar word in his Spanish/English dictionary. He gets bored and frustrated.

5. When he does his homework, he usually watches a TV program in Spanish at the same time.

6. When his teacher asks him a question in English, he always translates the question into Spanish before he answers.

Activity 23D

Use the present unreal conditional to ask how José's English could be better if he didn't have bad study habits. Your classmate will give a short answer with *yes* + subject + *would*.

Example

He speaks Spanish with his classmates during and after class. His fluency in English is poor.

If he *spoke English* with his classmates, *would his fluency be* better?

Yes it would.

Present Unreal Conditional

1. He arrives late to class all of the time. He doesn't understand what's happening in class.

    If he _____ on time, _____ better?

2. When he goes to a store, he doesn't try to speak English. His fluency in English is poor.

    _____ better if _____ to speak English when he goes to a store?

3. He always buys a newspaper in Spanish. His vocabulary in English is very limited.

    _____ larger if _____ a newspaper in English?

4. He always looks up every unfamiliar word when he reads a story in English, so he gets bored and frustrated.

    _____

5. He makes a lot of mistakes when he does his homework for English class because he watches TV programs in Spanish at the same time.

    _____

6. He always translates a question into Spanish before he answers it, so his comprehension in English is weak.

    _____

ACTIVITY 23E

Do you have any bad habits, or do you know someone who has bad habits? Tell the class about the habit and why you think it is bad. The class will offer advice or tell how things could be different using statements with the present unreal conditional.

ACTIVITY 23F

Look at the situations in Chapter 11 on page XXX. Ask a classmate a yes/no question using the present unreal conditional. For example, for item 1, would you look the other way if you were Ruth?

24 THE PASSIVE VOICE WITH THE SIMPLE PAST AND SIMPLE PRESENT TENSES

Top: Marie Curie, John F. Kennedy
Bottom: Gamal Abdel Nasser, Chou En Lai

Content Focus: KNOWLEDGE OF WORLD HISTORY

QUIZ

In 1987, E. D. Hirsch, Jr., wrote *Cultural Literacy*. In this book, he says that schools in the United States don't do a good job of teaching basic facts. He thinks that every educated person should know these facts, but he says that many U.S. high-school graduates don't know them. Knowledge of world history is part of cultural literacy. How much do you know about world history? Take this quiz to see if you know the basic facts. As you read the information, also pay attention to the verb forms in boldface type. You will find it helpful to use the vocabulary that appears at the beginning of each item of information.

Here is a list of famous people, dates, and countries. Use it to fill in the blanks as you read.

Simón Bolívar	King Edward	Queen Victoria
Chou En-lai	People's Republic of China	France
John F. Kennedy		the Bastille
Napoleon Bonaparte	the 1950s	Yasir Arafat
Queen Elizabeth I	the 1890s	Chiang Kai-shek
Vietnam	Notre Dame Cathedral	Charles de Gaulle
the 1920s	Gamal Abdel Nasser	Adolf Hitler
Fidel Castro	Mao Tse-tung	the United States
Deng Xiaoping	Jimmy Carter	the 1850s
Richard Nixon	Leonardo da Vinci	the Eiffel Tower
Benito Mussolini		

1. **conquer:** to use military force to put a group of people or a country under your control
   defeat: to conquer; to be the winner in a battle or a war

   Many countries of Europe were conquered by _____ during the late eighteenth and early nineteenth centuries. He was defeated by the British at the Battle of Waterloo.

2. **free:** to permit someone to go free. (Notice that *free* is used as a verb here.)
   Several areas in the northern part of South America were freed from Spanish control by _____ during the first half of the nineteenth century. Today these areas are called Venezuela, Colombia, Ecuador, Peru, and Bolivia.

3. **led:** guided, directed
   The Communist Revolution in China was led by

   _____.

4. During World War II, Italy was led by _____.

5. **rule:** to have the power to govern a country. Kings and queens rule. During the second half of the nineteenth century, Great Britain was the most powerful nation in the world. During this period, the country was

   ruled by _____.

6. During the 1970s, a better relationship between the United States and the People's Republic of China was formed. This was the work of two

   important political leaders, _____ of China and

   _____ of the United States.

7. During the Korean War of the 1950s, South Korea was helped by

   _____, and North Korea was helped by

   _____.

8. **overthrow:** to take away the power to govern by using force

   King Farouk of Egypt was overthrown by _____ in 1952.

9. **release:** to permit someone to go free
   destroy: to ruin; to break apart so that it cannot be used anymore
   Just before the French Revolution began, political prisoners were

   held at a famous prison in Paris. This prison was called _____

   _____. It was attacked by workers on July 14, 1789. The prisoners were released, and the building was destroyed.

   _____ Day is celebrated every July 14 in France.

10. **port:** a city on the coast where ships come in
    trade: commerce; buying and selling
    fleet: a group of ships
    put pressure on someone: to try to make someone do what you want him or her to do

    Japan's ports were opened to trade with the West in _____. Admiral Matthew C. Perry sailed a fleet of American ships into Tokyo Bay to put pressure on the Japanese emperor to trade with Western countries.

When you finish the quiz, compare your classmates' answers with yours. Turn to page 287 to find the correct answers.

THE PASSIVE VOICE WITH THE SIMPLE PAST AND SIMPLE PRESENT TENSES

Statements

To form the passive voice, you need the verb *be* (*is, are, was, were*) and the past participle (third form) of the verb.

The past participle of regular verbs is the same as the past tense: *-ed*.

For some irregular verbs, the past participle and the past tense are the same: *hold, held, held.*

For some irregular verbs, the part participle and the past tense are different: *know, knew, known.*

Look at the difference between the verbs in the active voice and the passive voice in the following sentences. Both sentences are in the past tense.

Active Voice: Queen Victoria **ruled** Great Britain during the second half of the nineteenth century.

Passive Voice: Great Britain **was ruled** by Queen Victoria during the second half of the nineteenth century.

In the sentence in which the active voice has been used, the subject of the verb is Queen Victoria. She performs (does) the action. We can call Queen Victoria the *doer* and Great Britain, the *receiver,* of the action. In the sentence in which the passive voice has been used, Great Britain (the receiver) has changed positions with Queen Victoria (the doer). Great Britain is the subject now, but it does not perform the action. It receives the action.

Why do we use the passive voice instead of the active voice? Here are some reasons.

1. We want to put more importance on the receiver. The receiver comes into our minds first, so we say it first.

   Napoleon was defeated at the Battle of Waterloo.

2. We all know who the doer is, so we don't need to say it.

   This prison was called the Bastille.

   We know that the doer is the French people. It is not necessary to say this.

   This prison was called the Bastille (by the French people).

3. Sometimes we know the doer, but we don't want to say it for some reason.

   During the 1970s, a better relationship between the United States and the People's Republic of China was formed.

   When we use the passive voice, we can omit the doer if we want to. In the above sentence, the author of this text chose to ask the students to supply the information about the doer by filling in the blanks in the next sentence.

   Sometimes we don't know the doer, so we can't name it. If somebody stole my car, but I didn't know who, I would probably say, "My car was stolen."

■ ACTIVITY 24A

Practice forming sentences with the past tense of the passive voice. Connect the receivers in the column on the left with the doers in the column on the right. Write the letter of the doer next to the receiver. Use the verb in parentheses to make a passive voice sentence. Work in groups so that you can share your knowledge. There are facts here about world history, including some about famous inventions. The first item has been done for you.

_f_ 1. Kubla Khan, the Mongol ruler of China
     (*visit*)
     Kubla Khan, the Mongol ruler of China, was visited by Marco Polo.

____ 2. Christopher Columbus
     (*support*)

____ 3. the Great Wall of China
     (*build*)

____ 4. Julius Caesar, the leader of ancient Rome
     (*kill*)

____ 5. the telephone
     (*invent*)

a. Abraham Lincoln
b. Ho Chi Minh City after the Vietnam War
c. Alexander Graham Bell
d. Pierre and Marie Curie
e. the French people during the French Revolution
f. Marco Polo
g. the Wright brothers
h. Mahatma Gandhi
i. Chiang Kai-shek
j. Guglielmo Marconi

The Passive Voice with the Simple Past and Simple Present Tenses _____ 283

_____ 6. parts of central and eastern Europe during the fifth century
(*conquer*)

_____ 7. the telegraph (a machine to send messages over long distances)
(*invent*)

_____ 8. Hangul (the characters that are used to write the Korean language)
(*create*)

_____ 9. radium
(*discover*)

_____ 10. the first successful airplane with a motor
(*build and fly*)

_____ 11. the fight for India's independence from Great Britain
(*win*)

_____ 12. the Republic of China (Nationalist China)
(*establish*)

_____ 13. Louis XVI and Marie Antoinette, the rulers of France
(*execute*)

_____ 14. the American slaves
(*free*)

_____ 15. Saigon
(*rename*)

k. Attila the Hun

l. an emperor of the Ch'in dynasty

m. Brutus and other members of the Roman Senate

n. King Ferdinand and Queen Isabella of Spain

o. King Sejong

Activity 24B

This exercise is the same as Activity 24A, but here the receivers in the left-hand column are from the world of art, architecture, literature, and music. Most of these famous works of art are a part of Western culture, but a few works from Eastern culture are included also. When you work in your groups, share your knowledge. Explain to your classmates what the receiver is: a famous statue, a famous book, a famous building, and so on. Then make a sentence in the passive voice to match the receiver with the doer. The first item has been done for you.

__1__ 1. the *Nutcracker Suite* (a famous piece of classical music) (*write/compose*)
   The *Nutcracker Suite* was composed by Pyotr Ilich Tchaikovsky.

_____ 2. *Hamlet, Othello,* and *Romeo and Juliet* (*write*)

_____ 3. the statue of *David* (*make/sculpt*)

_____ 4. the Taj Mahal (*build*)

_____ 5. *Guernica* (*paint*)

_____ 6. *Rashomon* (*direct*)

_____ 7. *The Tale of Genji* (*write*)

_____ 8. the Statue of Liberty (*give to the United States*)

_____ 9. *Madame Butterfly* (*write/compose*)

_____ 10. *The Last Supper* and the *Mona Lisa* (*paint*)

_____ 11. *The Blue Danube* waltz (*write/compose*)

_____ 12. *The Rubaiyat* (*write*)

_____ 13. the Ninth Symphony (the *Choral* Symphony) and the Third Symphony (the *Eroica*) (*write/compose*)

_____ 14. *Don Quixote* (*write*)

_____ 15. the Parthenon (*build*)

a. Akira Kurosawa
b. Ludwig van Beethoven
c. France
d. Omar Khayyám
e. Johann Strauss
f. Pablo Picasso
g. the ancient Greeks
h. Miguel de Cervantes
i. William Shakespeare
j. Michelangelo Buonarroti
k. Shāh Jahān, a ruler of India
l. Pyotr Ilich Tchaikovsky
m. Giacomo Puccini
n. Murasaki Shikibu
o. Leonardo da Vinci

Activity 24C

Share your knowledge of your country's history, art, music, literature, or film with the class. Choose five important facts that almost everyone from your country should know. Teach these facts to the class. Begin your sentence with the receiver so that your sentence will be in the passive voice.

Questions

Reverse the receiver and the verb *be* to form a question.

(Question word)   *was/were* + receiver + past participle?

Question: **Was** the Ninth Symphony **written** by Beethoven?
Answer: Yes, it **was.**
Question: **Were** *Othello* and *Hamlet* **written** by Shakespeare?
Answer: Yes, they **were.**
Question: When **was** India's fight for independence **won**?
Answer: It **was won** in 1947.

Activity 24D

Here are some famous wars and battles and a list of dates to go with them. Work with a classmate. One person will ask a question with *When* and the verb that is given, and the other person will try to answer the question. Use the passive voice for the questions and answers.

1815	1941	1914 to 1918	1588
1950 to 1953	1781	1947	1954
1955 to 1958	1973	September 1945	1910 to 1914
May 1945	1839 to 1842		

Example

Germany (*defeat*) in World War II

When was Germany defeated in World War II?

Germany was defeated in _May 1945_.

1. Japan (*defeat*) in World War II
2. the War of Independence in the American colonies (*win*)
3. Napoleon (*defeat*) at Waterloo
4. the treaty to end the Vietnam War (*sign*)
5. the French army in Vietnam War (*defeat*) at Dien Bien Phu
6. the Korean War (*fight*)
7. Russia (*invade*) by Germany
8. World War I (*fight*)
9. the Opium War (*fight*)

ACTIVITY 24E

In the preceding examples and activities, you've practiced the past tense of the passive voice. Next you will practice the present tense of the passive voice with *is/are* + the past participle.

> *Example*
>
> In the United States, a large percentage of the oranges **are grown** in Florida.

Do you know some facts about world production? Work with a classmate. One person will ask a question with *Where* and the verb that is given, and the other person will look at the list of countries and try to answer. Use the present tense of the passive voice for the questions and answers.

The Netherlands	Colombia	Japan	France
the United States	Cuba	South Africa	Spain
the USSR	India	Switzerland	Ghana
Saudi Arabia			

> *Example*
>
> coffee (*grow*)
>
> Where is a large percentage of the world's coffee grown?
>
> It is grown in Colombia.

1. wheat (*grow*)
2. electronic appliances (*manufacture*)
3. tea (*grow*)
4. diamonds (*mine*)
5. cars (*manufacture*)
6. cigars (*make*)
7. tulips (*grow*)
8. olive oil (*produce*)
9. champagne (*produce*)
10. watches (*manufacture*)
11. steel (*produce*)
12. cacao (*grow*)
13. sugar cane (*grow*)
14. high-fashion clothing (*design*)

ACTIVITY 24F

Tell the class about your country's economy. What are the most important products that are manufactured or produced in your country? What important minerals are mined? What are the most important crops (food plants) grown?

Answers

QUIZ

1. Napoleon   2. Simón Bolívar   3. Mao Tse-tung   4. Benito Mussolini   5. Queen Victoria   6. Chou En-lai; Richard Nixon   7. the United States; the People's Republic of China   8. Gamal Abdel Nasser   9. the Bastille; Bastille Day   10. the 1850s (1853)

ACTIVITY 24A

1.f Kubla Khan, the Mongol ruler of China—Marco Polo.   2.n Christopher Columbus—King Ferdinand and Queen Isabella of Spain.   3.l the Great Wall of China—an emperor of the Ch'in dynasty.   4.m Julius Caesar, the leader of ancient Rome—Brutus and other members of the Roman Senate.   5.c the telephone—Alexander Graham Bell.   6.k parts of central and eastern Europe during the fifth century—Attila the Hun.   7.j the telegraph—Guglielmo Marconi.   8.o Hangul—King Sejong.   9.d radium—Pierre and Marie Curie.   10.g the first successful airplane with a motor—the Wright brothers. 11.h the fight for India's independence from Great Britain—Mahatma Gandhi. 12.i the Republic of China—Chiang Kai-shek. 13.e Louis XVI and Marie Antoinette, the rulers of France—the French people during the French Revolution. 14.a the American slaves—Abraham Lincoln. 15.b Saigon—Ho Chi Minh City after the Vietnam War.

ACTIVITY 24B

1.l the *Nutcracker Suite*—Pyotr Ilich Tchaikovsky. 2.i *Hamlet, Othello,* and *Romeo and Juliet* (three of the greatest plays of the English language)—William Shakespeare. 3.j the statue *David* (one of the most famous sculptures of the Italian Renaissance)—Michelangelo Buonarroti. 4.k the Taj Mahal (one of the most beautiful buildings in India)—Shāh Jahān, a ruler of India. 5.f *Guernica* (a famous painting of a Spanish town during the civil war)—Pablo Picasso. 6.a *Rashomon* (a Japanese film, now a classic)—Akira Kurosawa. 7.n *The Tale of Genji* (a classic work of literature from Japan)—Murasaki Shikibu. 8.c the Statue of Liberty (the famous statue in New York harbor)—France. 9.m *Madame Butterfly* (a famous opera)—Giacomo Puccini. 10.o *The Last Supper* and the Mona Lisa (a famous painting of Jesus and the twelve disciples and *La Gioconda,* a famous painting of a lady with a rapturous smile)—Leonardo da Vinci. 11.e *The Blue Danube* waltz (a famous piece of music)—Johann Strauss. 12.d *The Rubaiyat* (a collection of love poems from Persia)—Omar Khayyám. 13.b the Ninth Symphony and the Third Symphony (two famous pieces of music)—Ludwig van Beethoven. 14.h *Don Quixote* (the most famous classic Spanish novel)—Miguel de Cervantes. 15.g the Parthenon (a beautiful example of classical Greek architecture)—the ancient Greeks.

ACTIVITY 24D

1. September 1945   2. 1781   3. 1815   4. 1973   5. 1954   6. 1950 to 1953   7. 1941   8. 1914 to 1918   9. 1839 to 1842 (a war between China and England over the right to sell opium to the Chinese)

ACTIVITY 24E

1. wheat—the United States and the USSR   2. electronic appliances—Japan   3. tea—India   4. diamonds—South Africa   5. cars—the United States and Japan   6. cigars—Cuba   7. tulips—The Netherlands   8. olive oil—Spain   9. champagne—France   10. watches—Switzerland   11. steel—the United States   12. cacao—Ghana   13. sugar cane—Cuba (and other Caribbean countries)   14. high-fashion clothing—France

25 INTEGRATION OF TENSES AND VERB FORMS

Content Focus: GETTING INTO SHAPE

In this chapter, you will practice using all of the verb forms that you have learned in this book.

Activity 25

☐ Fill in the blanks to tell what is happening in the cartoon strip about Bill and Ruth on page 289. Choose the verb forms carefully. When a sentence describes what is happening at the present moment in the picture, use the present continuous tense (be + -ing). When you see the word *modal*, choose from *can, could, should, have to,* and *must.*

Picture 1

In the first picture, Bill _____ his apartment. He _____
　　　　　　　　　　　　　　　(leave)　　　　　　　　　　　　　(wear)
a jogging suit and running shoes because he _____ when he
　　　　　　　　　　　　　　　　　　　　　　　(run)
_____ to the park. He _____ very happy about it. He
　(get)　　　　　　　　　　　(negative for **be**)
_____ but he _____ it because he is overweight.
(negative for **want, jog**)　　　(modal + **do**)
Last week he _____ to the doctor for a checkup, and the doctor
　　　　　　　　(go)
_____ a serious talk with him. He said, "Bill, you're about twenty
　(have)
pounds overweight, and you're out of shape.[1] I _____ you
　　　　　　　　　　　　　　　　　　　　　　　　　　　(tell)
_____ weight for a long time. If you _____ on a diet, you
　(lose)　　　　　　　　　　　　　　　　(negative for **go**)
_____ heart trouble. Your blood pressure is a little high already.
　(have)
You _____ games with your health. You _____ weight.
　　　(modal + **play**)　　　　　　　　　　　　　　(modal + **lose**)
Also, I _____ you _____ for half an hour three times a
　　　　　(want)　　　　　(jog)
week. If I _____ you, I _____ twenty pounds,
　　　　　　(be)　　　　　　(lose)
but it's okay if you try for only ten or fifteen pounds."

After Bill _____ the doctor's office last week, he decided to
　　　　　　(leave)
follow the doctor's advice. He _____ straight to a sporting goods
　　　　　　　　　　　　　　　　(go)

[1] *Out of shape* means "not in good physical condition."

store and _____ a jogging suit and some new running shoes. Then
         (buy)
he _____ home and _____ Ruth _____ out all of
      (go)   (ask)   (throw)
the cookies, cakes, and ice cream in the kitchen. Ruth _____,
                                                              (say)
"Fine," and she did it.

At this moment, Ruth _____ at the door and _____
                          (stand)   (say)
good-bye to Bill. She _____ because she's happy that
                              (smile)
Bill _____ in shape. She _____ a jogging suit,
        (get)   (negative for wear)
so we know that she _____ with Bill today. When she
                          (negative for plan, jog)
_____ back inside the apartment, she _____.
    (go)   (relax)

Picture 2

In the second picture, Bill is in the park. He _____.
                                                        (jog)
He _____ a lot, and he's hot and uncomfortable. He
        (sweat)
_____. He _____ at his watch and
 (negative for enjoy, jog)   (look)
thinking, "I can't believe it! I _____ for only fifteen
                                       (jog)
minutes. I _____ for fifteen more minutes. I
                (modal + run)
_____."
     (hate, jog)

Picture 3

In the third picture, Ruth _____ on the sofa. She
                                     (relax)
_____ the Sunday paper and _____ a
        (read)   (eat)
breakfast of coffee and two donuts. Her favorite time of the week is Sunday

morning. She always _____ it easy. She never _____ or
                          (take)   (clean)
_____ on Sunday morning.
   (plan, study)

Picture 4

In the fourth picture, Ruth is in the bathroom. She _____ on the scale. She is very upset because
              (stand)
she _____ herself four days ago, and she _____
     (weigh)   (weigh)
135 pounds. Today she _____ 140 pounds—five pounds in just
                        (weigh)
four days! If I _____ Ruth, I _____ upset too. She's
          (be)   (be)
thinking to herself, "Uh, oh. If I _____ careful, I _____
                    (negative for **be**)   (be)
as overweight as Bill is soon. I _____ on a diet too."
                             (need, go)

Picture 5

In the fifth picture, Ruth and Bill _____ together.
                           (jog)
Both of them _____. Bill _____ trouble
         (sweat)   (have)
_____ up with Ruth. She's really worried about _____
 (keep)   (lose)
weight, so she _____ faster than Bill right now. They
             (run)
_____ for almost ten minutes, so they are out of breath.
 (jog)
They are tired of _____, but they _____
            (jog)   (negative for **stop**)
yet. They're going to keep going for ten more minutes. When they
_____, they _____ a shower and have lunch. Bill
 (finish, jog)   (take)
and Ruth _____ now. Exercise always _____
        (starve)   (make)
people hungry. They would like _____ a giant pizza for lunch, but
                       (have)
they _____ that they _____ fattening
    (know)   (negative for modal + **eat**)
food like pizza because they're on a diet. If they _____ on a diet,
                              (negative for **be**)
they _____ pizza, but today rabbit food[2] is on the
     (have)
menu for lunch.

[2]*Rabbit food* means "lettuce, carrots, and other raw vegetables with few calories."

☐ Practice forming questions. Work with a classmate. Don't look back at the fill-in activity. Look at the appropriate picture. Then look at the answer below the unfinished question and decide what tense to use for the question.

Questions About Picture 1

1. (*go*)

   _____ now?
   To the park.

2. (*do*)

   _____ when he gets to the park?
   He's going to jog.

3. (modal + *jog*)

   _____?
   Because he's overweight.

4. (*go*)

   _____ to the doctor for a checkup?
   Last week.

5. (*have*)

   _____ heart trouble if he doesn't lose weight?
   Yes. The doctor says that he will.

6. (*lose*)

   How many pounds _____ if he were Bill?
   He'd lose twenty pounds.

7. (*do*)

   _____ after he left the doctor's office?
   He went to a sporting goods store.

8. (*buy*)

   _____ there?
   A jogging suit and new running shoes.

9. (*do*)

   _____ when he went home?
   He asked Ruth to throw out all of the cookies, cakes, and ice cream that were in the kitchen.

10. (*do*)

_____it?
Yes, she did.

11. (*jog*)

_____with Bill today?
No. She's going to go back inside and relax.

Questions About Picture 2

1. (*do*)

_____in this picture?
He's jogging in the park.

2. (*jog*)

_____?
For only fifteen minutes, but he's already tired and out of breath.

3. (*enjoy, jog*)

_____?
No, he doesn't.

Continue asking your partner questions about pictures 3, 4, and 5.

26 INVITATIONS WITH *WOULD YOU LIKE*

296 — English Alive

Use *would you like* ... when you want to offer something to someone.

WOULD YOU LIKE + NOUN?

How to Offer
Examples

1.

    Brrr.
    Would you like my jacket?

2.

    Would you like some help?

ACTIVITY 26A

Ask questions with "Would you like ... ?" Answer with "Yes, please" or "No, thank you."

1.

2.

Invitations with Would You Like — 297

3.

4.

5.

Other Ways to Accept or Refuse

Examples

1.

> Would you like my jacket?
>
> Thank you. That would be great.

2.

> Would you like some help?
>
> Thank you very much. That's very nice of you, but I'm okay.

3.

> Would you like a cup of coffee?
>
> Yes, I would, thank you.
>
> No, thank you. I don't drink coffee.

Invitations with Would You Like 299

ACTIVITY 26B

Look at the set of five pictures in Activity 26A. Accept or refuse with the following expressions.

That would be { great. / nice. / fantastic. }

WOULD YOU LIKE TO + (BASE FORM OF VERB)?

More Ways to Offer
Examples

1. Would you like to dance?

2. There's a good movie at this theater. Would you like to see it tonight?

ACTIVITY 26C

Ask questions with "Would you like to . . . ?" Answer with "Yes, I would, thank you. That would be nice/great/fantastic" or "Thank you, but I'm busy tonight/that night."

1.

2.

3. I'm going to have a party at my house next Saturday.

4. Hi. Are you going to the park?
Yes.

5. We're going to sit down and study English under that tree.

More Ways to Accept or Refuse
Examples

1. "Would you like to dance?"
   "Yes, thanks. I'd like to very much.[1]"

2. "There's a good movie at this theater. Would you like to see it with me tonight?"
   "Thanks for the invitation. I'd like to, but I'm busy tonight. I'm going to visit a friend."

ACTIVITY 26D

Look at the five pictures in Activity 26C again. Repeat the exercise, but this time use *I'd like to* for some of the answers.

ACTIVITY 26E

Fill in the blanks with one of the expressions used in this chapter.

1. (JOE, HIRO, and MARIA are eating dinner at DIANE's apartment.)

   JOE: This chicken is delicious.

   DIANE: _____ some more?

   JOE: Yes, _____, thanks. It's great.

   DIANE: What about you, Maria? Hiro?

   MARIA: No, thanks. It's delicious, but I'm on a diet.

   HIRO: Yes, please. That _____. You're a good cook.

2. (JOE is talking to BILL on the telephone.)

   JOE: Diane and I are going roller skating tonight. _____ you and Ruth _____ with us?

[1] *I'd like to* means "I would like to."

BILL: Thanks. We _____ very much. What are you going to do after skating? _____ you and Diane _____ to our place for coffee and cake? Ruth made a great chocolate cake today.

JOE: Sure. That _____.

3. (DIANE is inviting MARIA to dinner.)

DIANE: I'm going to have some friends to my place for dinner next Saturday. _____?

MARIA: I _____, but I'm busy on Saturday. Two weeks ago, a friend invited me to a party. But thanks for the invitation.

DIANE: I'm sorry you can't come. Next time.

ACTIVITY 26F

Role play these situations with your classmates. Use the expressions taught in this chapter.

1. Two friends are visiting you in your home. Offer something to drink.
2. You and some guests are sitting at your table eating dinner. Your guests' plates are almost empty. Offer some more food to them.
3. You're at a party. Invite someone to dance.
4. Your classmate is carrying a lot of heavy books. Offer your help.
5. You're sitting on a crowded bus. An old woman is standing near you. Offer her your seat.
6. You have a pack of cigarettes, and you're going to smoke. Offer cigarettes to the people who are sitting near you.
7. Invite someone to a party at your home. (Explain what you are planning and when you are having the party before you offer the invitation.)

27 GIVING DIRECTIONS

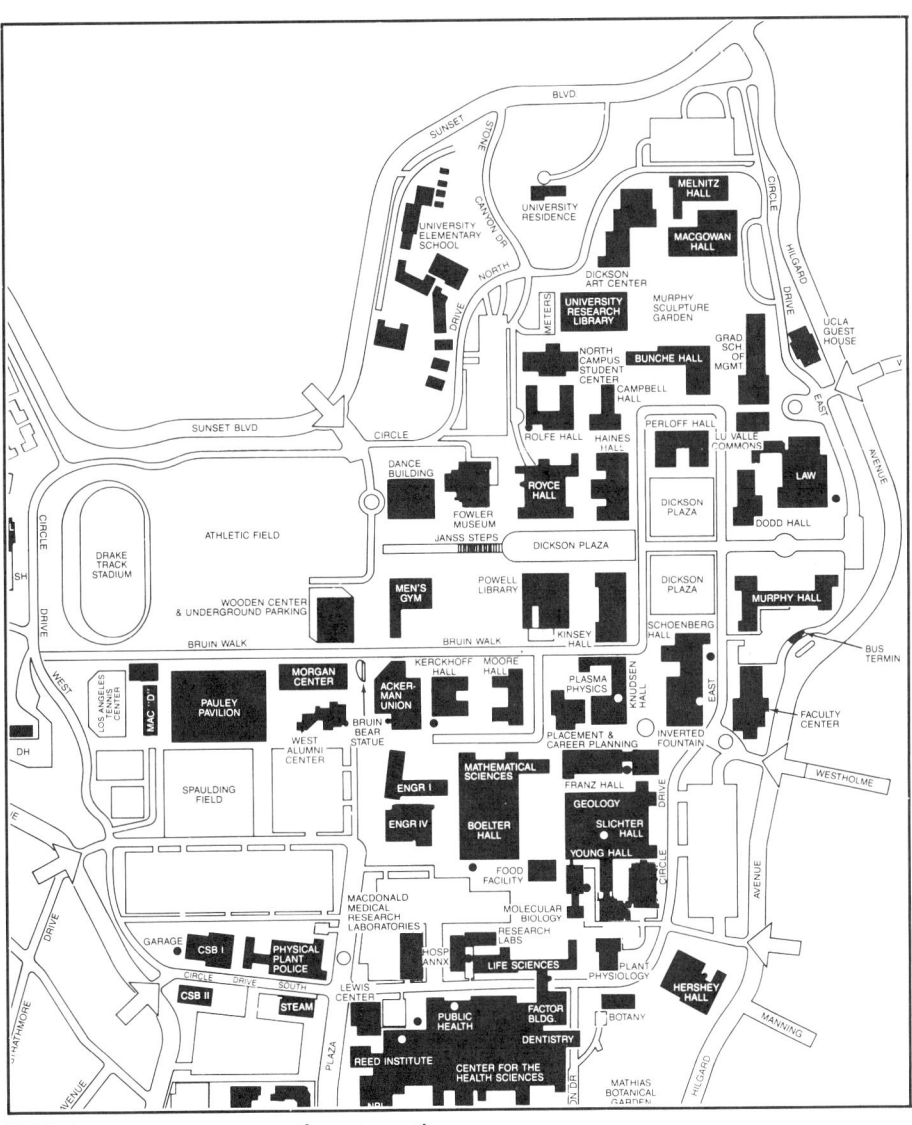

UCLA campus map, northeast section.

QUESTIONS AND ANSWERS

Use these questions to ask for directions.

How can I get to _____ from here?

Can you tell me how to get to _____ from here?

To answer, you need these different directions.

Take _____

$$\text{Take} \begin{cases} \text{the bus} \\ \text{the train} \\ \text{the George Washington Bridge} \\ \text{the Westside Highway} \\ \text{the elevator} \\ \text{Exit 7} \end{cases}$$

Go _____

Walk _____

$$\begin{matrix} \text{Go} \\ \text{Walk} \end{matrix} \begin{Bmatrix} \text{east} \\ \text{west} \\ \text{north} \\ \text{south} \\ \text{straight} \end{Bmatrix} \begin{Bmatrix} \text{one block} \\ \text{two blocks} \\ \text{four miles} \end{Bmatrix}$$

Turn _____

$$\text{Turn} \begin{Bmatrix} \text{left} \\ \text{right} \end{Bmatrix} \begin{Bmatrix} \text{at the corner} \\ \text{at the traffic light} \\ \text{at Main Street} \end{Bmatrix}$$

Examples

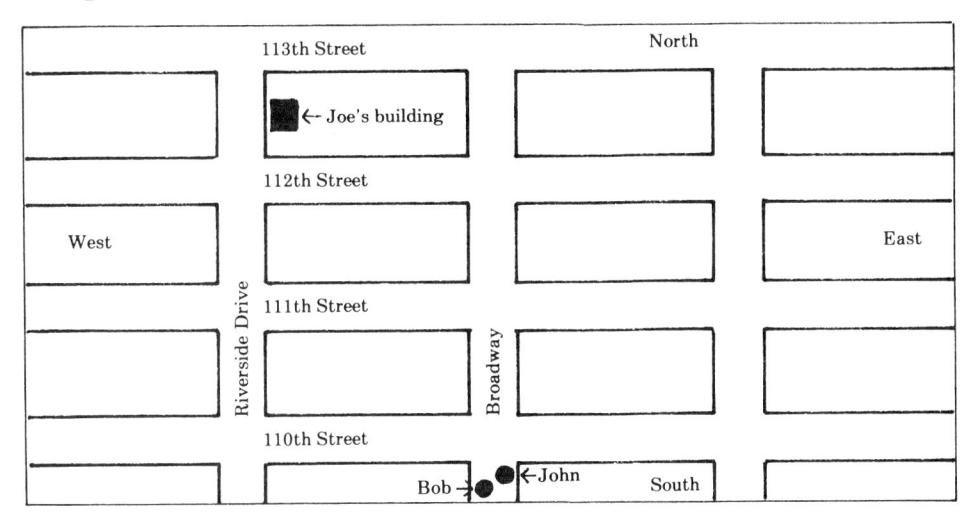

JOHN: How can I get to Joe's building from here?
BOB: Walk north on Broadway two blocks. Turn left at 112th Street and go west one block to Riverside Drive. His building is between 112th and 113th streets.

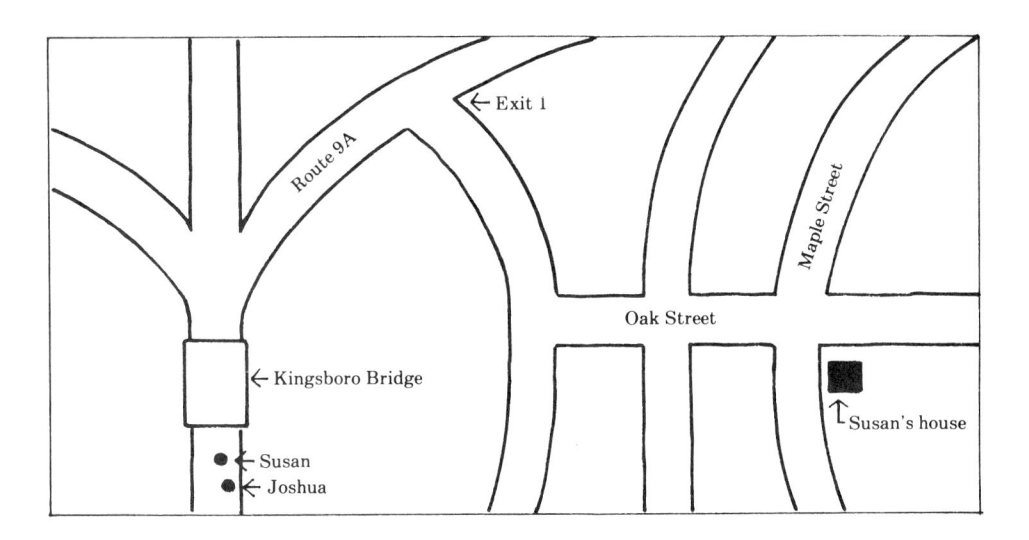

JOSHUA: How can I get to your house from here?
SUSAN: Take the Kingsboro Bridge. When you get off the bridge, take Route 9A. Take Exit 1 to the first traffic light. Turn left on Oak Street and go two blocks. Turn right on Maple Street. My house is number 83.

■ **ACTIVITY 27A**

Complete these questions and write the answers.

1.

```
                        North          The two people are here. →●●
                     37th Street

    West  Seventh  36th Street  Sixth   Fifth    Madison   East
          Avenue                Avenue  Avenue   Avenue
                     35th Street
              Macy's
                     34th Street
                        South
```

FIRST PERSON: Excuse me. Can you _____
               Macy's from here?

SECOND PERSON: _____

2.

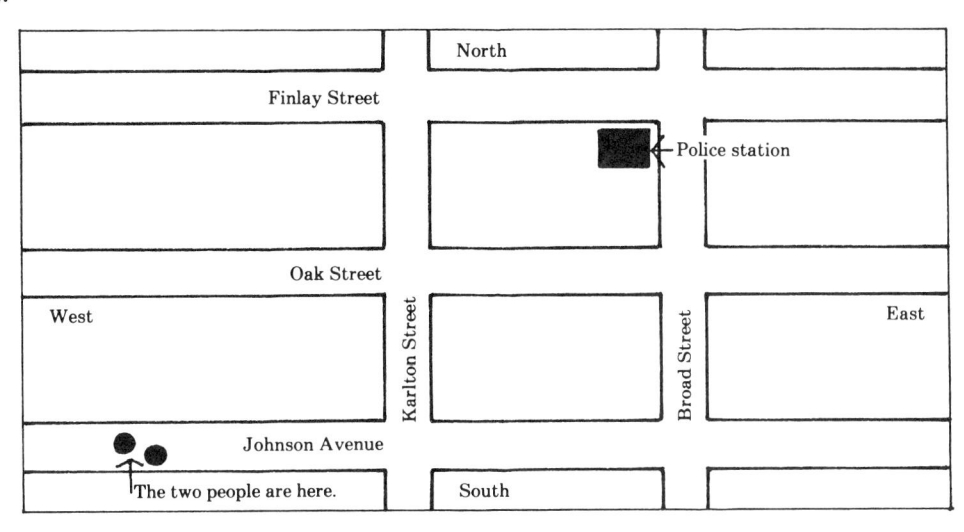

FIRST PERSON: Excuse me. How _____ the police station from here?

SECOND PERSON: _____

3.

BARBARA: How _____ your house from here?

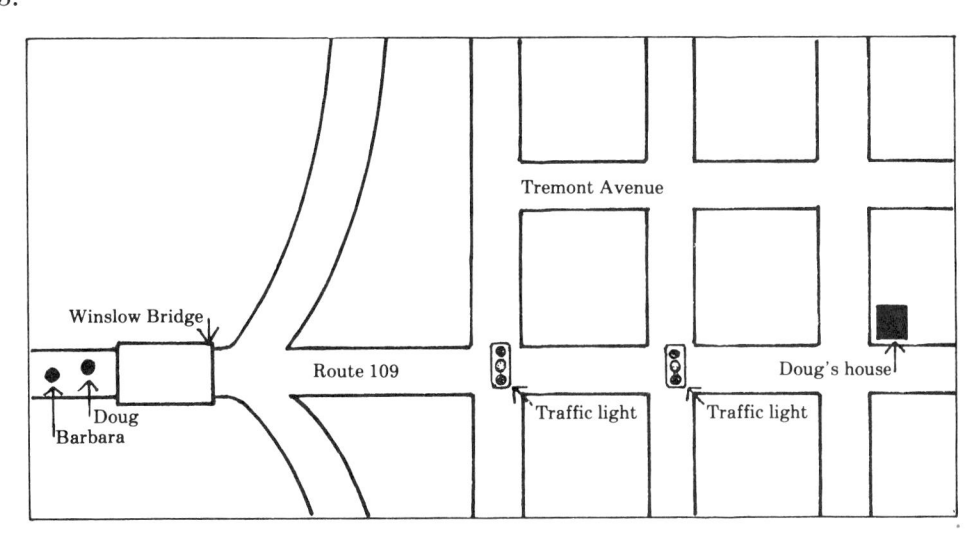

DOUG: _____

WORDS THAT TELL PLACE

Between
The supermarket is between the post office and the drugstore.

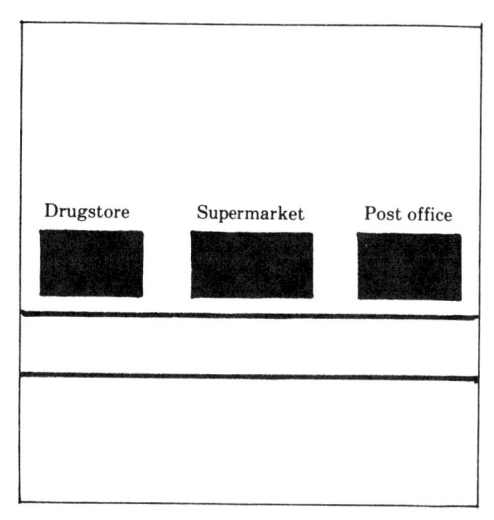

On the Corner of
The theater is on the corner of Sixth Avenue and 37th Street.

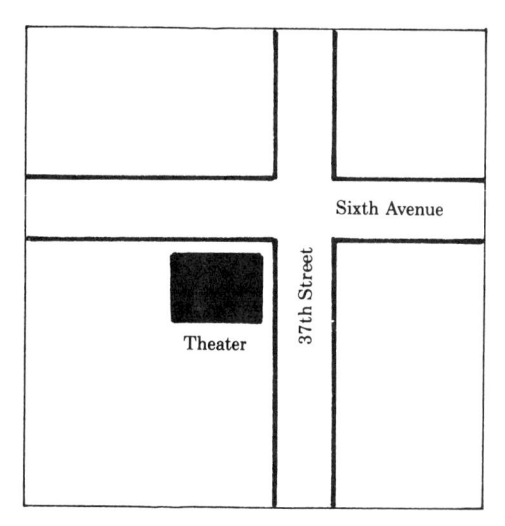

Across the Street from

The gas station is across the street from the supermarket.

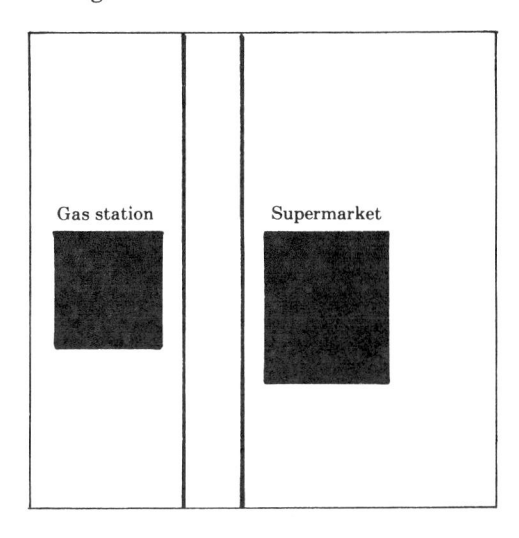

Around the Corner from

The library is around the corner from the theater.

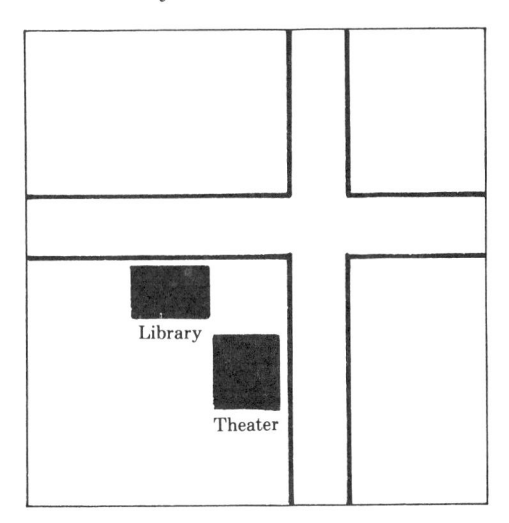

Next to
The library is next to Johnson Hall.

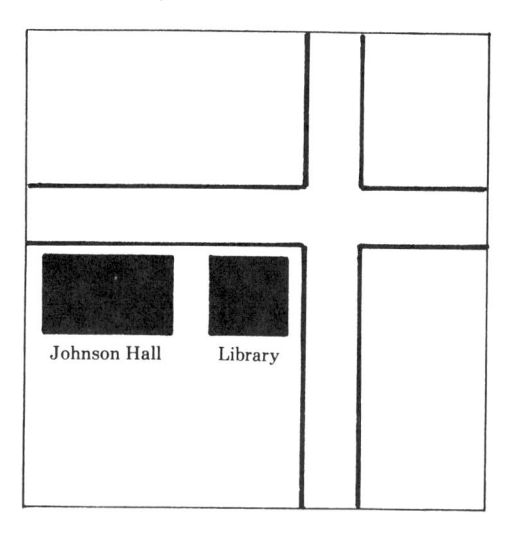

■ ACTIVITY 27B

Look at the map. Notice that you are at the east end of Pine Street. Give directions to get to the following places using expressions from this chapter.

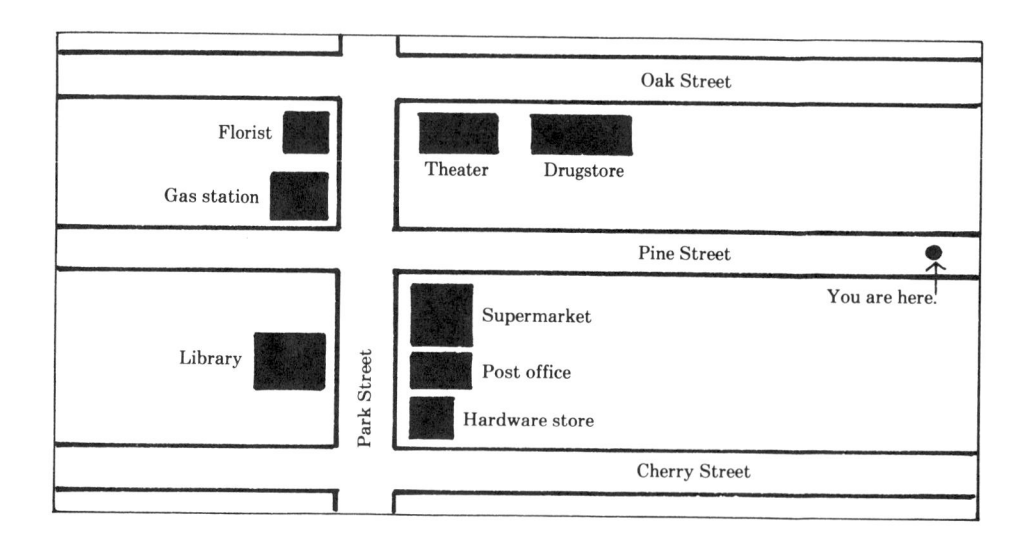

Giving Directions

1. the drugstore

2. the gas station

3. the library

4. the supermarket

5. the post office

28 MAKING SUGGESTIONS WITH *LET'S* AND *WHY DON'T*

Making Suggestions with Let's and Why Don't

When you want to make plans or make a suggestion for yourself and another person (or persons), you can use the following patterns.

Let's + base form
Let's not + base form

Why don't { you / we } + base form

Examples

See the chapter opening illustration for several examples.

Note: *Let's* means "Let us," but we almost always say, "Let's."

■ Activity 28A

Make suggestions with *let's* or *let's not*.

Examples

JOE: What do you want to do tonight?

DIANE: *Let's see the new Japanese movie by Kurosawa.*

JOE: That sounds great.

BILL: Hey, Ruth. Do you want to go over to see Joe and Diane tonight?

RUTH: Oh, *let's not go out tonight.* I'm really tired.

1. RUTH: I just spoke to my friend Linda. She's going to be alone on Thanksgiving. I feel bad about it.

    BILL: _____ with us.

    RUTH: Fine. I'll speak to her in the morning.

2. TEACHER: Everyone looks a little tired today.

    CLASS: _____

    TEACHER: Okay. That's not a bad idea.

3. MARIA: This looks like a good restaurant.

    HIRO: No, _____. It's too expensive.

4. JOE: How can we get to the hospital to visit your aunt?
   DIANE: We can take the bus or the subway. Or we can walk. It's not far.
   JOE: _____ because I'm tired.

5. RUTH: My God, I'm tired. How many cookies did we make? Do we have enough?
   DIANE: Yes. _____. It's hot in this kitchen.

6. BILL: This car is never going to start. What are we going to do?
   JOE: _____
   Maybe that will help.
   BILL: All right. If that doesn't work, _____.
   I'm tired of working on this car.

Activity 28B

Make suggestions using *Why don't you/we . . . ?*

> *Example*
> DIANE: I don't feel well. I feel very tired, and I have a terrible headache.
> JOE: *Why don't you go home and lie down?*
> DIANE: I think I'm going to do that.

1. MARIA: I'm bored. I'm tired of studying.
   HIRO: _____
   MARIA: That sounds like fun.

2. RUTH: I had a hard day at work today. I don't want to cook dinner tonight.
   BILL: _____
   RUTH: Okay. Great.

   HIRO: Tomorrow is Maria's birthday. What can I get her for a present?
   JOE: _____
   HIRO: Good idea.

4. BILL: Uh, oh. It's raining outside. I don't have an umbrella.
   JOE: _____ my umbrella?
   BILL: Thank you.

Making Suggestion With Let's and Why Don't _____ *315*

5. BILLY, JR.: Mommy, I don't understand my homework. Please help me.
   RUTH: I'm making dinner now, Billy. Your father is reading the newspaper in the living room. _____

6. MARIA: I'm out of shape.[1] I never get any exercise. I just sit all day studying.
   DIANE: _____

[1]Out of shape means "not in good physical condition."

29 REQUESTS AND FAVORS

When you want to ask someone politely for help or for a favor, you can use this pattern.

Will you (*please*) + base form?

Here are some other ways to ask.

> *Would you* (*please*) + base form?
> *Would you please help me?*
> *Could you* (*please*) + base form?
> *Could you please help me?*
> *Would you mind* + base form + *-ing*?
> *Would you mind helping me?*

Here are some ways to say that you will help the person who has asked you to do a favor.

I'll be happy to.

I would be glad to   or   I'd be glad to.

It's no trouble at all.

Sure.

Of course.

I wouldn't mind at all (this is in response to "would you mind...").

Here are some ways to refuse politely when you cannot help the person.

I'm really sorry, but I can't because....

I'd like to, but....

I can't do it right now. I'm in a hurry, but I'll be glad to do it later.

> ***Examples***
>
> 1. Bill is talking to one of his co-workers.
>
>   BILL: Are you going out for lunch now?
>   COWORKER: Yes, I am.
>   BILL: **Would you please bring me a chicken salad sandwich?** I don't have time to go out right now.
>   COWORKER: **I'll be glad to.**
>   BILL: **Would you mind getting me a soda too?**
>   COWORKER: **I wouldn't mind at all. It's no trouble.** I'll be back in about twenty minutes.
>
> 2. Bill is talking to one of the secretaries in the office. This secretary doesn't usually work for Bill, but Bill's secretary, Ms. Brown, is not in the office today because she is sick.
>
>   BILL: Ms. Thompson, Ms. Brown is out sick today. **Would you mind typing these letters for me?**
>   MS. THOMPSON: **I'm really sorry, Mr. Roberts, but I can't do it right now.** I have to finish this work for Mrs. Jones. **I'll be glad to do it later.**

Note: When you ask for a favor, you frequently need to use the words *lend* and *borrow*. Don't confuse them.

If your friend has a pen, but you don't have one, you *borrow* your friend's pen.

Your friend *lends* the pen to you.

When you want to use something that belongs to another person, you can ask:

May I please *borrow* your _____?

Would
Could } you please *lend* me your _____?
Will

Would you mind *lending* me your _____?

Requests and Favors _____ 319

■ **ACTIVITY 29**

Write short dialogs using these expressions to ask for help or a favor. Agree to help or politely refuse.

1. You have a car. A friend wants to borrow it for a few hours to move some things to a new apartment. You don't want to lend your car.

    FRIEND: I need to move a few things to my new apartment this afternoon.

    _____your car for a few hours?

    YOU: _____

2. You are in a restaurant Your hamburger is a little too rare for you. You want to ask the waiter to take it back to the kitchen to cook a little longer.

    YOU: This hamburger is a little too rare.

    _____a little longer?

    WAITER: _____

3. You broke your arm, and it's difficult for you to go shopping. You're talking to your neighbor. She is leaving to go shopping now.

    YOU: _____

    NEIGHBOR: _____

4. You lost your textbook, and you want to borrow a friend's book to photocopy some pages.

    YOU: _____

    FRIEND: _____

5. You're going to your doctor's office, and you're very nervous. You want your good friend to go with you.

    YOU: _____

    FRIEND: _____

30 TRAVEL

HOW TO ASK FOR DIRECTIONS FOR THE TRAIN AND BUS

Person 1: Excuse me. Does the Number 2 $\begin{Bmatrix} \text{train} \\ \text{bus} \end{Bmatrix}$ $\begin{Bmatrix} \text{stop at} \\ \text{go to} \end{Bmatrix}$ 23rd Street?

Person 2: Yes, it does
    or
No, it doesn't. Take the Number 1 $\begin{Bmatrix} \text{train} \\ \text{bus} \end{Bmatrix}$.
    or
No, it doesn't. Get off at 42nd Street, and change to the Number 1 $\begin{Bmatrix} \text{train} \\ \text{bus} \end{Bmatrix}$.

Person 1: Which train do I take to get to Times Square from here?
    or
How can I get to Times Square from here?

Person 2: Take the Number 1 train to 42nd Street.

Dialog Practice

Study the preceding dialogs for a minute or two. Then use the following guides to practice dialogs with a classmate. Don't look back at the preceding dialogs. Your classmate can help if you don't know an answer. Follow these same directions each time you practice with the dialog guides in this chapter.

1. Person 1: Excuse me. _____ the Number 2 bus _____ 23rd Street?

   Person 2: Yes, _____

2. Person 1: Excuse me, _____ train _____

   _____ 23rd Street?

   Person 2: No, _____ . _____ .

   _____ at 42nd Street and _____

   _____ the Number 1 train.

3. Person 1: Which _____ to get to Times Square from here?

   Person 2: _____ the Number 1 train to 42nd Street.

4. Person 1: How _____ Times Square from here?

   Person 2: _____ 42nd Street.

HOW TO ASK FOR AIRLINE INFORMATION

CUSTOMER: {Can you please tell me / I'd like to know} the schedule for flights to Hawaii.

RESERVATIONS CLERK: There's a flight every day at 7:00 A.M.

CUSTOMER: How much is a {round-trip / one-way} ticket?

CLERK: First class or economy class?

CUSTOMER: Economy class.

CLERK: It's $300.

Dialog Practice

CUSTOMER: _____ you please _____ the _____ for _____ to Hawaii?

CLERK: _____ every day _____ 7:00 A.M.

CUSTOMER: _____ ticket?

CLERK: First class or economy class?

CUSTOMER: Economy class.

CLERK: _____ $300.

HOW TO MAKE A RESERVATION WITH AN AIRLINE

CUSTOMER: I'd like to make a reservation on the 6:00 P.M. to San Francisco.

CLERK: Just a moment. I'll check the computer.
(A few minutes later.) I'm sorry. That flight is full. Would you like to make a reservation on the next flight at 8 P.M.?

CUSTOMER: Yes, thank you.

CLERK: All right. Just a minute, please. Your seat is confirmed on Flight 106 at 8:00 P.M. Please check in a half hour before departure time. Where would you like to pay for your ticket—at a travel agency or at the airport?

CUSTOMER: I'll pay at the airport.

Dialog Practice

CUSTOMER: I _____ on the 6:00 P.M. flight to San Francisco.

CLERK: Just a moment. I'll check the computer.

(A few minutes later.) _____ sorry. That flight _____. _____ a reservation on the next flight at 8 P.M.?

CUSTOMER: Yes, thank you.

CLERK: _____. Just a minute, please. Your seat is _____ on Flight 106 at 8:00 P.M. Please _____ a half hour before _____ time. Where _____ you _____ to _____ for your _____—at a travel agency or at the airport?

CUSTOMER: _____ at the _____.

HOW TO ASK FOR INFORMATION ABOUT A FLIGHT

CUSTOMER: What time does the plane arrive in Boston?

CLERK: It arrives at 11:30 P.M. There's a one-hour layover/stopover in Chicago.

CUSTOMER: Do they serve dinner on that flight?

CLERK: Yes, they do.

Dialog Practice

CUSTOMER: What time _____ in Boston?

CLERK: It _____ at 11:30 P.M. _____ a one-hour _____ in Chicago.

CUSTOMER: _____ dinner on that _____?

CLERK: Yes, they do.

CHECKING IN AT THE AIRPORT

CLERK: Is this all of your luggage?
CUSTOMER: Yes. May I carry this bag onto the plane with me?
CLERK: Yes. That's okay. Which section would you like—smoking or nonsmoking? And where would you like to sit?
CUSTOMER: Nonsmoking, please. I'd like a seat near the window.
CLERK: All right. Here's your seat number and boarding pass. Your flight departs from Gate 5 in thirty minutes.
CUSTOMER: Thank you.

Dialog Practice

CLERK: _____ all of your _____?

CUSTOMER: Yes. _____ this bag onto the plane with me?

CLERK: Yes. That's okay. Which section _____—

_____ or _____? And where

_____?

CUSTOMER: _____, please. _____ a seat

_____ the window.

CLERK: _____. Here's your seat number and

boarding _____. Your flight _____ from Gate 5

in thirty minutes.

CUSTOMER: Thank you.

HOW TO MAKE HOTEL RESERVATIONS

(telephone call)

RESERVATIONS
CLERK: Good afternoon. Hotel Bellview.
CUSTOMER: I'd like to reserve a room for the nights of July 12 and 13.
CLERK: Yes. We have a vacancy for those days. Would you like a double or a single room?

Travel 325

CUSTOMER: A double, please. How much is the room, please?
CLERK: Sixty dollars a night.
CUSTOMER: All right.
CLERK: What's your name, please?
CUSTOMER: Mr. and Mrs. Sansom. That's *S* as in *Sam*, *A*, *N* as in *Nancy*, *S*, *O*, *M* as in *Mary*.
CLERK: All right. Please send a twenty-dollar deposit by July 1. And, on the night of your arrival, please be here by 7:00, or you will lose your reservation.
CUSTOMER: Okay. Thank you.

Dialog Practice

CLERK: Good afternoon. Hotel Bellview.

CUSTOMER: I _____ a room for the nights of July 12 and 13.

CLERK: Yes. We have a _____ for those days. _____ a _____ or a _____ room?

CUSTOMER: A double, please. _____?

CLERK: Sixty dollars a night.

CUSTOMER: All right.

CLERK: _____?

CUSTOMER: Mr. and Mrs. _____. That's _____ _____.

CLERK: All right. Please send a twenty-dollar _____ by July 1. And, on the night of your _____, please _____ by 7:00, or you will _____ your reservation.

CUSTOMER: Okay. Thank you.

CHECKING IN AT THE HOTEL

CUSTOMER: Good evening. We have a reservation for a double room for Mr. and Mrs. Sansom.

CLERK: Yes. Good evening. Please sign the register.

(Mr. and Mrs. Sansom sign.)

The bellhop will show you to your room. Checkout time is 11:30 on the day of departure.

CUSTOMER: Thank you.

Dialog Practice

CUSTOMER: Good evening. We _____ a double room for Mr. and Mrs. Sansom.

CLERK: Yes. Good evening. Please _____ the register.

The bellhop will _____.

_____ time is 11:30 on the day of _____.

CUSTOMER: Thank you.

Role Playing

Role play these different situations.
1. Make a telephone call to an airline to get information about flights and the price of a ticket. Your partner will be the reservation clerk.
2. Make a reservation on a flight. Then find out what time the flight arrives and if they serve a meal on it. Your partner will be the reservation clerk.
3. Check in at the airport, and get your seat number. Your partner will be the reservation clerk.
4. Make a reservation for a hotel room.
5. Check in at the hotel.

31 IN A RESTAURANT

MAKING A RESERVATION BY PHONE

Headwaiter: Greensleeve's Restaurant. Good evening.
Joe: Good evening. I'd like to make a reservation for Friday night.
Headwaiter: Yes. For what time and for how many people?
Joe: Four people for eight o'clock. The name is Haley.
Headwaiter: All right. Thank you.

Dialog Practice

Study the above dialog for a minute or two. Then use the following guide to practice a dialog with a classmate. Don't look back at the dialog above. Your classmate can help if you don't know an answer. Follow these same directions each time you practice with the dialog guides in this chapter.

Headwaiter: _____.

Joe: Good evening. _____

reservation _____.

Headwaiter: Yes. _____?

Joe: Four people for 8:00. _____ Haley.

Headwaiter: _____. Thank you.

ENTERING A RESTAURANT

Headwaiter: Good evening. Do you have a reservation?
Joe: Yes, we do. For four people. The name is Haley.
Headwaiter: I'll show you to your table. Right this way, please.

Headwaiter: Good evening. Do you have a reservation?
Joe: No, we don't. We'd like a table for four people.
Headwaiter: There will be about a twenty-minute wait. Would you like to have a drink at the bar? We'll call you when a table is ready.

Dialog Practice

Headwaiter: Good evening. _____?

Joe: Yes, we do. _____.

HEADWAITER: _____ your table.

_____ , please.

HEADWAITER: Good evening. _____?

JOE: No, we don't. _____

four people.

HEADWAITER: _____ twenty-minute _____.

_____ at the bar?

We _____ when a table _____.

ORDERING

WAITER: Are you ready to order?
       or
May I take your order?
       or
Would you like to order now?

JOE: Yes. I'd like the roast chicken.

DIANE: I'll have the steak.

WAITER: How would you like your steak?

DIANE: Medium rare,[1] please.
       or
Rare[2], please.
       or
Well done[3], please.

JOE: And may I have a baked potato instead of french fries?

WAITER: Of course.
       or
I'm sorry, but there are no substitutions.

Would you like anything to drink?

JOE: I'll have a beer, please.

DIANE: Nothing for me. Just water, thank you.

WAITER: Would you like anything else?

[1]*Medium rare* means "pink in the middle."
[2]*Rare* means "red in the middle."
[3]*Well done* means "cooked completely."

JOE: No, that's all, thank you.
    or
That's it.
    or
That will be all.

Dialog Practice

WAITER: _____?

JOE: Yes. _____ the roast chicken.

DIANE: _____ the steak.

WAITER: _____?

DIANE: Medium rare, please.

JOE: _____ a baked potato _____ french fries?

WAITER: I'm sorry, but _____.

_____ to drink?

JOE: _____ a beer, please.

DIANE: _____. Just water, thank you.

WAITER: Would you like _____?

JOE: _____.

THE CHECK

JOE: May I have the check, please?
    or
Would you bring us the check, please?

WAITER: Here's your check. Did you enjoy your dinner?
    or
I hope you enjoyed your dinner.
    or
Was everything all right?

DIANE: Yes. It was delicious.

JOE: Excuse me, but I think there's a mistake. Would you check it again, please?

or

Excuse me, but we didn't order any dessert. There's a mistake here. Could you please take this off our check?

Dialog Practice

JOE: _____ the check, please?

WAITER: Here's your check. _____?

DIANE: Yes. _____.

JOE: Excuse me, but _____ a mistake.

_____, please?

or

Excuse me, but we _____ any dessert.

_____ a mistake here.

_____?

AMERICAN CUSTOMS

- ❑ In the United States, it's the custom to tip in a restaurant. In a good restaurant, most people leave between fifteen and twenty percent of the bill as a tip for the person waiting on you.
- ❑ When you want to call the person waiting on you, it is impolite to snap your fingers, clap your hands, or call across the room. You must wait until the person is close to call him or her (say, "Waiter, please") or try to catch his or her eye.

Role Playing

Role play these restaurant conversations. Begin with a telephone call to make a reservation. Then role play the conversation from the time you arrive until the time you leave.

32 VISITING A FRIEND'S HOME

Visiting a Friend's Home   333

WHEN THE GUEST ARRIVES

Host
or Hostess: Hi. Come on in. Let me take your coat.
Guest: Thanks. What a nice apartment you have! It's really beautiful.
Host: Thank you. Can I get you something to drink? What would you like?
Guest: I'd like some white wine if you have it.
Host: Sure. Help yourself to the hors d'oeuvres,[1] and then let me introduce you to some of my friends.

Here are some common cocktails (alcoholic drinks) or drinks that Americans offer before dinner.

a martini (vermouth and gin)

a gin and tonic (gin and tonic water)

a daiquiri (a rum and lime juice cocktail)

a scotch and soda

a screwdriver (orange juice and vodka)

If you do not drink alcohol, feel free to tell your host this and ask for fruit juice or a soft drink (soda; for example, Coca-Cola or 7-Up).

Dialog Practice

Study the above dialog for a minute or two. Then use the following guide to practice a dialog with a classmate. Don't look back at the dialog above. Your classmate can help if you don't know an answer. Follow these same directions each time you practice with the dialog guides in this chapter.

Host: Hi. _____ in. _____ your coat.

Guest: Thanks. _____! It's really beautiful.

Host: _____. Can _____ to drink? What _____?

Guest: _____ some white wine if _____.

[1] *Hors d'oeuvres* means "before-dinner snacks, for example, cheese and crackers."

Host: Sure. _____ the hors d'oeuvres, and then _____ some of my friends.

AT THE DINNER TABLE

Guest: Everything looks delicious.
Host: Thank you. Would you like some turkey?
Guest: Yes, thanks.
Host: Help yourself to some potatoes, and pass them around.
(Later.)
Host: Your plate is almost empty. Would you like some more turkey? Are you ready for a second helping?
Guest: Yes, thanks. It's very good.
Host: Joe, please pass the turkey to Hiro.
Host: What else can I get you? How about some more vegetables?
Guest: No, thank you. Everything was very good, but I can't eat another bite. I'm full.[2]

Dialog Practice

Guest: Everything _____.

Host: Thank you. _____ some turkey?

Guest: _____.

Host: _____ yourself _____ some potatoes, and _____ them _____.

(Later.)

Host: Your plate _____. _____ some more turkey? Are you ready for a _____?

Guest: Yes. thanks. _____.

[2] *I'm full.* We frequently use this expression when we are with friends, but we don't use it at a formal dinner party.

Visiting a Friend's Home

Host: Joe, please _____the turkey _____Hiro.

Host: What else _____? _____some more vegetables?

Guest: No, thank you. Everything _____, but I

_____. I'm _____.

WHEN THE GUEST LEAVES

Guest 1: Thank you for inviting me. I had a wonderful time.
Guest 2: I really enjoyed myself. You're a wonderful cook.
  Host: Thank you. And thank you for coming. I'm glad you enjoyed yourselves.

Dialog Practice

Guest 1: Thank you _____ me. _____

a wonderful time.

Guest 2: I really _____. You _____.

  Host: Thank you. And thank you _____. I'm glad

_____.

Role Playing

Role play a conversation between a host and two or three guests beginning when the guests arrive, including the conversation at dinner, and ending with the conversation at the door when the guests leave.

33 A VISIT TO THE DOCTOR

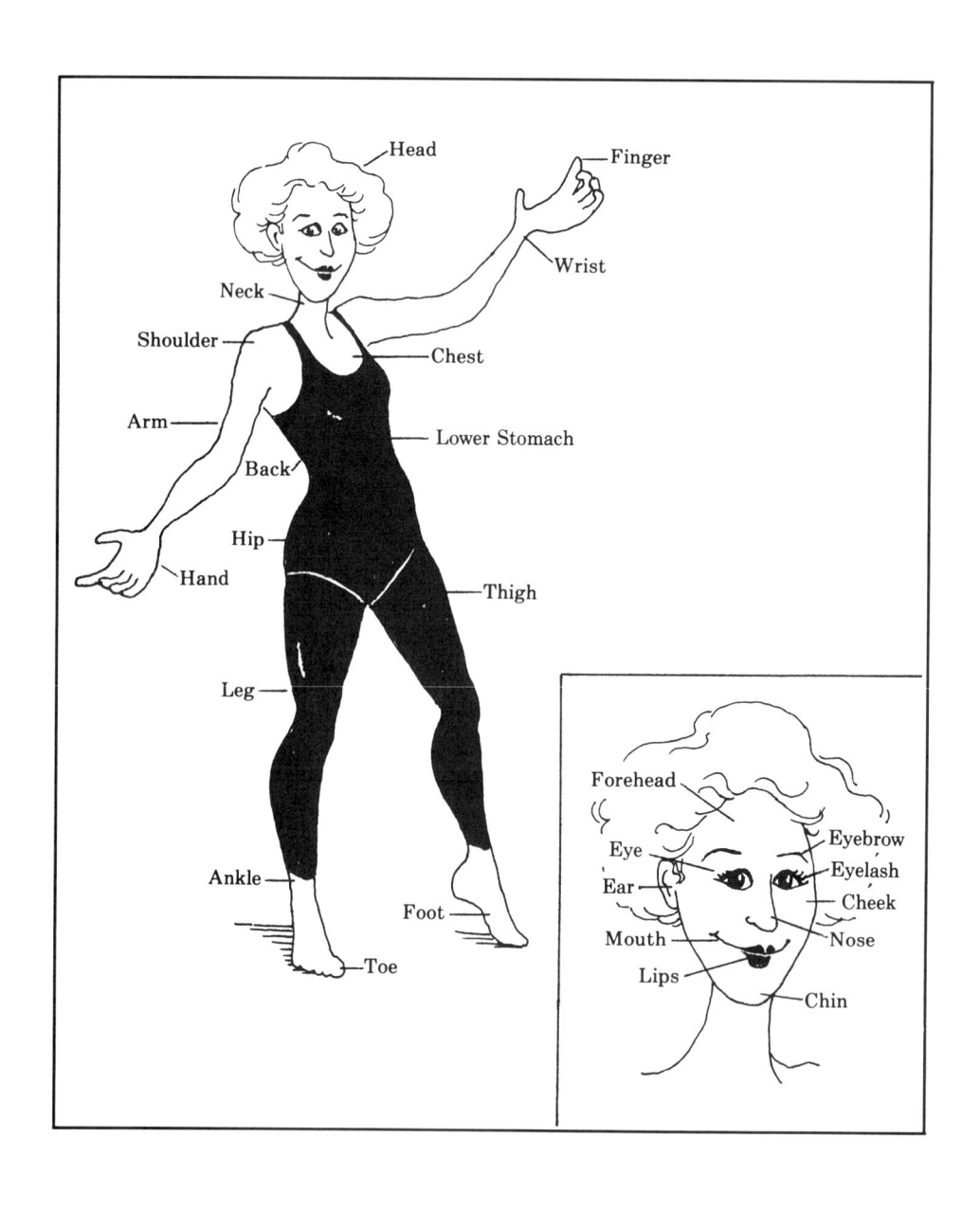

A Visit To the Doctor 337

HOW TO DESCRIBE MEDICAL PROBLEMS

The parts of the body and the parts of the face are shown and clearly labeled on the preceding page.

■ Activity 33A

☐ Study the parts of the body as shown on page 000. Then test yourself on the vocabulary.

☐ Study the following illustrations and their captions for each of these medical problems.

Ruth is waiting to see the doctor. She *doesn't feel well.*

She *has a cold.* She *has a sore throat.*

She *has a cough*.   She *has a fever*.

There are several other patients in the doctor's office.

This man *has a broken leg*.

        or

This man *broke his leg*.

A Visit to the Doctor

This child *has a stomachache.*

This man *has an earache.*

This man dropped a heavy box on his foot. His foot *is swollen.* It *hurts* very badly.

This woman works too hard. She feels *tired* and *run-down* all of the time.

ACTIVITY 33B
What's wrong with these people?

1. _____

2. _____   3. _____

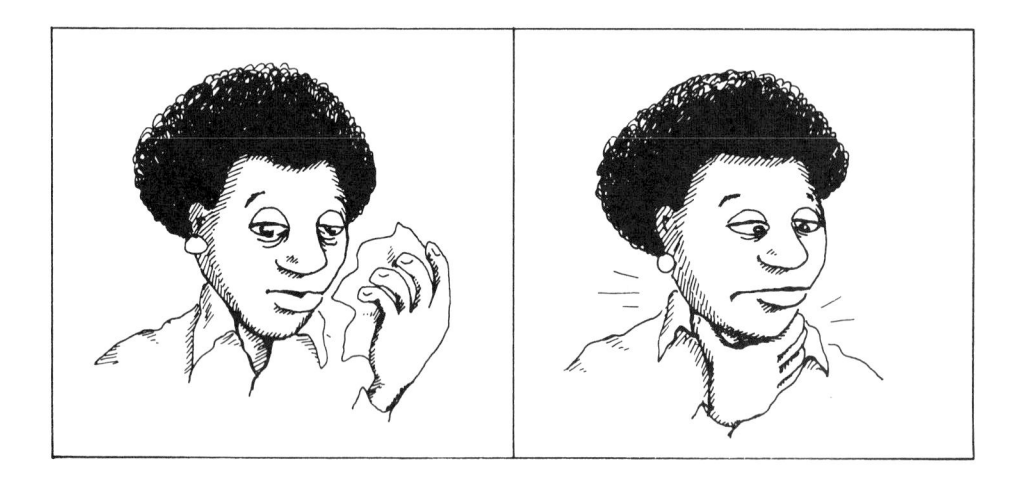

A Visit to the Doctor _____ 341

4. _____   5. _____
   _____   _____

6. _____
   _____

7. _____   8. _____

9. _____   10. _____

HOW TO MAKE AN APPOINTMENT

RECEPTIONIST: Good afternoon. Dr. Smith's office. May I help you?

PATIENT: Yes. I'd like to make an appointment to see the doctor as soon as possible.

RECEPTIONIST: All right. The next available appointment is next Monday at 4:30.

PATIENT: I'm sorry, but this is urgent. I can't wait until next week. I have a high fever and a very bad stomachache. Is it possible to see the doctor today?

RECEPTIONIST: Yes, if it's urgent. Come in about 2:00. What is your name, please?

PATIENT: Joe Haley. Thank you very much.

Activity 33C

Study the dialog above. When you are ready, practice with a classmate. Use this guide to help you remember.

RECEPTIONIST: Good afternoon. Dr. Smith's office. _____ help you?

PATIENT: Yes. _____ an appointment _____ the doctor _____.

RECEPTIONIST: All right. The _____ appointment _____ next Monday at 4:30.

PATIENT: I'm sorry, but _____. I _____ until next week. I _____ fever and _____ stomachache. _____ the doctor today?

RECEPTIONIST: Yes, if _____. _____ about 2:00. _____, please?

PATIENT: _____. Thank you very much.

❑ Now role play without looking at the above dialog guide.

34 USING THE TELEPHONE

LONG-DISTANCE CALLS

STATION-TO-STATION

OPERATOR: May I help you?
CUSTOMER: Yes. I'd like to make a station-to-station call to Miami.
OPERATOR: You can dial that call direct. Hang up and dial 1, then the area code for Miami, and then the number. It's cheaper if you dial direct.
CUSTOMER: Oh, okay. Thanks.

Dialog Practice

Study the above dialog for a minute or two. Then use the following guide to practice the dialog with a classmate. Don't look back at the dialog. Your classmate can help if you don't know an answer. Follow these same directions each time you practice with the dialog guides in this chapter.

OPERATOR: _____?

CUSTOMER: Yes. _____ to Miami.

OPERATOR: You can _____. Hang up and _____ 1, then the _____ code for Miami, and then the number. It's cheaper if _____.

CUSTOMER: Oh, okay. Thanks.

PERSON-TO-PERSON AND COLLECT

OPERATOR: May I help you?
CUSTOMER: I'd like to make a person-to-person call.
OPERATOR: What's the person's name and number, please?
CUSTOMER: It's Henry James at 813-555-7510. Also, operator, I'm calling collect.
OPERATOR: What's your name and number, please? Area code first.
CUSTOMER: My name is Tom Johnson, 212-555-0183.
OPERATOR: Thank you.
HENRY: Hello?
OPERATOR: I have a person-to-person call for Mr. Henry James from Tom Johnson. Will you accept the charges?
HENRY: Oh, all right.
OPERATOR: Go ahead, please.
CUSTOMER: Hi, Uncle Henry. Sorry I called collect again, but I'm broke.

Dialog Practice

OPERATOR: _____?

CUSTOMER: _____.

OPERATOR: _____ name and number, please?

CUSTOMER: It's Henry James at 813-555-7510. Also, operator, _____ collect.

OPERATOR: Your name and number, please? _____ first.

CUSTOMER: My name is Tom Johnson, 212-555-0183.

OPERATOR: Thank you.

HENRY: Hello?

OPERATOR: I _____ for Mr. Henry James from _____. _____?

HENRY: Oh, all right.

OPERATOR: _____, please.

CUSTOMER: Hi, Uncle Henry. Sorry I called collect again, but I'm broke.

INFORMATION

OPERATOR: Directory Assistance.
CUSTOMER: Can you give me the number of Richard Faust on Riverside Drive, please?
OPERATOR: How do you spell *Faust*?
CUSTOMER: *F* as in *flower, a, u, s* as in *Sam, t* as in *Tom*.
OPERATOR: Is this a new listing?
CUSTOMER: I don't know.
OPERATOR: I'm sorry. I can't find any such name.
CUSTOMER: All right. Thanks.
OPERATOR: Have a nice day.

Dialog Practice

OPERATOR: _____

CUSTOMER: _____ the number of Richard Faust on Riverside Drive, please?

OPERATOR: _____ Faust?

CUSTOMER: _____

OPERATOR: _____ a new listing?

CUSTOMER: I don't know.

OPERATOR: I'm sorry. I _____ any such name.

CUSTOMER: All right. Thanks.

OPERATOR: _____ day.

WRONG NUMBER

HELEN: Hello?
LISA: Hello. Is Carl there?
HELEN: Who?
LISA: Carl.
HELEN: I think you have the wrong number.
LISA: Oh. Is this 555-0923?
HELEN: No, it isn't.
LISA: I'm sorry.
HELEN: That's okay.

Dialog Practice

HELEN: Hello?

LISA: Hello. _____ Carl _____?

HELEN: Who?

LISA: Carl.

HELEN: I think _____.

LISA: Oh. _____ 555-0923?

HELEN: No, _____.

LISA: _____

HELEN: _____

BUSY SIGNAL

EVA: Hello?
MEREDITH: Hello. This is Meredith calling. Is Kim there?
EVA: Yes. I'll get him for you. Hold on.
KIM: Hi, Meredith. What's up?[1]
MEREDITH: I can't reach Gaby. Her phone is always busy. Maybe I have the wrong number. Do you know her number?
KIM: Her number is 555-2531.
MEREDITH: That's the number I have.
KIM: Maybe her phone is out of order.
MEREDITH: Maybe. I'll ask the operator to check.

Dialog Practice

EVA: Hello?

MEREDITH: Hello. _____ Meredith _____.

_____ Kim _____?

EVA: Yes. I _____ for you. _____

KIM: Hi, Meredith. _____?

MEREDITH: I can't _____ Gaby. Her phone is always _____.

Maybe I have _____. _____

you _____ her number?

KIM: Her number is 555-2531.

MEREDITH: That's the number I have.

[1] *What's up?* means "How are you? Why are you calling? What's new?" This expression is informal.

Kim: Maybe her phone _____.

Meredith: Maybe. I _____ the operator to _____.

LEAVING A MESSAGE

Judy: Hello?
Henrietta: Hello. May I speak to Jack, please?
Judy: He isn't here now. May I ask who's calling? Can I take a message?
Henrietta: Yes. This is Henrietta. Would you ask him to call me at 555-3585?
Judy: Sure. I'll give him the message.
Henrietta: Thanks a lot.

Dialog Practice

Judy: Hello?

Henrietta: Hello. _____ Jack, please?

Judy: He isn't here now. May I _____ who _____?

_____ a message?

Henrietta: Yes. This is Henrietta. _____

me at 555-3585?

Judy: Sure. I _____.

Henrietta: Thanks a lot.

SOME IMPORTANT TELEPHONE NUMBERS

    0: to get the operator

  411: to get a telephone number from Directory Assistance

area code +
  555-1212: to get a long-distance telephone number from Directory Assistance

  911: to report an emergency to the police

ROLE PLAYING

Study all of the telephone conversations again. Then role play these situations.

1. You want to speak to a friend, but he or she isn't at home. Leave a message.
2. You want to make a person-to-person call.
3. You want to make a collect call.
4. You are calling Directory Assistance to get a phone number.
5. You answer the phone, and it's the wrong number.

35 SHOPPING FOR CLOTHES

MAY I HELP YOU?

SALESPERSON: May I help you?
CUSTOMER: No, thank you. I'm just looking.
SALESPERSON: All right. My name is _____. Call me if you need help.
CUSTOMER: Okay. Thank you.

SALESPERSON: Do you need any help?
CUSTOMER: Thank you, but someone is helping me.

SALESPERSON: Is anyone helping you?
CUSTOMER: No. Maybe you can help me. I'm looking for a jacket.

Dialog Practice

Study the above dialog for a minute or two. Then use the following guide to practice the dialog with a classmate. Don't look back at the dialog. Your classmate can help if you don't know an answer.

Follow these same directions each time you practice with the other dialog guides in this chapter.

SALESPERSON: _____ I _____ you?

CUSTOMER: No, thank you. I'm just _____.

SALESPERSON: All right. My name is _____. _____ if you need _____.

CUSTOMER: Okay. Thank you.

SALESPERSON: _____ help?

CUSTOMER: Thank you, but someone _____.

SALESPERSON: _____ anyone _____?

CUSTOMER: No. Maybe you _____. I _____ a jacket.

WHAT SIZE? WHAT OTHER COLORS?

Customer: I'm looking for a jacket. Can you help me?
Salesperson: What size are you?
      or
What size do you wear?
Customer: I'm size 40.
      or
I wear size 40.
Salesperson: These jackets are your size.
Customer: I like this one. Does it come in blue?
Salesperson: Yes, but we don't have it in your size.
Customer: What other colors does it come in?
Salesperson: It comes in beige, red, and gray.

Dialog Practice

Customer: I _____ a jacket. _____ help me?

Salesperson: What size _____?

Customer: _____.

Salesperson: These jackets _____ your size.

Customer: I like this one. _____ blue?

Salesperson: Yes, but we _____ your size.

Customer: What other colors _____?

Salesperson: _____ beige, red, and gray.

TRYING ON

Customer: {May / Can} I see this jacket in gray, please?
Salesperson: Yes. Here it is. Would you like to try it on?
Customer: Yes, I would.

(The customer tries on the jacket.)

Salesperson: That jacket looks very nice on you.
Customer: Well, I'm not sure. I don't think it's my style.

Dialog Practice

CUSTOMER: _____ this jacket in gray, please?

SALESPERSON: Yes. Here _____. Would you _____?

CUSTOMER: Yes, I would.

(The customer tries on the jacket.)

SALESPERSON: That jacket _____ nice on you.

CUSTOMER: Well, I'm not sure. I don't think _____.

THE FIT

SALESPERSON: How do these jackets fit?
CUSTOMER: The blue one fits well, but this one doesn't fit very well.
It's too tight.
    or
It's too loose.
    or
It's too small.
    or
It's too big.
    or
It's too short.
    or
It's too long.
SALESPERSON: Would you like me to bring a larger size?
    or
Would you like me to bring a smaller size?
CUSTOMER: Yes, please.
    or
No, thanks.

Dialog Practice

SALESPERSON: How _____ these jackets _____?

CUSTOMER: The blue one _____ well, but this one _____ very well. It's too _____.

Shopping for Clothes / 355

SALESPERSON: Would you like _____ a _____ size?

CUSTOMER: _____

PAYING

CUSTOMER: How much is this shirt? There isn't any price tag on it.
SALESPERSON: It's on sale. It's marked down from twenty-five dollars to eighteen dollars and ninety-eight cents.
CUSTOMER: I'll take it.
SALESPERSON: Cash or charge?
CUSTOMER: Do you accept personal checks?
SALESPERSON: Yes, if you have two pieces of identification.
CUSTOMER: Here's my driver's license and a credit card.
SALESPERSON: Thank you. I'll be back in a moment.

(After a few minutes.)

Thank you for waiting. Here's your shirt. Have a nice day.
CUSTOMER: Thank you. You too.

Dialog Practice

CUSTOMER: How _____ ? _____ any price tag on it.

SALESPERSON: _____ sale. It _____ from twenty-five dollars to eighteen dollars and ninety-eight cents.

CUSTOMER: I _____ .

SALESPERSON: Cash or _____ ?

CUSTOMER: _____ personal checks?

SALESPERSON: Yes, if you _____ identification.

CUSTOMER: _____ my driver's license and a credit card.

SALESPERSON: Thank you. I _____ back in a moment.

(After a few minutes.)

      Thank you for _____. Here's your shirt.

      _____ nice day.

Customer: Thank you. You too.

AMERICAN SIZES

Women's Sizes

For dresses, blouses, pants, and jackets, American sizes are 5/6, 7/8, 9/10, 11/12, 13/14, 15/16, and larger.

 American shoes are sizes 5 through 11, generally. There are different widths: A is narrow, B is medium, and C is wide, generally.

Men's Sizes

Men buy pants according to the size of their waist and height in inches. [*inseam*] A slim man of about six feet probably wears pants size 32 waist, 33 length.

 Men buy shirts according to the size of their neck in inches and the length of their arms, for example, 15½, 33.

 Men's average shoe sizes are 7 through 14.

 What about you? What American sizes do you wear? If you can't decide from the preceding information, go to some stores after school and find your correct size for shirts, blouses, pants, skirts, and shoes.

For More Practice

1. Study this chapter at home. The next day, role play a shopping situation with a classmate.
2. Write a dialog between a salesperson and a customer.

APPENDIX: IRREGULAR VERBS IN ENGLISH

Here is an alphabetical list of most of the irregular verbs in English. Some of the less common verbs are not included in this list.

Base Form	Past	Past Participle
be (am, is, are)	was, were	been
bear	bore	born
beat	beat	beat
become	became	become
begin	began	begun
bend	bent	bent
bet	bet	bet
bite	bit	bitten
bleed	bled	bled
blow	blew	blown
break	broke	broken
bring	brought	brought
build	built	built
burst	burst	burst
buy	bought	bought
catch	caught	caught
choose	chose	chosen
come	came	come
cost	cost	cost
cut	cut	cut
deal	dealt	dealt
do	did	done
dig	dug	dug

draw	drew	drawn
drink	drank	drunk
drive	drove	driven
eat	ate	eaten
fall	fell	fallen
feed	fed	fed
feel	felt	felt
fight	fought	fought
find	found	found
fit	fit	fit
fly	flew	flown
forbid	forbade	forbidden
forget	forgot	forgotten
forgive	forgave	forgiven
freeze	froze	frozen
get	got	got (or) gotten
give	gave	given
go	went	gone
grow	grew	grown
hang	hung	hung
have	had	had
hear	heard	heard
hide	hid	hidden
hit	hit	hit
hold	held	held
hurt	hurt	hurt
keep	kept	kept
kneel	knelt	knelt
know	knew	known
lay	laid	laid
lead	led	led

leave	left	left
lend	lent	lent
let	let	let
light	lit	lit
lose	lost	lost
lie	lay	lain
make	made	made
mean	meant	meant
meet	met	met
pay	paid	paid
put	put	put
quit	quit	quit
read	read[1]	read
ride	rode	ridden
ring	rang	rung
rise	rose	risen
run	ran	run
say	said	said
see	saw	seen
sell	sold	sold
send	sent	sent
set	set	set
shake	shook	shaken
shine	shone	shone
shoot	shot	shot
shut	shut	shut
sing	sang	sung
sink	sank	sunk
sit	sat	sat
sleep	slept	slept

[1] Pronunciation change.

speak	spoke	spoken
speed	sped	sped
spend	spent	spent
split	split	split
spread	spread	spread
stand	stood	stood
steal	stole	stolen
stick	stuck	stuck
sting	stung	stung
strike	struck	struck
swear	swore	sworn
sweep	swept	swept
swim	swam	swum
swing	swung	swung
take	took	taken
teach	taught	taught
tear	tore	torn
tell	told	told
think	thought	thought
throw	threw	thrown
understand	understood	understood
wake	woke	woken
wear	wore	worn
win	won	won
wind	wound	wound
write	wrote	written

Appendix

In the following section, the verbs from the alphabetical list of irregular verbs are grouped into different categories. Some of the verbs in the alphabetical list do not fall into a special category and therefore do not appear in this section.

begin	began	begun	bleed	bled	bled
run	ran	run	feed	fed	fed
sing	sang	sung	lead	led	led
ring	rang	rung	speed	sped	sped
sink	sank	sunk	read	read	read
swim	swam	swum	feel	felt	felt
drink	drank	drunk	keep	kept	kept
			leave	left	left
bring	brought	brought	mean	meant	meant
buy	bought	bought	sleep	slept	slept
catch	caught	caught	sweep	swept	swept
fight	fought	fought	meet	met	met
teach	taught	taught	deal	dealt	dealt
think	thought	thought	kneel	knelt	knelt
grow	grew	grown	break	broke	broken
know	knew	known	choose	chose	chosen
throw	threw	thrown	freeze	froze	frozen
blow	blew	blown	speak	spoke	spoken
draw	drew	drawn	steal	stole	stolen
fly	flew	flown	wake	woke	woken
			bear	bore	born
drive	drove	driven	swear	swore	sworn
rise	rose	risen	tear	tore	torn
ride	rode	ridden	wear	wore	worn
write	wrote	written			

shake	shook	shaken	pay	paid	paid
take	took	taken	say	said	said
			lay	laid	laid
hide	hid	hidden			
bite	bit	bitten	sell	sold	sold
			tell	told	told
sting	stung	stung			
swing	swung	swung	find	found	found
hang	hung	hung	wind	wound	wound
stick	stuck	stuck			
strike	struck	struck (or) stricken			
dig	dug	dug			

INDEX

Ability, using *can* and *could* to express special, 125, 128
Active voice, 281
  doer and receiver in, 281
Adjectives
  comparative form of, 174, 176–178
    formation of, 176–178
    irregular, 178
    questions with, 188
  defined, 176
  expressing equality, 182
  expressing inequality, 185
  long, 177, 197
  and nouns, 176, 178
  short, 177, 197
  superlative forms of, 194, 196–199
    formation of, 196–198
    irregular, 197–198
  two-syllable, 177–178
Adverbs
  comparative form of, 174, 176, 180
    formation of, 180
    irregular, 180
    questions with, 188
  defined, 180
  expressing equality, 182
  expressing inequality, 185
  formation of, 180
  of frequency, 77–78
A few, 103, 104
Affirmative statements, 4
  with *can, could,* 124, 125, 128
  in future tense with *will,* 113, 265–266
  with *going to,* 20, 265
  in past continuous tense, 225, 226
  in present continuous tense, 4, 10
  in present perfect continuous tense, 238
  in present unreal conditional, 272
  with *should,* 135
  in simple past time, 31–32
    time clauses, 210, 212
  in simple present tense, 205–206
    time clauses, 205–206
  with *there is, are, was, were,* 59, 63
  with *was, were,* 48
A great deal of, 100
A great many, 100
Airline
  how to make reservations with, 322
  information, how to ask for, 322
Airport, checking in at, 324
A little, 103, 104
All, present perfect continuous tense with, 240–241
A lot, a lot of, 100, 101
American history, 46–55, *passim*
Answers, short, 101 n. 1
  with *can, can't,* 124–125
  with containers or measurements, 106
  in present continuous tense, 10, 16, 17
  in present perfect continuous tense, 239
  to questions with *how often,* 78
  in simple past tense, 34
  in simple present tense, 73
  with *was, were,* 49
Article, indefinite *(a, an),* 100, 101, 103, 104, 106

Bad habits, 270–277
Be
  past tense of, 48–49
  simple present perfect tense of, 244–245
  simple present tense of, 4, 20
  with *there,* 56, 59, 63–64
  use of, in passive voice, 281–282, 285
Birthday dinner, 110–114
Borrow vs. *lend,* 318
Bus, how to ask directions for, 321

California, Disneyland and, 56–57, 59–61, 63

Can and *could*, 121
  errors in using, 125
  and *may*, 125
  negative of, 152
  in past tense, 128
  in present tense, 124
  in questions, 124, 125, 128
  in short answers, 124–125
  in statements, 124, 125, 128
  uses of, 124–125, 128
Cartoon strips, 1–6, 8–15, 33, 37–39, 146–147, 170–171, 253–257, 290, 295–301, 336–342
Characters, introduction of, 3–6, 8–15
Checking in
  at airport, 324
  at hotel, 326
Clauses
  main, 205, 206, 212, 252, 265
  time, 204–206, 210, 212, 225–227, 250, 252
Clothes, shopping for. *See* Shopping for clothes
Comma, 272
Comparative form, of adjectives and adverbs, 174, 176–178, 180
Conditional, present unreal, 270, 273
  correct tense in, 272
  formation of, 272
  position of *if* clause in, 275
Conditional, real (*if* . . . , *will* . . .), 262
  correct tenses for, 265–266
  position of *if* clause in, 266
  questions in, 266
Consonants, 177
Contractions, 5, 10, 48, 61, 70, 73, 100, 101, 114, 122 n. 1, 124, 128, 135, 150, 152–153, 273
Could/would, 128, 272, 273, 275, 317. *See Can* and *could*
Customs and manners, in the United States, 204–209

Dialogs, 19, 20, 29, 30, 57–59, 69, 111, 112, 122, 123, 133, 134, 139–141, 152, 160–162, 223, 224, 263, 264, 271, 272, 321–326, 328–331, 333–335, 343, 345–349, 352–356
Did, in questions, 33–34
Did not (didn't), in negative statements in simple past tense, 33
Different country or culture, difficulties in living in, 132–135, 137

Directions
  asking for, 304–305
  giving, 303–305, 308–310
  how to ask for train and bus, 321
  and words that tell place, 308–310
Disneyland and California, 56–57, 59–61, 63
Doctor, visit to, 340–342
  how to describe medical problems, 336–339
  how to make appointments, 343
Doer
  in active voice, 281
  in passive voice, 281–282
Don't have to and *must not*, 150, 152–153
Dreams, 87–89

-ed and *-d* past tense endings, 32
Equality, adjectives and adverbs expressing, 182
Extended present, 14

Famous people, 194–203
Favors and requests, 316–318
Flights, how to ask for information about, 323
Food, cooking of and shopping for, 96–108
For, present perfect continuous tense with, 240–241
Frequency adverbs, 77–78
Friend's home, visiting a. *See* Home, visiting a friend's
Future tense with *going to*, 18, 20, 26
  contrast of *will* and, 113, 117, 265, 266
  integration of, with present continuous tense, simple present tense, and simple past tense, 90–95
  and time clauses, 252
  time expressions with, 21
Future tense with *will*, 110
  in affirmative statements, 113, 265–266
  contrast of *going to* and, 113, 117, 265, 266
  in negative statements, 114, 115
  in questions, 115, 266, 317
  and time clauses, 252
Future time clauses, 250, 252

Gerund, verb +, 159, 163, 165–166, 168
Getting into shape, 290–294

Ghosts, poltergeists and, 222–227, 230–235
Going to, future tense with. See Future tense with *going to*

Had to, 155
Have
  simple present tense of, 70
  simple present perfect tense of, 244–245
Have to, 138
  and *must,* 152–153
  must not and *don't have to,* 150
  negative of, 150, 152–153
  past tense of, 155
  questions with, 142–143
History, American. See American history
Henry VIII, King, 233–235
Holidays in the United States, 68–77, 79–80, 82–84
Home, visiting a friend's, 332
  at dinner table, 334
  when guest arrives, 333
  when guest leaves, 335
Hotel
  checking in at, 326
  reservations, how to make, 324–325
How many, 106
How much, 106
How often, questions with, 78

Idioms, 15, 40 n. 1, 42, 73, 82 n. 1, 101 n. 1, 102 nn. 3–5, 103 n. 7, 111 nn. 1–4, 127 n. 2, 133 n. 1, 164 n. 1, 184 n. 1, 233 n. 1, 228 n. 4, 230 n. 5, 271 nn. 1–3, 273 n. 4, 290 n. 1, 313 n. 1, 329 nn. 1–3, 333 n. 1, 334 n. 2
If, and *when,* 265
If . . . , will . . .
  correct tense for, 265–266
  position of *if* clause, 266
  questions in, 266
Infinitive
  verb +, 159, 163, 168
  verb + object +, 169
Information
  how to ask for airline, 322
  how to ask for, about flights, 323
  how to ask for telephone, 346

-ing
  as ending of gerund, 163, 165, 166, 168, 317
  in past continuous tense, 225, 226
  in present continuous tense, 4, 9, 16, 82
  in present perfect continuous tense, 238, 239
International Living, The Experiment in, 135 n. 2
Interrupted action, past continuous tense with, 225–226
Interviews, 26, 47–48, 52–53
Invitations with *would you like,* 295
  + base form of verb, 299
  + noun, 296
  ways to accept or refuse, 298, 301
Irregular comparative of some adjectives, 178
Irregular verbs. See also *be, have*
  categories of, 361–362
  list of most of the, in English, 357–362
  past participle of, 281, 357–362
  past tense of, 281, 357–362

Know, simple present perfect of, 244–245
Knowledge of world history, 278–288

Language, difficulties of learning a foreign, 133–134
Lend vs. *borrow,* 318
Let's, making suggestions with, 310–311

Main clause, 205, 206, 212, 265
Many, 100, 101
Marriage, 90–95
  vs. career or children, 159–163, 166, 169–173
May, and *can,* 125
Measurements (or containers), for nouns, 106
Moral, story with a, 251–253
Much, 100, 101
Mugging, 28–37
Must
  and *have to,* 152–153
  negative of, 152–153
  past tense of, 155
Must not and *don't have to,* 150, 152–153

Negative statements
  with *can, could,* 124, 125, 128

Negative statements (*continued*)
  with *did not (didn't)*, 33
  in future tense with *won't*, 114, 115
  with *going to*, 20
  in past continuous tense, 275, 276
  in present continuous tense, 4, 10
  in present perfect continuous tense, 238
  in present unreal conditional, 272
  with *should*, 135
  in simple past tense, 33
  in simple present tense, 70
  with *there is, are, was, were*, 59, 63
  using *have to*, 150, 151–153
  with *was, were*, 48
Noun(s), 61, 63
  and adjectives, 176, 178
  count and noncount (or mass), 96, 99–101, 103, 104, 106, 107
  definition of, 99
  examples of, 99–101, 103, 104, 106, 107
  large quantities of, 100
  list of, 107
  and the plural form, 99
  in questions, 101, 106
  small quantities of, 100–101, 103, 104
  would you like +, 296

Object, verb +, + infinitive, 169
One of the, 199
Only a few, 104
Only a little, 104

Parents and teenagers, 217–221
Participles, past. *See* Past participles
Passive voice
  doer in, 281–282
  formation of, 281–282
  questions in, 285
  reasons for using, 281–282
  receiver in, 281–282
  with simple past tense, 278, 281–282, 285
  with simple present tense, 278, 281–282, 285
Past continuous tense, 222
  formation of, 225
  with interrupted action, 225–226
  + *when* clauses, 225
    questions with, 226–227
  while +, 226

Past participles, 281, 285
  list of, of most English irregular verbs, 357–362
Past tense
  of *be*, 46, 48–49, 272
  could in, 128, 272
  list of, of most irregular verbs in English, 357–362
  there was, were in, 63–64
  would in, 272
People, famous. *See* Famous people
Permission, using *can* to express, 125
Picture stories, 236, 237, 241–243
Place, words that tell, 308–310
Plurals, of nouns, 99, 103, 199
Poltergeists and ghosts, 222–227, 230–235
Possibility, using *can* to express, 125
Prepositions (e.g., *of, about, in*) + gerund form of verb, 166
Present continuous tense, 2, 5, 10
  affirmative statements in, 4
  contrast of simple past tense, present perfect continuous tense, and, 248
  formation of, 4, 82
  integration of simple present tense, simple past tense, simple future tense (*going to*), and, 90–95
  negative statements in, 4
  questions in, 9, 16
  simple present tense and, 82
  use of, 4, 82
  use of, to talk about future, 26
Present moment, 82
Present perfect continuous tense, 236
  contrast of simple past tense, present continuous tense, and, 248
  formation of, 238, 239
  practice with, 239–240
  and simple present perfect tense of *be, have, know*, 244–245
  time expressions with, 240–241
Present tense
  of *be*, 272
  can in, 124
  there is, are in, 59
Present tenses of English. *See* Present continuous tense; Simple present tense
Present unreal conditional, 270, 273
  correct tense in, 272

formation of, 272
position of *if* clause in, 275
Pronunciation
change in, for past tense, 359 n. 1
for *-ed* past-tense ending, 32
Proverbs, 251, 259–261
Punctuation, 272

Questions
with *can, could,* 124, 125, 128
with comparative adjectives and adverbs, 188
count and mass nouns in, 101, 106
did in, 33–34
in future tense with *will,* 115, 266
with *going to,* 20
with *have to,* 142–143, 155
with *how often,* 78
in passive voice, 285
in past continuous tense, 226–227
in present continuous tense, 9, 16
in present perfect continuous tense, 239
in present unreal conditional, 275
in real conditional, 266
with *should,* 135
in simple past tense, 33–34
beginning with *who,* 34
time clauses, 212
in simple present tense, 72–74, 78
time clauses, 206
with *there is, are, was, were,* 61, 63–64
with *was, were,* 48–49
with *when* clauses, 206, 212, 226–227
yes/no questions, 115, 124–125, 135, 143, 188, 249, 275, 285

Real conditional (*if* . . ., *will* . . .), 262
correct tenses for, 265–266
position of *if* clause in, 266
questions in, 266
Receiver
in active voice, 281
in passive voice, 281
in questions, 285
Regular verbs, simple past tense of, 30–32
Religions, stories from great, 210–216
Requests and favors, 316–318
Reservations
with airline, 322
with hotel, 324–325
with restaurant, 328

Restaurant, 327
American customs in, 331
asking for check in, 330–331
entering, 329
making reservation in, 328
ordering in, 329–330
Robbery, 42–43
Role playing, 43, 50, 59, 94, 134, 141, 162, 165, 173, 326, 331, 335, 343, 350

School life, 138–152, 154–158
Shape, getting into, 290–294
Shopping for clothes, 351, 355
American sizes, 356
fitting, 354
help in, 352–353
paying, 355
trying on, 353
Short answers. *See* Answers, short
Should, 132, 134–135
Simple past tense, 28
affirmative statements in, 31–32
contrast of present continuous tense, present perfect continuous tense, and, 248
integration of present continuous tense, simple present tense, future tense (going to), and, 90–95
irregular verbs in, 30, 32, 34, 44–45
negative statements in, 33
with past continuous tense, 225, 226
questions in, 33–34
regular verbs in, 30–32
formation of, 32
time clauses and, 210, 212, 225
time expressions with, 31
use of, 31
Simple present perfect tense of *be, have,* and *know,* 244–245
Simple present tense, 68, 69
affirmative statements in, 70
formation of, 70, 82
and frequency adverbs, 77–78
integration of, with present continuous tense, simple past tense, and future tense *(going to),* 90–95
negative statements in, 70
and present continuous tense, 82
questions in, 72–74, 78
in real conditional with *if,* 265
time clauses, 204–206, 252
uses of, 82

Since, present perfect continuous tense with, 240–241
Singular, of nouns, 99–100
Special abilities, 121–123, 125, 128, 129, 131
Spelling rules
　for forming comparative of adjectives, 177–178
　for forming superlative of adjectives, 197
　for regular simple past tense, 32
Statements. *See* Affirmative statements; Negative statements
Stereotypes
　about different nationalities, 190–193
　about men and women, 174–190
Subject, 4, 9, 16, 17, 20, 33, 34, 113, 114, 124, 128, 135, 155, 225, 226, 239, 265, 272, 273, 281, 282
Suggestions, making, with *let's* and *why don't,* 310–311
Superlative forms, of adjectives, 194, 199
　formation of, 196–198
　irregular, 197–198

Teenagers, and parents, 217–221
Telephone, using, 344, 350
　busy, 348
　information, 346
　leaving a message, 349
　long-distance calls, 345
　　person-to-person, 345
　　station-to-station, 345
　making reservations by, 328
　some important telephone numbers, 349
　wrong number, 347
Tenses. *See also* Future tense with *going to;* Future tense with *will;* Past continuous tense; Past tense; Present continuous tense; Present perfect continuous tense; Present tense; Simple past tense; Simple present tense
　integration of, 289–294
There is, are, was, were, 56
　in past tense, 63–64
　in present tense, 59
　use of, 59, 63–64
Time clauses
　future, 250, 252
　with past continuous tense, 225, 226

　position of, 205–206, 212, 225, 226
　questions with, 206
　and simple past tense, 210, 212, 225
　and simple present tense, 204–206
　words beginning, 205, 212
Time expressions
　used in answers to *how often* questions, 78
　used with future tense, 21
　used with present perfect continuous tense, 240–241
　used with simple past tense, 31
To, with infinitive, 163, 168, 169
Train, how to ask directions for, 321
Travel, 320
　checking in at airport, 324
　checking in at hotel, 326
　how to ask directions for train and bus, 321
　how to ask for airline information, 322
　how to ask for information about flights, 323
　how to make hotel reservation, 324–325
　how to make reservation with airline, 322

Verb(s). *See also* Tenses
　base form of, 4, 9, 20, 30–34, 44, 45, 70, 82, 113, 114, 124, 128, 135, 142, 155, 163, 165, 166, 168, 169, 225, 226, 248, 249, 265, 272, 312, 317, 357–362
　+ gerund, 159, 163, 165–166, 168
　+ infinitive, 159, 163, 168
　integration of forms of, 217–221, 289–294
　irregular, 4, 20, 30, 34, 44–45, 48, 281, 357–362
　+ object + infinitive, 169
　regular, 30, 32
　would you like + base form of, 299
Visiting a friend's home. *See* Home, visiting a friend's
Voice
　active, 281
　passive, 278, 281–282, 285
Vowels, 177

Was, were, 46, 272
　in questions, 48–49
　in statements, 48

Washington, D.C., a trip to, 19, 20, 22–27
What questions, in present continuous tense, 17
When, and *if*, 265
When clauses
  past continuous tense with, 225, 226
  questions with, 226–227
  simple past tense with, 212
  simple present tense with, 205–206
  and *while* clauses, 226
While
  past continuous tense with, 226
  and *when*, 226
Who questions
  in present continuous tense, 16
  in simple past tense, 34
Who, *whose*, and *which* questions, when comparing things, 188

Why don't, making suggestions with, 310–311
Will, future tense with. *See* Future tense with *will*
Won't, negative statements in future tense with, 114, 115
Words, that tell place, 308–310
World history, knowledge of, 278–288
Worry, 262–269
Would/could, 128, 272, 273, 275, 317
Would you like, invitations with, 295
  + base form of verb, 299
  + noun, 296
  ways to accept or refuse, 298, 301

Yes/no questions, 115, 124–125, 135, 143, 188, 249, 275, 285